# QUOTES

*They were chosen, both for their elegant decor and because they possess an ambience like that of a fine residence.*
—Washington Post

*Thank you, Pamela for your unerring good taste for quality and for your talent in telling us about it.*
—Peter Balas, President
International Hotel Association

*It is indeed very good and full of fascinating addresses for people who travel as much as we do.*
—Duchess of Bedford

*My schedule is so hectic that when I can steal a few days for myself, they are very precious to me. I always choose small, out-of-the-way places, which give me and my family privacy, while providing excellent service and luxury accommodations.*
—Donna Karan

*The elegant ones make staying in hotels a little more bearable. The elegant ones don't seem like hotels at all.*
—Philip Glass

*Elegant Small Hotels makes a seductive volume for window shopping. . . . Handsomely illustrated. Hotels that provide the atmosphere of a fine residence: beauty in design, color and furnishings, fresh flower, luxurious toiletries and linens. Other considerations are select business and physical fitness facilities, excellence of cuisine and concierge services.*
—Chicago Sun Times

*The entries for each hotel include rates, service and facilities available, as well as a short description of the style and mood of the establishment.*
—San Francisco Chronicle

*Every great hotel in this guide is unique . . . handsome photographs.*
—Hideaways International

*The switchboard operator knows your name, the people at the desk say welcome back when you come through the door, and they try to give you your favorite room if you've stayed there a long time, and its fine to have dinner in the dining room if you're there alone. My favorite is the Hotel Bel Air because that's where I spent my honeymoon. . . . We all know small hotels are sexy because they are small and intimate.*

—Helen Gurley Brown

*It's a great adventure to read.*

—Roger Horchow

*A small hotel is your home away from home.*
—Caroline Hunt Schoelkopf

*The author and Peter Duchin, who wrote the introduction, make a very persuasive case for staying at small elegant hotels . . . these hotels lived up to the author's description. Fortunately the author covers a range of rates from affordable to expensive and more.*

—St. Louis Post-Dispatch

*Each hotel is described in detail with a side listing that includes everything . . . this is an excellent guide for the traveler who is looking for European style tradition in the U.S.*

—The Armchair Traveler

*America's finest! . . . An abundance of places to stay; that rival any European hotel in warmth, charm and service.*

—The Horchow Collection

*If you've enjoyed the charming personalized hotels of Europe, you will love Pamela Lanier's selection of . . . outstanding hotels here at home. The information and photographs will allow the discerning traveller to choose from among the best. . . .*

—Traveller's Bookstore

*It happens I always stay at a fine small hotel when given the choice. I'm familiar with quite a few of your selections and must commend you upon the realistic assessments you provide.*

—Tom Shane

# ELEGANT

## SMALL HOTELS

### BOUTIQUE & LUXURY ACCOMMODATIONS

by

PAMELA LANIER

A division of the Lanier Travel Guides Network

The interactive version of this book
may be found on the Internet
(www.elegantsmallhotel.com)

E-mail: elegant@TravelGuideS.com

Cover picture:  Hotel Makanda By The Sea, Costa Rica, page 131

Author: Pamela Lanier & Marie Lanier-Castro
Editor: Vivian Sturdavant
Typesetter: John Richards
Cover Designs by: Laura Lamar of MAX Design Studio, Middletown,
    CA 95461

First Edition September 1986
Twenty-Fifth Silver Anniversary, Collectors Edition, March 2011

Published by Lanier Publishing International, Ltd.
PO Box 2240
Petaluma, CA 94953 USA
Phone: 707-763-0271
Fax: 707-763-5762
Email: Elegant@TravelGuides.com

Distributed to the trade by National Book Network
    Blue Ridge Summit PA 17214

Library of Congress Cataloging-in-Publication Data
Lanier, Pamela
 Elegant small hotels: a connoisseur's guide/Pamela Lanier.
      p.  cm.—(A Lanier guide)
    ISBN: 978-0-9843766-9-8    ISBN10: 0-9843766-9-0
    1. Hotels, taverns, etc.—United States—Guidebooks.
    2. United States—Guidebooks.
    I. Title.      II. Series.
Library of Congress Cataloging in Publication data is on file with the
publisher.

# ADDITIONAL WORKS

*22 Days in Alaska*
*Cinnamon Mornings*
*Cinnamon Mornings and Raspberry Tea*
*Elegant Small Hotels – Pacific Rim*
*The Back Almanac*
*Bed and Breakfast Getaways – in the South*
*Bed and Breakfast Guide – For Food Lovers*
*Moving Mom and Dad*
*Golf Resorts International*
*Golf Courses – The Complete Guide*
*Golf Resorts – The Complete Guide*
*Bed and Breakfast Cookbook*
*The Bed and Breakfast Chronicle Magazine*
*Family Travel & Resorts*
*Condo Vacations*
*Bed & Breakfasts Inns & Guesthouses International*
*Bed & Breakfasts Inns & Guesthouses - Midwestern*
*Bed & Breakfasts Inns & Guesthouses - Northeastern*
*Bed & Breakfasts Inns & Guesthouses - Southern*
*Bed & Breakfasts Inns & Guesthouses - Western*
*All - Suite Hotel Guide*

---

Lanier Publishing has facilitated the
planting of nine trees for every tree
used in the production of this book.

---

Printed on recycled paper.

# DEDICATION

This is truly a special time for me—our twenty-fifth Silver Anniversary year. Looking back over the years to all the people we have met along this journey (hoteliers, staff and traveling guests), we dedicate this collectors edition to you. For without each of your contributions and continued support we would not be here today and poised to embark towards our next twenty-five years.

# INTRODUCTION

. . . And then there was the time that my band (eight men and one woman) and myself travelled all day changing planes twice to get from New York to a small town in the West where we had to play that night. It had been that kind of travelling day—replete with rudeness, abruptness, computer mix-ups and a complete lack of attention or care for the individual. So somehow it didn't really surprise us when we found upon reaching our ultimate destination that all our instruments and other bags had been mis-routed and sent to Kalamazoo, Chattanooga or some other strange Indian-sounding city. This meant that only those of us who had carried our clothes on board (something I've learned to do) had anything to wear that evening and only me on piano (it doesn't travel with us, thank God) and the trumpet player (who had carried his instrument with him) had anything to play that night—a most unlikely duet! What to do? One could rage uselessly at the cipher in back of the airlines desk, or one could attempt to be cunning.

Opting for the second alternative, I remembered that we were staying in an elegant small hotel which had a reputation for service and attention to the individual; so with fading hope I called the hotel. I was immediately switched to a polite concierge whom I belabored with our seemingly insoluble problem. He listened attentively, asked intelligent questions (a first that day, I'll tell you) and told me to come directly to the hotel and see him there. When we arrived and assembled numbly around his desk, we found that this wonderful man had done the following: he had contacted the local music store which was standing by to hear the specifications of the instruments we needed and would deliver them to the job on time: he had contacted the local evening wear store, which was waiting to hear our sizes and would deliver to the hotel; he had contacted the airlines and traced our bags; he had pre-registered us in our rooms; and finally, he had set up a private room for us in which he had arranged to serve us dinner before we left for the job. Furthermore, it all worked!

Believe me, I need no further inducement to stay in elegant small hotels for the rest of my days. When I travel, which I do a great deal of the time (we played in 41 states in the last three years). I really do appreciate those wonderful qualities that can be found in these hotels: politeness, attentiveness and really an old-fashioned attention to detail and to the needs of the client. Sadly, these qualities are quite lacking in everyday life as we prepare for the 21st century. I'm glad to see, though, that these hotels are returning to a sense of service and style . . . I just hope that with the publication of this book my band and I will be able to get reservations whenever we need them!

—*Peter Duchin*

# A NOTE FROM PAMELA

Elegant Small Hotels offer exclusivity, sophistication and personalized service. The discriminating traveler looking for a five-star hotel experience will find this world-wide boutique guide and our www.ElegantSmallHotels.com website, indispensable. Our Elegant Small Hotels guidebook provides details on luxury small hotels, inns and resorts with premier amenities and services in locations with first-class recreational and dining facilities.

For over 25 years we have been providing you with quality information about the hotel/lodging industry. During those years many travelers have asked me how we identify and select the elegant small hotels from the many hotels/lodging facilities that are offered around the world today. For us to even consider a particular hotel, it must first have met our level of standards. Other factors we have kept in mind, while separating the exceptional from the merely first-class, relate to the individual traveler's needs. For example . . . .

By "elegant" we mean décor—and also something more. If a hotel is to be one's home away from home its atmosphere should be like that of a fine residence. The feeling should be reflected not only in design, color and furnishings, but also in those little touches that really matter; fresh flowers, nightly turn down (with a chocolate!), overnight shoe shine, luxurious toiletries and over sized towel ...all the myriad details that add up to the intangible quality we call elegance.

When we say "small" we generally mean fewer than 400 guest rooms; in fact, the typical hotel selected for inclusion in this our printed guide (or our Internet directory) has approximately half that number. We have found that small hotels are best able to offer the high staff-to-guest ratio enabling a genuine concern for each guest's comfort and pleasure.

If you are among those travelers for whom fine cuisine is a top priority, we agree completely! We have chosen our hotels with excellent dining in mind. If you conduct business while traveling, such facilities as teleconferencing and Internet access and perhaps an appropriately sized meeting or conference room, will be essential; and, if you are among the growing number of people to whom physical fitness is a personal must, your hotel should provide in house facilities such as swimming pool, tennis, spa and massage room, and perhaps weight training equipment. Many of our recommended hotels also arrange guest privileges at prestigious private country clubs and health centers.

An important key to getting the most out of your Elegant Small Hotel experience is to allow the concierge to assist you whenever possible. The hotels described in this guide are small enough to permit a degree of personal attention rarely encountered in modern life. Accordingly, the function of the concierge is to cater to the individual needs (and whims) of each guest. Rather than attempted a detailed description of services and amenities the concierge can arrange –which would leave no space in this guide for the hotels themselves—we have presented "A Concierge's Day," the viewpoint of one outstanding concierge, on the following page.

If you are among those discerning travelers who understand that the essence of the good life is quality, this book is designed especially to enhance your travel enjoyment. Our promise to you is that we will continue to bring you the best of the best in hotel/lodging accommodations in *Elegant Small Hotels*. Whether you travel for business, pleasure, or a bit of both, each elegant small hotel described on our Internet directory or in our annually printed *Elegant Small Hotels: Boutique & Luxury Accommodations"* will deserve a special place in your travel plans and your memories!

—*Pamela Lanier December 2010*

# A CONCIERGE'S DAY

"I am absolutely certain we can have the car and driver here in twenty minutes, sir. I only need to know what sort of car and what sort of driver you would prefer. And yes, I expect your day in the wine country will be splendid; the weather is perfect."

The 20-minute wait for the special car and driver to arrive will not be wasted. The concierge first calls ahead for luncheon reservations at a spot that normally requires two weeks' notice. Next, he will call the wineries for any special considerations that might be possible for his guest. After all, everything must be the best. (It will soon become evident that perfect weather is the only thing the concierge has not arranged—the sunshine being courtesy of a somewhat higher power.)

The larger day's work begins for the concierge at this small Nob Hill hotel (the Huntington) in San Francisco with a review of the arriving guest list and of their special requests noted in his log. He opens that delicious document with the same excitement felt by a maestro opening the score of a beautiful symphony.

Appreciating that not everyone who travels in America is yet fully acquainted with the full range of services he can provide, the concierge will promptly call each guest within minutes of arrival to extend a personal introduction and a warm invitation to take full advantage of his skills and resources. To him and his hotel, every guest is a Very Important Person.

The concierge next turns his attention to a couple at his desk, eager to begin a day of sightseeing. Shopping, museum-hopping and general about-towning are the plan, with a lovely lunch along the way. The concierge will not only point them in the right direction, but also enhance their day with helpful hints and local insights.

The couple will return with happy faces and tired feet, to swap a few stories with the concierge and then retire for a nap or workout followed by tea.

Afterward they will consult the concierge once again to plan an evening grand finale to a delight-filled day. Knowledgeable and sensitive to his territory, he can advise them concerning matters of cuisine, attire, entertainment, transportation and adventure; then he will make the necessary arrangements.

You see, living vicariously is the route to concierge heaven. As the concierge plans the guests' daytime and evening activities with them, striving to maximize their pleasure, and as he takes the necessary measures to bring the plan to reality, and as he hears guests tell of their experiences afterwards, he feels something beyond professional pride. He actually enjoys it.

—Jeremy Dove

Included with the purchase of this guide

# $\mathcal{C}$ertificate for a
# FREE *night stay*

This certificate entitles the bearer to a free night,
with the purchase of one or more nights.
at any one of the participating Elegant hotels.

*Valid through May 31, 2012. Certificate must be attached to the guidebook.*
*See details on back.*

# $\mathcal{D}$reams $\mathcal{D}$o
# $\mathcal{C}$ome $\mathcal{T}$rue

## Terms & Conditions

The Certificate is good for one free consecutive night stay with the purchase of one or more nights at the hotel's regular rate. Each certificate is valid for no more than 2 people and no more than 1 room. This offer is only valid at specially marked participating hotels, as indicated on page xiii, and is not valid at all times. Check with the participating hotel, in advance, for availability, rates, reservations, cancellation policies and other hotel requirements, terms and conditions as other restrictions regarding occupancy may also apply. Bed tax, sales tax, alcoholic beverages, food, and gratuities are not included. Reservation requirements vary from property to property, so please check with the individual hotel for applicable details.

This certificate may not be reproduced and cannot be used in conjunction with any other promotions offers unless specifically authorized by the hotel itself. This Certificate has no cash value and is redeemable only for the offer as described above. The Certificate must be redeemed no later than May 31, 2012. Lanier Publishing International is not responsible for any changes in the hotel's operations or policies, each of which can occur without notice and affect this Certificate offering.

The section below is to be completed by the lodging property upon presentation/acceptance. Hoteliers, please complete the information as listed below and mail to:

ATTN: Dreams Do Come True Awards
Lanier Publishing International
PO Box 2240
Petaluma, CA 94953

Name of Guest: _____

Email of Guest: _____

Name of Hotel: _____

Authorized Hotel Agent: _____

# MEMBERS ACCEPTING THE DREAMS CERTIFICATE

To celebrate our 25th Silver Anniversary, many of our Elegant Small Hotel members have joined our Dreams Do Come True, gift certificate offering. Listed below are those participating members. As a courtesy, please be sure to acquaint yourself with the terms and conditions on the back of the certificate and let the booking agent know that you will be utilizing the certificate when you place the reservation for your hotel stay. This is our gift to you!

## Participating Members

| Property Name | Page | Restrictions |
| --- | --- | --- |
| Albergo Villa Marta | 139 | Subject to availability. Not valid from June to September; December 24th-31st; during special events and holidays. |
| Casa Grandview Historic Luxury Inn, Cottages & Suites | 51 | Subject to availability, not valid during black out dates or holidays. Room Upgrade. |
| Danfords Hotel & Marina | 82 | Check at time of reservations |
| Golden Plough Inn at Peddler's Village | 87 | Valid January–April 2011 and Valid January–April 2012 (Sunday–Friday) |
| Groveland Hotel at Yosemite National Park | 10 | Valid October 15th–April 15th (excluding holidays and special events) |
| Hotel Hana-Maui and Honua Spa | 54 | Anytime. Subject to availability / Valid only 30 days before intended usage. |
| Hotel Makanda by the Sea | 131 | Valid September–October. New reservations only. |
| Lakeside Illahee Inn | 125 | Anytime. Valid January 1, 2010–June 30th, 2011 and September 6, 2011–May 31, 2012. |
| Marcus Whitman Hotel | 108 | Valid January–March and November–December. |
| New Harmony Inn | 57 | Valid Sunday–Thursday. |
| Old Monterey Inn | 19 | Valid Monday–Thursday, November 1–April 30th; excluding holidays or special events. |
| Posh Palm Springs | 23 | Subject to availability. |
| Strater Hotel | 38 | Valid Jan 1–May 15 and October 15–December 15. |
| The Washington House Inn | 109 | Valid Sunday–Thursday/ Valid on Room Rates $148–236. Holidays & Festivals excluded). |

# HOW TO USE THIS GUIDEBOOK

For ease of use our guidebook is divided into two sections. All of the **USA** based hotels are grouped in the first section and all **International** properties in the second section. Within each section are further divisions for your convenience. For example: in the USA section, the hotels are grouped by state first, then within each state – by city or town– and last by alpha order within each city. Within each page you will find a wealth of information about the hotel that you are researching. Such as:

**1** **Description** – this is a brief overview of of the type of experience you should expect to receive when you visit our member hotel.

**2** **Basic Information** – From address to website URL. All the basics are here for you to contact the property. Though rates are subject to change without notice — we have even provided a gauge for budgeting purposes when planning your trip. Unless otherwise noted all prices are in US dollars.

**3** **Attractions, Business Facilities, Concierge, Restaurant, Services,** even the **Restrictions** and closest **Airport**. (This information has been expanded on our web site. See page 162 for additional information about our SEARCH BY icons.) Other services and sundries are often available. When you call to book reservations, ask whether the hotel offers those items you desire. Traveling with children, pets or handicaps can be a challenge.

**4** It's very hard to limit our members to just one photo for the guidebook when we see so many beautiful photos. We invite you to visit our web site to see the complete information on each of our members and view their whole array of photos.

## HOTEL MAKANDA BY THE SEA, VILLAS AND STUDIOS

Makanda by the Sea is the ideal location for visitors wishing to experience Costa Rica's natural splendor and variety while enjoying the comforts of first-class jungle lodging. All of the Villas are contoured into the jungle and descending mountain terrain with the abruptly inclining hillsides allowing dramatic ocean views from all locations. **1**

In July 1985, Makanda by the Sea was started by the designer and owner, Joe McNichols. Inspired by his dream, Makanda has been built in balance with its natural surroundings. Using nature as the backdrop, the architectural openness allows the rich tropical flora to become a part of the living environment. Selection of flora was based on the ability to attract a mix of butterflies, birds, monkeys, sloths and other local fauna, making a stay here a heightened jungle experience.

**Address:** 3K Main Road 2, Manuel Antonio Park, Puntarenas
**Phone:** 506-2777-0442 **2**
**Tollfree:** 888-625-2632
**Fax:** 506-2777-1032
**Email:** info@makanda.com
**Web:** www.makanda.com/EN/
**Room Rates:** 200 – 460 US$
**Suite Rates:** 200 – 460 US$
**No. of Rooms:** 11
**No. of Suites:** 11
**Credit Cards:** Most CCs Accepted
**Attractions:** • Manuel Antonio Park Hike • Mangrove Boat • Whitewater Rafting • Canopy **3** Zipline • Jet Skis • Snorkel/Dolphin & Whale Tour • Horseback Riding • ATV Tour • Kayak Excursions • Butterfly/Reptile Farm • Vanilla Spice Farm • Surfing • Inshore/Offshore Sportfishing
**Services:** • Welcome Cocktail • Breakfast In-Room • Coffee Maker • A/C • Cable TV • Stereo & iPod dock • Mini Bar • Full Kitchen • Safe • Secure Parking • Free Internet/Int Calls • Tour Desk • Wedding Plan
**Restrictions:** Adults Only – Regretfully we do not accept children under the age of 14 yrs.
**Concierge:** Available 7am to 8pm
**Room Service:** Available 7am to 10pm Daily
**Restaurant:** Sunspot Bar & Grill, located poolside.
**Bar:** Sunspot Bar & Grill
**Business Facilities:** Available
**Conference Room:** No
**Sports Facilities:** No
**Spa Services:** We are proud to offer a complete range of Spa Services in the comfort of your luxury Villa.
**Location:** Manuel Antonio-Quepos

**4**
Dazzling late-afternoon sunsets and tantalizing tropical breezes greet you as you stroll the beaches of Costa Rica's Pacific Coast. A splash of color catches your eye as an unnamed species of bird or butterfly wings it's way through the rain forest. A challenging hike through the jungle paths lead to a secluded rocky beach cove where guests can explore the tide pools as well as rare pre-Columbian fish traps.

At Makanda by the Sea you will find a number of ways of keeping comfortable on even the hottest of tropical days. The geometrically designed infinity pool. Spacious viewing decks. Enjoy delicious poolside appetizers.

Or, unwind in the Jacuzzi while the wildlife watches you! These are only a few of the many wonders that have captured the imaginations of visitors from around the world as they are quietly seduced by the natural splendor of a visit to Hotel Makanda by the Sea. Makanda, the name once said to mean "essence" or "nectar" in ancient Sanscrit, is a paradise found!

EWW 979 25TH ED

www.ElegantSmallHotel.com

*. . . devoted to pleasing the most discriminating. The photos put you on the scene while the text and side notes offer explicit answers.*
—*Los Angeles Times*

# CONTENTS

**SECTION THREE – International Members**

---

## DISCLAIMER

    Every attempt has been made to be absolutely current. Some information contained in this guide has been provided by the hotels' management, and management policies may change. If you feel that anything in this book is even slightly inaccurate, please inform us so we can put it right in future editions. We appreciate reader comments; including any hotel we have overlooked which you feel deserves to be included.

**Contact us at: elegant@travelguides.com**

# KACHEMAK BAY WILDERNESS LODGE

Kachemak Bay Wilderness Lodge is an exclusive private hideaway for only 10 to 14 guests per week, offering 2, 3 or 5 night packages starting on Monday and departing by Saturday.

Your all-inclusive rate includes daily naturalist guide service, gourmet meals and private cabins with views of the ocean and mountains. Wine, flowers, fruit basket with chocolates are placed in the room daily. All your special birthdays, anniversaries, or special events are honored with requested menu, wines, champagne, and dessert.

The staff is attentive, friendly, thorough and experienced. The eight staff at this award-winning lodge are experienced in providing personalized guiding and hospitality services. Your visit may include viewing wildlife, glaciers, birding, fishing, hiking, tide pooling, sea kayaking, and relaxing surrounded by mountains and ocean in a fantastic wilderness setting.

Kachemak Bay Wilderness Lodge is the winner of more national and international awards than any other lodge in Alaska. This all-inclusive world class lodge features classic accommodations and gourmet meals.

Warmth and charm, inspiration, presentation and a truly enchanting environment make Kachemak Bay Wilderness Lodge a unique world class vacation destination.

**Address:** China Poot Bay Homer AK 99603
**Phone:** 907-235-8910
**Fax:** 907-235-8911
**Email:** info@alaskawildernesslodge.com
**Web:** www.alaskawildernesslodge.com
**Suite Rates:** 750 per person
**No. of Suites:** 5
**Credit Cards:** Visa, MC
**Attractions**: World class wildlife viewing: birds, marine life & terrestrial animals. Kayak & boat in protected waters. Hike beaches, forests, glaciers, alpine & tide pools. Fishing, local harvest of berries, clams & mussels.
**Services:** Staff can personalize all activities for you. All excursions are with professional and experienced guides. Chef takes special requests. Fine quality wines and beers are complimentary. All seafood is fresh caught wild Alaskan.
**Restrictions:** Sorry, no pets or handicap facilities
**Concierge:** Available 24/7
**Room Service:** On request
**Bar:** Complimentary wine and beer
**Business Facilities:** Phone, cell reception, WiFi
**Conference Room:** Yes. Lounge and dining for 18.
**Sports Facilities:** Help us haul, cut and split firewood.
**Spa Services:** Relax in private sauna & outdoor hot tub. Your personal hot tub and sauna await you. Massages upon advance request. Robes available.
**Airport:** Homer, Alaska
**Location:** Seaside facility surrounded by mountains, estuary and glaciers.

# THE HERMOSA INN

**Address:** 5532 North Palo Cristi Road, Scottsdale AZ 85253
**Phone:** 602-955-8614
**Tollfree:** 800-241-1210
**Fax:** 602-955-8299
**Email:** mgildersleeve@hermosainn.com
**Web:** www.hermosainn.com
**Room Rates:** 199–520
**Suite Rates:** 349–780
**No. of Rooms:** 34
**No. of Suites:** 4
**Credit Cards:** Most CCs Accepted
**Attractions:** Golfing and hiking, Desert Hummer Tours and Balloon tours. Multiple art galleries and shopping centers.
**Services:** In room fireplaces, secluded patios, antique pedestal tubs, Free High-speed wireless Internet, Jacuzzi, walk-in showers, skylights, flat panel TVs, vaulted ceilings.
**Restrictions:** A Non-Smoking Hotel, Pets excepted
**Concierge:** Front desk assistance
**Room Service:** Available 7am until 10pm
**Restaurant:** LON's has an organic garden just outside the kitchen that provides fresh food and training ground for the culinary team.
**Bar:** The Last Drop Bar
**Business Facilities:** Audio/visual support, High-speed Internet.
**Conference Room:** Indoor and Outdoor Facilities available.
**Sports Facilities:** Guest passes at nearby 24 Hour Fitness
**Spa Services:** An alluring menu of treatments featuring the Hermosa's signature citrus sage scent with a variety of custom massages, reflexology, ashiatsu, and a deep cleansing facial.
**Airport:** Phoenix Sky Harbor
**Location:** Desert

The Hermosa Inn offers the perfect Arizona vacation experience, ideal for relaxation, meetings, weddings, shopping, entertainment, dining and golf.

The Hermosa Inn features 34 hacienda-style, single-story accommodations on more than six acres of lush desert landscaping in view of famous Camelback Mountain. Lon's at The Hermosa is Arizona's only remaining authentic hacienda. Its elegant adobe dining room is surrounded by some of the most spectacular scenery Arizona has to offer.

Since the 1930s, The Hermosa Inn has been a recognized destination in the desert Southwest offering exclusive lodging accommodations in one of the city's most affluent suburbs, Paradise Valley. It is an ideal retreat for meetings, social gatherings (weddings, birthdays, and holidays) and , of course vacations!

Magargee, a native of Philadelphia, came West at the turn of the century. He earned his way as a cowboy, bronco buster, poker dealer and commercial artist and home builder. This is the place that Megargee created as a uniquely Southwestern home and that he dubbed "Casa Hermosa" which means Beautiful House. To supplement his art income he began running "Casa Hermosa" as a guest ranch. Though the inn has had several owners over the years it still retains the ambiance of the 1930s. It has even been said that Megargee, who passed away in 1960, still visits from time to time.

# EL PORTAL SEDONA HOTEL

From the breathtaking mountains, sky and earth to the serenity and intimate peacefulness they offer, from the historic haciendas and hospitality of eras gone by, to the warm, often unspoken, calm of the present, this spirit of Sedona, this spirit of timelessness and natural wonders which surround and fill us with a feeling of oneness. This spirit is the essence of El Portal Sedona Hotel, a luxury boutique hotel.

Going beyond the ordinary, the architecture and adobe construction of El Portal is completely authentic. Nowhere else in Sedona will you find a luxury inn or hotel, with 18-inch thick adobe walls, that provides both quiet and history. It's truly an architectural masterpiece.

Painstakingly, the finest builders of today have created this extraordinarily beautiful hacienda with a traditional center courtyard and fountain. All work was performed by hand and eye. As a result, the subtle, inviting sense of culture forms a wonderful link to the spirit of the past. Just as carefully, building materials were taken from nature wherever possible. This, too, forms a spiritual connection, a blending, if you will, with the earth. Watch magnificent sunrises through some of our windows framed in recycled 200-year-old wood. Experience the calm and peace that hand-sculptured walls and niches subtly offer. As with the architecture and construction, the interior design of each room is uniquely historical. Twelve spacious rooms have been created in accordance with the simplicity and function of turn-of-the-century architecture.

Guests aren't just handed a key at El Portal, the staff at El Portal offers a wealth of knowledge about all there is to see and do in Sedona and the surrounding area, and will sit down with guests every morning, get the maps out and get them started.

**Address:** 95 Portal Lane Sedona AZ 86336
**Phone:** 928-203-9405
**Tollfree:** 800-313-0017
**Fax:** 928-203-9401
**Email:** info@elportalsedona.com
**Web:** www.elportalsedona.com
**Suite Rates:** 199–459
**No. of Suites:** 12
**Credit Cards:** Most CCs Accepted
**Attractions**: Hiking, rafting, kayaking, wine tours, balloon rides, and jeep tours, an hour to the Grand Canyon.
**Services:** Each guest suite includes a private entrance, fireplace, whirlpool bath, entertainment center with DVD, WiFi; cashmere blankets, Egyptian cotton sheets & bath towels, down pillows & comforters.
**Restrictions:** Pets Welcome (no fees), Children Welcome, Smoke-Free Indoor Environment,
**Concierge:** Yes: Individualized Service
**Room Service:** Yes: Mornings until 10am
**Restaurant:** For a special dining experience, we recommend René at Tlaquepaque, offering classic French menu with Southwestern touches, comprehensive wine list.
**Bar:** Yes
**Business Facilities:** Free broadband cable high-speed Internet and free wireless.
**Conference Room:** Spacious Great Room
**Sports Facilities:** No: Accessibility (next door) to full gym
**Spa Services:** There is a spa next door with a hot tub, 2 saltwater pools and more. We can arrange an in room massage for you as well.
**Airport:** Phoenix Int'l Airport
**Location:** Located in the heart of Sedona

# BERNARDUS LODGE

**Address:** 415 Carmel Valley Road
Carmel CA 93924
**Phone:** 831-658-3400
**Tollfree:** 888-648-9463
**Fax:** 831-658-3584
**Email:** reservations@bernardus.com
**Web:** www.bernardus.com
**Room Rates:** 295–605
**Suite Rates:** 485–1,990
**No. of Rooms:** 57
**Credit Cards:** Most CCs Accepted
**Attractions:** Wine tasting and
antique shopping in Carmel Valley
Village, Mazda Laguna Seca
Raceway, Monterey Bay Aquarium,
Cannery Row, Carmel-by-the-Sea,
17-Mile Drive, Carmel Mission
Basilica, Point Lobos State Rese
**Services:** All rooms include a
stone fireplace, private deck,
double bathtub, Feather bed,
wine pantry, remote cable TV,
CD players, coffee makers, fresh
flowers, plush robes, hair dryers
and WiFi.
**Restrictions:** No Pets
**Concierge:** 24 hour service
**Room Service:** 7:00am–10:00pm
**Restaurant:** Marinus serves
Dinner Wed through Sun,
6:00pm to 10:00pm. Wickets
serves Breakfast daily, 7:00am to
10:30am, Lunch from 11:00am to
2:30pm, and Dinner from 2:30pm
to 10:00pm.
**Bar:** Wickets Bistro serves
cocktails 11:00am–Midnight
**Business Facilities:** high-speed
Internet and WiFi available in
guest rooms and public space.
**Conference Room:** 4 meeting
rooms.
**Sports Facilities:** Workout
Facility, Croquet, Bocce Ball,
Swimming Pool, Tennis Courts.
**Spa Services:** The Spa offers
7 treatment rooms and uses
indigenous herbs, flowers and
oils.
**Airport:** Monterey Peninsula
**Location:** Carmel Valley.

Nestled on twenty-two verdant acres with stately pines and California oak trees, surrounded by a vineyard and the Santa Lucia mountains rising majestically in the background, Bernardus Lodge is a premier luxury resort that combines the simple elegance of fine country living, with the high quality of service and luxury amenities found in only the choicest European hotels. Here, discriminating travelers experience the finest accommodations, cuisine, viticulture, spa services and recreational venues in a singular environment.

For your culinary experience, acclaimed chef, Cal Stamenov, has created cuisine that is distinctively California Natural and the menu is designed to take you on an exciting gastronomical journey that will tempt your palate and keep you wanting more. To accompany the culinary delights select something from wine list. Each year, since 2001, the *Wine Spectator* magazine has awarded the Marinus Restaurant their "Grand Award" for the generous, balanced wine list that was created to enhance the innovative California Natural Cuisine.

Carmel Valley enjoys moderately warm temperatures year round. Such fine weather allows for many outdoor activities such as golf, tennis, swimming or perhaps Croquet or Bocce Ball as well as discovering the local attractions which abound for all types of new experiences. At the end of a day, The Spa is a haven designed for pure indulgence and luxury pampering.

Experience life as you have never before!

# CARMEL MISSION INN

Breathtaking beaches, world-class golf courses, an endless variety of leisure and cultural activities and a wealth of unique shops are a primary part of the Monterey Bay experience. And there is no better way to experience a Monterey Bay retreat than to stay at the Carmel Mission Inn.

With our Carmel, CA hotel's quaint, yet stylish setting and array of gracious amenities that include a heated pool, fitness center and room service, we've truly created a destination within a destination. Additionally, we offer fantastic facilities for weddings, business meetings and special events.

First rate Carmel accommodations can make a good trip, a great one. From the soothing décor and plush furnishings to the unbelievable attractions and exhilarating activities just minutes away, our Carmel, California, hotel delivers the type of stay that makes a vacation feel complete.

Our property has recently undergone renovation with your comfort reigning as our utmost concern through every step of the transformation. The Carmel area is an unparalleled vacation destination, but we don't see why your vacation should stop when you come back to our hotel in the evening. We offer a number of amenities, from indulgent massage services, a heated pool and room service to the touches of home that include luxury bath amenities, a refrigerator and in-room coffeemaker. This is the lodging experience in Carmel, CA that you deserve.

**Address:** 3665 Rio Road Carmel CA 93923
**Phone:** 831-624-1841
**Tollfree:** 800-348-9090
**Fax:** 831-624-8684
**Email:** reservations@carmelmissioninn.com
**Web:** www.carmelmissioninn.com
**Room Rates:** 99–509
**Suite Rates:** 159–559
**No. of Rooms:** 165
**No. of Suites:** 2
**Credit Cards:** Most CCs Accepted
**Attractions**: The Monterey Bay area provides the perfect backdrop for your ideal vacation or business meeting—combining small town charm with the large scope of attractions, shopping spots and dining destinations of any big city.
**Services:** We offer a number of amenities, from indulgent massage services, a heated pool and room service to the touches of home that include luxury bath amenities, a refrigerator and in-room coffeemaker. We also offer free WiFi and complimentary parking.
**Restrictions:** Call ahead about restrictions regarding pets
**Concierge:** Front Desk Staff
**Room Service:** Yes
**Restaurant:** The restaurant/bar is roomy and open with bamboo flooring, stacked stone fireplace and columns, comfortable, over-sized chairs, a sleek mahogany bar, two large flat screen TVs and walls of windows.
**Bar:** Yes
**Business Facilities:** Services
**Conference Room:** Yes
**Sports Facilities:** Workout Room
**Spa Facilities:** Massages available
**Airport:** Monterey Peninsula
**Location:** Hwy 1 at Rio Road

# TICKLE PINK INN

**Address:** 155 Highland Drive
Carmel CA 93923
**Phone:** 831-624-1244
**Tollfree:** 800-635-4774
**Fax:** 831-626-9516
**Email:** mkurtow@ticklepink.com
**Web:** ticklepinkinn.com
**Room Rates:** 231–469
**Suite Rates:** 351–569
**No. of Rooms:** 35
**No. of Suites:** 12
**Credit Cards:** Most CCs Accepted
**Attractions**: Carmel and
Monterey Aquarium, hiking
trails, wine tasking, sightseeing,
Maritime museum, Monterey
Mission, Big Sur, golfing, whale
watching, motorcycle & car racing
**Services:** Wet bar, Fireplace,
Balcony, Whirlpool bath (some),
Robes, Cable TV, DVD and CD
players, Phones, Radios, Hot tubs,
ocean views, newspaper, 100%
Egyptian cotton bedding
**Restrictions:** No pets allowed,
Children not recommended,
Designated Smoking area
**Concierge:** Yes: available (daily)
8:00am–10:00pm
**Room Service:** Yes: available
(daily) 8:00am–10:00pm w/limited
menu
**Restaurant:** Our complimentary
continental breakfast is prepared
fresh each morning.
**Bar:** No: Wine & Cheese
reception 4:30pm–6pm (daily)
**Business Facilities:** Computer,
Printer, Presentation boards, Fax,
Audio-Visual
**Conference Room:** 1 room,
capacity 10
**Sports Facilities:** Outdoor hot
tub
**Spa Services:** Our staff will
assist you with an in-room
massage appointment or
recommendations to local full-
spa facilities.
**Airport:** Monterey Airport
**Location:** 4 miles south of
Carmel/Monterey airport

Established and operated by the Albert Gurries family, the
Tickle Pink Inn at Carmel Highlands has graced this setting high atop rugged cliffs, overlooking the untamed Pacific
Ocean and the lush Carmel Highlands, since 1956. The Inn
has a history and reputation that are founded on gracious
hospitality, personal service, indulgent comfort, and an attention to detail that is evident from the moment you arrive.

The Inn is intimate and private and offers the discriminating guest a variety of personal touches and extra amenities,
such as plush robes, slippers, fresh ground coffee service in
your room, and continental breakfast with fresh squeezed
orange juice and fresh pastries baked on the premises. The
guestrooms are tastefully decorated with traditional furnishings and European details orchestrated in a natural, eclectic
style. There are rough-hewn night tables, handcrafted armoires, stone fireplaces and the view from each room's private balcony is breathtaking!

With seating for up to ten people, the Terrace Board Room
provides all of the materials and services, including catering, computer and printer, slide and overhead projectors, flat
screen TV, DVD player, presentation boards, fax and copier,
essential to a successful and enjoyable private business
meeting.

A complimentary guest reception is held each evening in
the Terrace Lounge, featuring Monterey County wines and
an assortment of cheeses, breads, and fruits. Guests have
the opportunity to chat with the friendly staff, play a game of
chess, or just unwind in front of the fireplace and enjoy the
music.

The outdoor Cliffside Deck offers the perfect setting to
toast a beautiful lazy sunset as the day draws to an end.

# GOLDEN DOOR

Crossing a long, camellia-shaded wooden footbridge at the Golden Door, guests enter a serene, luxurious destination spa closely patterned after Japan's historic Honjin travelers' inns. Inside, one of the finest Japanese-style gardens in the world, the walkway weaves through the Golden Door's many sheltered courtyards, creating a sense of peace and beauty unmatched in the spa world.

Known for its complete attention to the needs of mind, body, and spirit, the small yet hugely famous "Door" cultivates an atmosphere of serenity and congeniality coupled with the most personalized instruction and service found in the spa world. Only 39 guests a week partake of fitness classes, hikes, beauty treatments, distinguished guest lecturers and class leaders, and world-class cuisine created by Golden Door's master chefs. Most of each meal's ingredients come direct from a 3-acre organic garden on the grounds. A full-time nutritionist gives advice and recommendations.

Primarily a women-only spa ("Founded by a woman for women"), the Golden Door makes an exception for men during five annual men-only weeks, as well as four annual coed weeks. All guests enjoy private single rooms, even during couples' weeks. Each generously sized accommodation becomes a peaceful, deeply comfortable retreat, complete with garden view and deck, flitting hummingbirds, and sumptuous furnishings. Guests receive a freshly laundered set of spa exercise wear daily, plus a beautiful flowered Japanese yukata (robe) suitable for wearing to meals and around the grounds.

The outside world seems far away from the 377-acre site with its many mountain trails. Guests choose from more than 80 different fitness classes and activities in a given week, and are encouraged to do as much or as little as they like during their stay.

**Address:** 777 Deer Springs Road, San Marcos, Escondido CA 92069
**Phone:** 760-744-5777
**Fax:** 760-471-2393
**Email:** reservations@goldendoor.com
**Web:** www.goldendoor.com
**Room Rates:** 7,995 per 7-day week
**No. of Rooms:** 39
**Credit Cards:** Most CCs Accepted
**Attractions:** Distinguished guest lecturers and class leaders.
**Services:** Valet service, boutique, library, laundry service, newspaper, CD player w/radio, hair dryer, makeup lights, complimentary skin care products, complete set of spa clothing daily. Complimentary transportation to and from the San Diego airport.
**Restrictions:** No pets allowed, not appropriate for children under 17
**Concierge:** Yes
**Room Service:** Available 6am–11pm
**Restaurant:** Award winning cuisine
**Bar:** No
**Business Facilities:** Limited
**Conference Facilities:** Limited
**Sports Facilities:** Tennis courts, 3 pools, 377 acres, 4 gyms (including weight training), yoga pavilion
**Spa Services:** Full-scale luxury spa, fitness classes, hikes, beauty treatments. Primarily a women-only spa but 5 annual men-only weeks, and 4 annual coed weeks.
**Airport:** San Diego
**Location:** Rural area; Guests are requested to remain on premises during their stay.

# CARTER HOUSE INNS & RESTAURANT 301

**Address:** 301 L Street
Eureka CA 95501
**Phone:** 707-444-8062
**Tollfree:** 800-404-1390
**Fax:** 707-444-8067
**Email:** reserve@carterhouse.com
**Web:** www.carterhouse.com
**Room Rates:** 159–250
**Suite Rates:** 309–615
**No. of Rooms:** 32
**No. of Suites:** 10
**Credit Cards:** Most CCs Accepted
**Attractions**: Fort Humboldt, Sequoia Park and Zoo, Old Town Eureka, Humboldt Bay harbor cruises, Humboldt Redwoods State Park, Avenue of the Giants, structures of historical interest, boutiques, art galleries, museums, antique shops
**Services:** Valet, Laundry, Baby-sitting service w/prior arrangements, Wine & Gift shop, Breakfast, Cable TV, DVD, Radio, Whirlpool baths, toiletries, wine, & hors d'oeuvres, Cookies & tea.
**Restrictions:** Pets allowed in some rooms; No smoking
**Concierge:** Availability from 7:00 a.m.-10:00 p.m. daily
**Room Service:** Yes during restaurant hrs: 7:30–10am & 6pm–9pm
**Restaurant:** Guests may order a la carte or enjoy chef's prix fixe menu, a memorable five course feast complete with wine pairings.
**Bar:** Yes—open daily from 5:00–10:00pm
**Business Facilities:** Message center, Copiers
**Conference Room:** 2 rooms, capacity 35 people
**Sports Facilities:** Privileges to Adorni Center (fee)
**Spa Services:** Massages can be booked; Whirlpools in some rooms; Jacuzzi in suites
**Airport:** Eureka/Arcada Airport
**Location:** Northern border of Old Town.

**B**uilt in 1986, the Hotel Carter is modeled after Eureka's Old Town Cairo Hotel. The Carter House is a renovated 1880s Victorian residence. The lobby of the brand-new Victorian Hotel Carter features unshaded windows, ceramic urns, oriental rugs, and antique pine furniture imported from England.

Rooms are decorated in a cocoa brown and ivory color scheme with bleached pine antiques. Original contemporary artwork and fresh flowers add a tasteful touch. The queen-size beds with comforters and overstuffed lounge chairs are reminiscent of a Victorian bed and breakfast, but these accommodations have all the modern conveniences: desks, telephones, clock-radios, and cable TV in the armoires. Spacious modern bathrooms are done in black and white tile. Many have whirlpool baths.

Each afternoon, guests enjoy complimentary wine and appetizers before a crackling fire in the lobby's marble fireplace.

The Hotel Carter is located at the gateway to Eureka's Old Town, with its charming brick-and-flower-lined streets, art galleries, antique shops, and boutiques. It is also only two blocks from Humboldt Bay and the Marina. Before sitting out in the morning to explore, be sure to savor the homemade muffins and tarts offered with the complimentary continental breakfast.

At the Hotel Carter's Restaurant 301, tables are formal, with white linens, fresh flowers, and crystal candlestick holders. Live music enhances the romantic ambiance and a large selection of fine regional wines if available.

Stay and explore the natural surroundings and history of Northern California.

ESH 563 25TH ED

# BENBOW HOTEL & RESORT

The historic Benbow Inn, built in 1926, is listed on the National Register of Historic Places. Its distinctive Tudor architecture and beautiful setting has intrigued travelers for over eight decades.

Completely renovated, all rooms are graced with antique furniture, fine prints, a basket of mystery novels and poetry, a decanter of sherry, coffee and teas. Each private bath has a basket of herbal soaps. All terrace rooms have private patios, antiques, televisions, WiFi, VCR's and CD players, some have fireplaces and one has a private Jacuzzi. The lobby and other common rooms are filled with antiques, paintings, needle-point and objets d'art—a perfect setting for reading, games, puzzles, and delicious afternoon tea and scones.

Our beautiful, romantic and elegant dining room, which offers fine cuisine and excellent wines, is light and airy with half timbering accents on white walls, Windsor chairs, fresh flowers and antique sideboards. French doors lead out to the terrace dining area where magnificent black oak trees shade lush flower and herb gardens. Our cozy lounge serves a full array of fine spirits, imported and domestic beers.

Open all year, The Benbow Inn is a special, luxurious destination for romance ... special occasions ... and it's also a perfect setting for weddings, meetings and executive retreats. Stroll along the river, go hiking, birding, fishing or cycling.

Located in the heart of the redwoods, The Benbow Inn's unique, enchanting atmosphere and gracious hospitality invites you to relax, renew, and savor life's pleasures.

**Address:** 445 Lake Benbow Drive Garberville CA 95542
**Phone:** 707-923-2124
**Tollfree:** 800-355-3301
**Fax:** 707-923-2879
**Email:** benbow@benbowinn.com
**Web:** www.benbowinn.com
**Room Rates:** 145–300
**Suite Rates:** 300–605
**No. of Rooms:** 54
**No. of Suites:** 3
**Credit Cards:** Most CCs Accepted
**Attractions**: Avenue of The Giants, Redwood State Parks, Victorian Village in Ferndale, Golf, Bicycling, Hiking, Birding, Winter Steelhead Fishing, Kayaking, Pacific Coast Beaches, Shelter Cove, Lost Coast and King Range; Nearby fitness and tennis club.
**Services:** Complimentary hors d'oeuvres in evening, afternoon tea & scones, decanter of sherry, herbal toiletries, newspaper, chocolate with turn down, WiFi, CD/Radio alarm clock, phone, hair dryer, iron and board
**Restrictions:** No Smoking.
**Concierge:** Front Desk—24hrs.
**Room Service:** No
**Restaurant:** Our Executive Chef, Kenneth Aldin, uses only the freshest herbs and locally grown produce and has created a fabulous menu.
**Bar:** Full Cocktail Service
**Business Facilities:** Fax, Message Center, and Copy Services. Conference & A/V Equipment.
**Conference Room:** 3 rooms. Capacity 35–140 people
**Sports Facilities:** Heated pool & spa, 9-Hole golf course.
**Spa Services:** Massage services available by appointment.
**Airport:** Eureka / Arcata Airport
**Location:** Benbow Valley borders the quiet town of Garberville.

# GROVELAND HOTEL AT YOSEMITE NATIONAL PARK

**Address:** 18767 Main Street
Groveland CA 95321
**Phone:** 209-962-4000
**Tollfree:** 800-273-3314
**Fax:** 209-962-6674
**Email:** info@groveland.com
**Web:** www.groveland.com
**Room Rates:** 145–285
**Suite Rates:** 235–285
**No. of Rooms:** 17
**No. of Suites:** 3
**Credit Cards:** Most CCs Accepted
**Attractions**: World-class river rafting on the Tuolumne River, hike and bike in the Stanislaus National Forest, cast a line in a multitude of rivers and streams.
**Services:** Dining available at hotel, high-speed Internet, phones with voice mail, coffee grinders and brewers, European antiques, and down comforters, extensive wine list.
**Restrictions:** Children and Pets Welcome! 4 rooms handicap accessible
**Concierge:** Yes—available from 7:00am until 11:00pm
**Room Service:** Yes—available daily: 8–11am & from 4–10pm
**Restaurant:** Menus feature organic seasonal ingredients. Dishes have subtle, unusual and delicious flavors.
**Bar:** Full bar in the restaurant.
**Business Facilities:** Copies, Faxes, Wireless Internet & some admin assistance
**Conference Room:** 1 room / 20 people
**Sports Facilities:** No
**Spa Services:** We offer a variety of experiences in the privacy of your room or with local professional therapists in their studios.
**Airport:** San Francisco, Oakland.
**Location:** Near Yosemite National Park

The Groveland Hotel is an ideal romantic Yosemite lodging getaway featuring 17 uniquely decorated rooms. Our Groveland B&B inn is the perfect place to stay for your Tuolumne River rafting expedition and Yosemite adventure. We are located on the most direct, scenic route to Yosemite National Park from the San Francisco Bay area on Highway 120. We are but a brief, awe-inspiring journey from Yosemite's year-round Northern entrance.

Our Groveland accommodations feature plush featherbeds, private baths, delicious California cuisine, a *Wine Spectator* award-winning wine list and a full-service saloon. Free WiFi Internet access in all rooms. We also offer free use of a computer for our guests.

Savor a lazy morning in the most luxurious featherbed you'll never want to get out of, snuggle into one of our cozy bathrobes, enjoy a cup of freshly brewed coffee on our veranda and permit a gracious staff member to indulge your every request. Each of our unique Victorian-style rooms includes a private bath, free wireless Internet access, telephone & voice mail, down comforters, European antiques, a coffee grinder & brewer, a CD player and an alarm clock.

Included with your room is a morning feast we nicknamed the Innkeeper's Breakfast. It's available to you from 7:30am to 10:00am, and it features a variety of fresh-baked goods, made to order egg dishes with bacon, sausage or ham, waffles, cereals, yogurt, freshly brewed coffee and tea, juices and fruits. Relish your Yosemite adventure and leave the details to us.

# APPLEWOOD INN SPA & FINE DINING

Located near Guerneville, California in Sonoma County's Russian River Valley, Applewood Inn Bed & Breakfast is on a knoll in the shelter of towering redwoods; this romantic inn has two distinct types of accommodations. Those in the original Belden House are comfortable but modest in scale. The 10 rooms in the newer buildings are larger and airier, decorated in sage green and terra-cotta tones that recall a Mediterranean villa. Whether you choose a comfortably cozy room in the inn's historic Belden House Mansion or a romantic fireplace room in the Piccola Casa & Gate House, you're sure to be pleased with your choice of accommodations here at Applewood Inn.

Life is meant to be enjoyed! Here at Applewood, we give you many ways to find relaxation and pleasure . . . from reading by the fire with a glass of wine, soaking up rays at the pool, easing tired muscles in a whirlpool tub or taking advantage of our many massage therapies. Applewood Inn offers world-class fine dining in their delightfully upscale restaurant. This Sonoma / Russian River Restaurant is highly regarded for its exquisite cuisine, soothing atmosphere, polished guest services, and its mellow earthy ambiance.

Applewood Inn is ideally located only minutes from the dramatic Sonoma Coast, the majestic old growth Redwoods of the Russian River Valley's Armstrong state park. Our knowledgeable staff can map out a special wine country itinerary just for you.

**Address:** 13555 Highway 116 Guerneville CA 95446
**Phone:** 707-869-9093
**Tollfree:** 800-555-8509
**Fax:** 707-869-9117
**Email:** relax@applewoodinn.com
**Web:** www.applewoodinn.com
**Room Rates:** 165-295
**Suite Rates:** 295-375
**No. of Rooms:** 19
**No. of Suites:** 10
**Credit Cards:** Most CCs Accepted
**Attractions:** Ancient redwoods, trail rides, California coastline, canoeing the Russian River, hot air balloon rides, golf, wineries, Fort Ross
**Services:** Outdoor hot tub, fine Italian linens & European down comforters, plush monogrammed robes, hair dryers, Cable TVs, phones, CD players/clock radios, WiFi internet access.
**Restrictions:** Non-smoking, max. 2 people per room
**Concierge:** (daily) 9am – 8pm
**Room Service:** No
**Restaurant:** Fine dining, upscale atmosphere. Blending French Cuisine with California sensibilities. Open seasonally (11/15-4/30: Thurs–Sun) & (5/1-11/14: Tues–Sun)
**Bar:** Yes: local wines/beer - located in the restaurant/ 5:30pm – Closing (daily)
**Business Facilities:** Computer, fax, copies, WiFi, high speed internet
**Conference Room:** 1 room / capacity: up to 20 people
**Sports Facilities:** Swimming pool
**Spa Services:** Spa services by appointment.
**Airport:** San Francisco Int'l
**Location:** The Russian River

# MADRONA MANOR WINE COUNTRY INN & RESTAURANT

**Address:** 1001 Westside Road
Healdsburg CA 95448
**Phone:** 707-433-4231
**Tollfree:** 800-258-4003
**Fax:** 707-433-0703
**Email:** info@madronamanor.com
**Web:** www.madronamanor.com
**Room Rates:** 265–485
**Suite Rates:** 290–625
**No. of Rooms:** 22
**No. of Suites:** 5
**Credit Cards:** Most CCs Accepted
**Attractions**: Shopping and dining in historic downtown, local Plaza with seasonal music and farmers market, wine festivals, world class cycling, California Redwoods, 150 local wineries.
**Services:** Buffet breakfast, individual climate controls, fireplaces, balconies, Aveda toiletries, Frette linens, pillow-top mattresses, private bathrooms, high-speed Internet access.
**Restrictions:** No pets, Children over 12 are welcome. No smoking indoors
**Concierge:** Yes: available (daily) from 8:00am–5:00pm
**Room Service:** No
**Restaurant:** Inventive cuisine, a stunning backdrop and impeccable service.
**Bar:** Yes: open (Wed—Sunday) 6:00pm–11:00pm
**Business Facilities:** Copier, Fax, Administrative Assistance, Audio-visual by prearrangement
**Conference Room:** 3 rooms / capacity up to 14 people
**Sports Facilities:** Outdoor heated swimming pool (open May thru Oct)
**Spa Services:** Professional massage therapists. Advance arrangement needed.
**Airport:** San Francisco & Oakland
**Location:** Sonoma wine country.

Planning a drive through the Sonoma County wine country? Madrona Manor, located in Healdsburg, is a must.

Built in the 1880s by a wealthy San Franciscan, and fully restored a century later, Madrona Manor achieved National Historic Registry status in 1987. In 2007 *Travel & Leisure* recognized Madrona Manor as one of the top 10 hotels in the Continental US and Canada, and again in 2008 as one of the top 100 Worldwide.

Eight elegant rooms are located in the Carriage House. The two luxurious School House Suites each have a Jacuzzi tub for two and the remaining five suites, on this eight acre romantic hideaway all feature fireplaces and separate sitting rooms. All the accommodations are uniquely furnished with Victorian antiques. All have private baths. No televisions interrupt the secluded peace of this retreat. The pleasures are those of earlier times: fresh flowers from the garden, freshly baked cookies in every room, and a vast kitchen garden which supplies the restaurant with fresh herbs, fruits and vegetables throughout the year.

Aah, how those Victorians did enjoy meals! Breakfast at the Manor is a bountiful style buffet. Dinner offers a choice of a la carte, Chef tasting menu of 7 courses, or the option to build your own 3, 4 or 5 course menu. Well orchestrated wine pairings are available with each course.

Come join us at the Madrona Manor Wine Country Inn & Restaurant. A visit here is an elegant step back in time!

# BED & BREAKFAST INN AT LA JOLLA

This romantic, historic inn voted "San Diego's Best" has been showcased in the *Los Angeles Times, Sunset Magazine, Travel and Leisure, New York Times, Glamour Magazine, Cooking Light* and *Country Inns.*

The inn abounds in priceless antiques. Hardwood floors with one of a kind Oriental and European area rugs and original works of art and antique prints add to the luxurious decor and European ambiance. Designed by the Cubist" architect Irving Gill in 1913 and home to the John Philip Sousa family in the 1920s, the inn exudes European charm with wood burning fireplaces in some of the select rooms. Some rooms have an ocean view.

Bask in the sun on the bougainvillea draped, second floor patio or make your way to the garden.

Take a leisurely stroll along the beach and explore the wonders of the tide pools. You may order a picnic basket for two and enjoy a romantic evening watching the sun set from the La Jolla cliffs.

.... Or, just relax with a cup of tea and a good book in the light and airy library. There are fresh flowers throughout the inn to embrace the senses; fresh fruit and fine sherry to soothe a weary body; and the beauty of the nearby sea to heal the soul.

So take a break from the ordinary and experience a more relaxing and gracious style of travel. Enjoy being our guest.

**Address:** 7753 Draper Avenue La Jolla CA 92037
**Phone:** 858-456-2066
**Tollfree:** 888-988-8481
**Fax:** 858-456-1510
**Email:** bedandbreakfast@innlajolla.com
**Web:** www.innlajolla.com
**Room Rates:** 199–339
**Suite Rates:** 369–469
**No. of Rooms:** 15
**No. of Suites:** 2
**Credit Cards:** Most CCs Accepted
**Attractions**: Enjoy the Stephen Birch Aquarium, Sea World, San Diego Zoo, Sea Port Village, Balboa Park, LegoLand, Wild Animal Park, Old Town, Gas Lamp District Downtown, Mexico, Wineries in North County, the Del Mar racetrack, Whale Watching.
**Services:** Limited Free parking/ Compacts only. Car hire, Beauty shop, House doctor, fireplaces, balconies, and Cable TV. in select rooms. Wireless Internet. Phones/ data ports, Robes, Hair dryers, Complimentary toiletries
**Restrictions:** Pets accepted with restrictions. Not for children under 12.
**Concierge:** Yes: 7 – 8pm (daily)
**Room Service:** No
**Restaurant:** No, but an afternoon reception is enjoyed daily, fresh fruit and sweet treats are available throughout the day.
**Bar:** No: (daily) Wine & Cheese Reception
**Business Facilities:** Fax and copier, WiFi, Computer accessible
**Conference Room:** 3 rooms space—up to 10 people
**Sports Facilities:** No on site gym or workout room
**Spa Services:** Arrangements can be made at a number of California's finest day spas.
**Airport:** San Diego Int'l Airport
**Location:** One block from the beach.

# GRANDE COLONIAL HOTEL LA JOLLA

**Address:** 910 Prospect Street La Jolla CA 92037
**Phone:** 858-454-2181
**Tollfree:** 888-530-5393
**Fax:** 858-454-5679
**Email:** info@gclj.com
**Web:** www.gclj.com
**Room Rates:** 255–500
**Suite Rates:** 259–1,500
**No. of Rooms:** 52
**No. of Suites:** 41
**Credit Cards:** Most CCs Accepted
**Attractions**: Miles of beaches and an abundance of watersport activities, shopping, dining, museums and galleries. San Diego's visitor attractions within 15-30 minutes from hotel.
**Services:** 32" LCD Televisions, Complimentary Bottled Water & refreshments, High-Speed Wired & Wireless Internet Goose down beds & pillows/ KashwTre Bathrobes/Twice Daily Housekeeping/iPod Docking/radio & stereo/Kitchens or Kitchenettes
**Concierge:** Yes: available (daily) 9:00am–5:00pm
**Room Service:** Yes: provided by NINE-TEN from 6am–11pm
**Restaurant:** The award-winning NINE-TEN's.
**Bar:** Yes: located in NINE-TEN from 6am–11pm
**Business Facilities:** Limited: computer, fax, copies, WiFi & high-speed Internet
**Conference Room:** 6 areas / capacity: up to 120 people
**Sports Facilities:** Swimming Pool
**Spa Services:** Spa services are available at world-class spas within walking distance.
**Airport:** San Diego Int'l Airport
**Location:** 1 Block from Ocean in the Village of La Jolla

Situated in the seaside Village of La Jolla and commanding views of the California coastline, the Four Diamond Grande Colonial offers classic European styling in the intimate setting of a boutique hotel.

The hotel boasts 93 guestrooms and suites (18 of which are extended-stay suites with full kitchens), all non-smoking and featuring iPod docking clock-radios, 32" LCD TVs, Kashware bathrobes, complimentary bottled water, free high-speed wired and wireless Internet access, daily newspaper and comfortable bed with goose-down comforter and pillows. Comfortable furnishings, enhanced and contemporary amenities and artwork reflect La Jolla's priceless ocean views.

The hotel's award-winning, Zagat-rated restaurant, NINE-TEN, regularly receives rave reviews for its market-based menu. Breakfast and lunch are served daily and dinner is served nightly. Seating is available indoors or al fresco on the sidewalk patio or ocean-view terrace.

With its ideal location, gracious service and environment of extraordinary comfort, the Grande Colonial provides the ideal destination for vacation or business travelers to San Diego.

# THE GRAFTON ON SUNSET

Arouse your senses at this sleek, modern hotel located on the legendary Sunset Strip. Relax by the Mediterranean garden & salt water pool or enjoy our seductive lounge & restaurant—renowned for its exquisite cuisine. Party like a rock star at night or sleep in during the day at one of West Hollywood's premier boutique hotels.

Fueled by the electricity of the legendary Sunset Strip and all of LA's beauties, the Grafton on Sunset is in the heart of West Hollywood's perpetual buzz. Just a hop, skip, and a jump from the hottest restaurants, studios, events and nightlife, our unique boutique hotel accommodations are a haven for Hollywood hipsters. Boasting 102 spacious guestrooms and six ultra-glam guest suites, The Grafton has spread its lavishness over four expansive floors. Each of the guest accommodations has been specially designed with ergonomic furnishings and luxury amenities to ease guests into a blissful state of mind.

At the Grafton, service is our hallmark and hospitality our commitment. Whether you are seeking a stylish suite for your business trip to the nearby Hollywood studios, or an enviable Sunset Blvd. locale to accompany your Los Angeles vacation, the Grafton on Sunset is your tranquil hideaway in the center of pure star studded radiance. We look forward to welcoming you to West Hollywood. And you'll look forward to coming back.

**Address:** 8462 West Sunset Blvd Los Angeles CA 90069
**Phone:** 323-654-4600
**Tollfree:** 800-821-3660
**Fax:** 323-654-5918
**Email:** sfarias@outrigger.net
**Web:** www.graftononsunset.com
**Room Rates:** 199–499
**Suite Rates:** 350 -650
**No. of Rooms:** 104
**No. of Suites:** 4
**Credit Cards:** Most CCs Accepted
**Attractions**: Trendy restaurants, bars, clubs & tourist attractions, positioned between Beverly Hills and world-renowned Hollywood.
**Services:** Italian linens, feather top mattress, organic/Eco-friendly bath products, bathrobes, spacious ergonomic writing desk, 37" LCD flat-screen plasma TV, DVD & VCR, on-demand movies, CD stereo player, iPod docking.
**Restrictions:** Pet Friendly, Children Welcome, Smoking rooms available
**Concierge:** Yes: available 24/7
**Room Service:** Yes: available (daily) from 7:30am–Midnight/ varies
**Restaurant:** Olive at Grafton on Sunset- Open Friday & Saturday from 7:30am–11:00pm. Sunday-through Thursday from 7:30am–10:30pm. Cali-Italian cuisine.
**Bar:** Yes: 5pm – closing
**Business Facilities:** Full Business Center/ accessible 24/7
**Conference Room:** 1 room / capacity: up to 15 people
**Sports Facilities:** Yes: Full fitness room / available 24/7
**Spa Services:** Our concierge will assist you with recommendations.
**Airport:** Burbank or Los Angeles Int'l Airports
**Location:** On Sunset Strip in West Hollywood

# THE STANFORD INN BY THE SEA

**Address:** 44850 Comptche Ukiah Road, Mendocino CA 95460
**Phone:** 707-937-5615
**Tollfree:** 800-331-8884
**Fax:** 707-937-0305
**Email:** info@stanfordinn.com
**Web:** www.stanfordinn.com
**Room Rates:** 198–288
**Suite Rates:** 228–526
**No. of Rooms:** 41
**No. of Suites:** 10
**Credit Cards:** Most CCs Accepted
**Attractions**: The Mendocino Art Center classes and galleries. Hike or mountain bike State Parks. Canoe or kayak Big River. Certified Organic Big River Nursery.
**Services:** Parking lot, game area, laundry, exercise room, TVs VCR, DVD players, CD player, radio, fireplaces, balconies, refrigerators, coffee makers & gourmet coffee, complimentary toiletries, wireless Internet.
**Restrictions:** Pets & Children Friendly!
**Concierge:** Yes: available (daily) 7:30 am–11:00pm
**Room Service:** Yes: available during breakfast and dinner hrs
**Restaurant:** The Ravens, breakfast — 7:30–11:00am and dinner— 5:30–9:00pm.
**Bar:** Yes: full bar in restaurant w/ Award winning wine list
**Business Facilities:** Message center: Computers, Admin assist, Copiers, Audio-visual, Teleconferencing
**Conference Room:** 3 rooms / capacity: up to 100 people
**Sports Facilities:** Indoor pool, whirlpool, sauna, and workout room
**Spa Services:** Massage and yoga lessons are offered guests at Massage in the Forest.
**Airport:** San Francisco, Oakland, and Sacramento Airports
**Location:** South of Mendocino's historic district

Nothing is left to chance at the Stanford Inn By The Sea! You are welcomed with chocolates, cold drinks in your room's refrigerator and the inn's own blend of organic coffee ready to brew. A compact stereo/CD system plays classical music, while the VCR and DVD players awaits a recent release from the inn's library. Traditional and antique furnishing grace rooms which feature luxurious bedding and the amenities found in the most expensive of luxury hotels. A fireplace laid with real wood enhances the romantic ambiance.

Breakfast is included with your stay and is served in the inn's dining room cooked to order from organic ingredients. And for the pet owner, pets are welcomed! There are areas to walk with your faithful friend and a special seating area in the lobby is available to owners and their dogs during breakfast or dinner. The staff provides treats, food and water bowls, blankets to protect furniture, and even pet beds should you require them.

If you have never tried yoga, you might sign up for classes. The inn's Massage in the Forest offers bodywork in Esalen, Shiatsu, Thai and other techniques. You can canoe or kayak, or take a mountain bike and explore coastal trails and back-roads. After a day's exploring, join other guests in the expansive lobby for a complimentary selection of cheeses and hors d'oeuvres. An outstanding selection of wines by the glass is also available. Dinner at The Ravens features vegetarian and vegan cuisine and has received national acclaim. The menu is inspired by the Stanford's California Certified Organic Farm.

At the days end retire to your room where each of the Stanford's wood-paneled rooms has French doors leading to a deck from which to enjoy the sunset over the Pacific.

# HOTEL PACIFIC

Hotel Pacific is a boutique hotel conveniently located in downtown Monterey, California just steps away from the Monterey Conference Center and a few minutes from the Monterey Bay Aquarium and other top area attractions. Hotel Pacific offers luxury all-suite accommodations with fireplaces, complimentary continental breakfast and afternoon refreshments, luxurious feather bedding, and unique vacation packages. Hotel Pacific is the perfect hotel choice for your next romantic weekend getaway, vacation or business trip to the Monterey Bay area.

Hotel Pacific is located just minutes away from the spectacular Monterey Bay Aquarium, Cannery Row, Monterey's best beaches, and other top area attractions. Our inviting boutique hotel offers a distinctive lodging experience combined with a convenient location for memorable vacations and weekend getaways on the Monterey Bay.

**Address:** 300 Pacific Street Monterey CA 93940
**Phone:** 831-373-5700
**Tollfree:** 800-554-5542
**Fax:** 831-373-6921
**Email:** reservations@hotelpacific.com
**Web:** www.hotelpacific.com
**Suite Rates:** 159–499
**No. of Suites:** 105
**Credit Cards:** Most CCs Accepted
**Attractions:** Old Fisherman's Wharf, Cannery Row, Monterey Bay Aquarium, Maritime Museum of Monterey, Monterey Museum of Art, Laguna Seca Raceway, Pacific Grove Monarch Sanctuary, 17 Mile Drive, Carmel Mission, Pebble Beach Golf Courses
**Services:** All suite hotel with spacious, luxury bathrooms; Gas fireplaces; Featherbeds; Private patios or balconies; Covered parking (fee).
**Restrictions:** No pets allowed. No Smoking.
**Concierge:** Yes—front desk, 24/7
**Room Service:** Available from 11:00am–10:00pm (daily)
**Restaurant:** Complimentary deluxe continental breakfast and afternoon tea service served daily in our Salon.
**Bar:** No
**Business Facilities:** Business Center w/faxing, copying services available at front desk
**Conference Room:** 3 rooms—capacity: up to 72 people.
**Sports Facilities:** No
**Spa Services:** Our hotel staff will be happy to assist you with an "in room" spa appointment.
**Airport:** Monterey Peninsula
**Location:** Historic downtown Monterey

Stay in one of 105 all-suite rooms, and enjoy an intimate hide-away in the heart of downtown Monterey. The authentic Spanish style adobe hotel offers lush private gardens, balcony and patio rooms, double, queen or king beds, down feather bedding, fireplaces, complimentary continental breakfast and afternoon refreshments. Enjoy friendly service, a relaxing atmosphere and convenient downtown location when you choose Hotel Pacific.

# MONTEREY BAY INN

**Address:** 242 Cannery Row
Monterey CA 93940
**Phone:** 831-373-6242
**Tollfree:** 800-424-6242
**Fax:** 831-373-7603
**Email:** reservations@innsofmonterey.com
**Web:** www.montereybayinn.com
**Room Rates:** 229–339
**No. of Rooms:** 49
**No. of Suites:** 0
**Credit Cards:** Most CCs Accepted
**Attractions**: Monterey Bay
Aquarium, Cannery Row,
Monterey Conference Center,
Carmel galleries and shopping,
Carmel Mission Basilica,
Fisherman's Wharf, Golf, Whale
watching, Kayaking, SCUBA
diving, Wine tasting, Laguna Seca
Raceway
**Services:** Plush feather beds and
pillows, Aveda bath products,
DVD players with a new 27" TVs,
locally inspired DVD's, stereo
CD players, cordless telephones,
laptop computer safes, wireless
Internet, and evening turn down
service, self parking $13 per day.
**Restrictions:** No pets allowed,
2 night minimum stay on most
weekends
**Concierge:** Yes: Available 24/7
**Room Service:** Yes: available
(daily) from 11am–10pm
**Restaurant:** Our sister restaurant,
the Sardine Factory.
**Bar:** No
**Business Facilities:** Wireless
Internet, voicemail, copy, fax
**Conference Room:** 1 room /
capacity up to 18 people
**Sports Facilities:** No
**Spa Services:** Indulge in a
relaxing spa service in our
Serenity Spa or a massage in the
comfort of your own guest room.
The rooftop, bay-view hot tub is
the perfect hideaway.
**Airport:** Monterey Airport & San
Jose Int'l Airport
**Location:** On the water at the
quiet end of historic Cannery Row.

Set in one of Northern California's most scenic locations, the Monterey Bay Inn is a luxurious retreat where the newly remodeled guestrooms and lobby take their design from the natural beauty of the Monterey Bay Marine Sanctuary. Here guests will enjoy nature's splendor in one of the world's richest marine regions.

The Monterey Bay Inn's forty-seven guestrooms feature plush king feather beds with elegant 310 thread-count Pima cotton bed linens for an extra touch of luxury. Spacious bathrooms provide sophisticated comfort, with fine linens, marble floors, double lavatory granite vanities, Aveda bath products, make-up mirrors, and handheld hair dryers.

Your private balcony provides the perfect setting to experience the invigorating ocean air and enjoy a complimentary continental breakfast for two which is served to your room, presented on a beautiful tray with fine china and linens. Complimentary fresh-baked cookies are also served each afternoon in the lobby. Other conveniences include two Cuisinart coffee pots per room with Café Novo coffee, DVD players with a new 27" Phillips televisions, stereo CD players, iron and ironing boards, laptop computer safes, and wireless Internet connection.

A short stroll down Cannery Row finds you at the Monterey Bay Aquarium, in the midst of lively restaurants, eclectic shops and a variety of recreational activities. Guest will enjoy our sister restaurant, The Sardine Factory, Monterey's premier seafood restaurant and lounge.

This unforgettable oceanfront environment and convenient location provide the ultimate escape.

# OLD MONTEREY INN

The Old Monterey Inn Bed and Breakfast of Monterey, CA, is a historic, boutique hotel bed and breakfast inn which boasts luxurious rooms and suites perfect for travelers headed to the Monterey Peninsula, Carmel and those seeking bed and breakfast accommodations near Pacific Grove and Big Sur.

Recently featured on The Today Show as a romantic rendezvous destination loved by the editors of *Travel and Leisure* Magazine and set in a beautiful garden, this 4-Diamond AAA rated Monterey bed and breakfast was recently awarded a position on the coveted *Condé Nast Traveler* Reader's Choice Gold List and is a popular choice for those seeking a romantic honeymoon destination or a Monterey vacation.

Each room at Old Monterey Inn offers a private bath and relaxing sitting area. Many have wood-burning fireplaces, stained glass windows and skylights. Thoughtful details abound: plush featherbeds and down duvets with superb quality linens, soft terry lined robes along with perfumed bath salts, thick towels, current magazines and candles.

Golfers will enjoy this Monterey bed and breakfast inn's proximity to some of the best golf courses in the world. For the rest of us there are beaches to explore, wineries to visit, tennis courts, hiking and bike trails and a luxurious spa to relax away your cares before enjoying some of the local dining and theaters.

**Address:** 500 Martin Street Monterey CA 93940
**Phone:** 831-375-8284
**Tollfree:** 800-350-2344
**Fax:** 831-375-6730
**Email:** omi@oldmontereyinn.com
**Web:** www.oldmontereyinn.com
**Room Rates:** 250–330
**Suite Rates:** 365–430
**No. of Rooms:** 10
**No. of Suites:** 4
**Credit Cards:** Most CCs Accepted
**Attractions**: Monterey Bay Aquarium, Monterey's Wharf, Monterey State Park, Monterey Museum of Art, Adventures by the Sea, Monterey Sports Center, Pebble Beach, Pacific Grove, Big Sur, Ano Nuevo & Elkhorn Slough Reserves, Forest (outdoor)& Golden Bough Theaters
**Services:** Rooms have private bath and sitting area, some wood-burning fireplaces, stained glass windows and skylights, plush featherbeds and down duvets with quality linens, terry lined robes, bath salts, thick towels, current magazines.
**Restrictions:** No Smoking, Minimum stay requirements.
**Concierge:** Yes: available 8–8.
**Room Service:** Limited: Champage, chocolate & roses by request
**Restaurant:** We always have a current list of "Guest Restaurant Favorites" available.
**Bar:** No: Wine & Cheese reception (daily) 4–6pm
**Business Facilities:** Yes: computer, fax, copies, WiFi & high-speed Internet
**Conference Room:** No
**Sports Facilities:** No
**Spa Services:** Treatments from 10am to 6pm in our SpaRetreat Salon. Appointments are necessary.
**Airport:** Monterey Airport & San Jose Int'l Airport
**Location:** California coast

# SPINDRIFT INN

**Address:** 652 Cannery Row
Monterey CA 93940
**Phone:** 831-646-8900
**Tollfree:** 800-841-1879
**Fax:** 831-646-5342
**Email:** reservations@innsofmonterey.com
**Web:** www.spindriftinn.com
**Room Rates:** 239–449
**No. of Rooms:** 45
**Credit Cards:** Most CCs Accepted
**Attractions**: Monterey Bay
Aquarium, Fisherman's Wharf,
Cannery Row, Carmel, Carmel
Mission Basilica, National
Steinbeck Center, Big Sur, whale
watching excursions, local
galleries and shops
**Services:** Valet parking ($16),
dry cleaning/laundry, turn
down service, complimentary
continental breakfast w/
newspaper, afternoon wine &
cheese reception, large TV, DVD,
radio, CD players, honor bar,
fireplace, phone in bath, robes,
Aveda bath products
**Restrictions:** No pets allowed.
2 rooms handicapped access.
2 night minimum on most
weekends.
**Concierge:** Available 24/7
**Room Service:** Yes: Available
11:00am–10:00pm (daily)
**Restaurant:** The Sardine Factory
is only a short, scenic, walk away.
**Bar:** No
**Business Facilities:** Copier, Fax,
Computer usage
**Conference Room:** No
**Sports Facilities:** No on-site gym
or workout room
**Spa Services:** To sooth the mind
and body, indulge in a relaxing
spa service in our Serenity Spa or
a massage in the comfort of your
own guest room.
**Airport:** Monterey Airport & San
Jose Int'l Airport
**Location:** Historic Cannery Row,
1 mile from downtown

In 1927 the Ocean View Hotel, then the only hotel on
Monterey Bay, opened as an ornate and opulent contender
for the San Francisco carriage trade.

In later years, as the area's fishing and canning industry
flourished, the grand hotel deteriorated to a shadow of its
former splendor. The once exclusive "Ocean View Avenue" was
renamed "Cannery Row." As the fishing industry declined in
the 1970s and the last operating cannery was converted into
an aquarium, the area known as "Cannery Row" underwent
major restoration and redevelopment as an historic district. In
1985 the original Ocean View Hotel was given a new name—
the Spindrift Inn and reopened its doors, after renovation,
as an intimate 42-room luxury hotel surpassing even its own
past glory!

The hotel is located directly on the beach, in the heart of
Cannery Row and only two blocks from the Monterey Bay
Aquarium. The lobby is a four-story atrium focusing on a fireplace flanked by large candelabras. A 20 × 30-foot sculpture in
22-karat gold leaf is mounted above the lobby on the atrium
wall.

Each romantic guestroom features a wood-burning fireplace, down comforters and pillows, draped or canopied
feather beds, oriental carpets over hardwood floors, and built-
in armoires. Baths are done in marble with brass fixtures and
handcrafted tile floors. Many of the rooms have spectacular
ocean views. A silver tray with a continental breakfast is delivered each morning to your room. In the Lobby—afternoon
tea, wine and cheese are served daily.

Come experience luxury!

# CHURCHILL MANOR
# BED & BREAKFAST

This grand 3-story mansion was built in 1889 and was the first Napa residence listed on the National Historic Registry. Surrounded by an extensive covered veranda and flanked by large white columns, the building rests amid a private-enclosed acre of beautiful trees, expansive lawns and lush gardens. As visitors pass through the massive, beveled-glass doors, they step back in time to a less hurried way of life. The first floor boasts four large parlors, each with a fireplace and magnificently carved redwood moldings and a solarium with an original mosaic floor of over 60,000 marble tiles. The mansion has been refurbished and is furnished with fine European antiques, oriental rugs, brass and crystal chandeliers, and a grand piano in the music room.

All 10 guestrooms are individually and uniquely decorated. The Stags Leap room is the original owner's master bedroom and features a magnificent antique French matching 7-piece bedroom set of carved walnut and marble and ample comfortable seating for relaxing. It also features original gold-leaf bathroom and fireplace tiles, a giant bathtub mounted on a mahogany pedestal, a two-person tiled shower, and the original pedestal sink.

A complimentary, bountiful breakfast including homemade muffins, nut breads, croissants, a fruit course, and daily changing sweet and savory entrees, is served each morning. Each afternoon there are freshly baked cookies. Coffee and tea are available all day long. Each evening there is a two-hour Napa Valley varietal wine-and-appetizer reception.

Churchill Manor is an ideal place for a romantic wedding or reception for any festive occasion. The inn hosts weddings each year with in-house catering, equipment and coordination. Croquet and tandem bicycles are provided complimentary to guests to enhance the Victorian charm of a stay at Churchill Manor.

**Address:** 485 Brown Street Napa CA 94559
**Phone:** 707-253-7733
**Tollfree:** 800 799-7733
**Fax:** 707-253-8836
**Email:** be@churchillmanor.com
**Web:** www.churchillmanor.com
**Room Rates:** 165–335
**No. of Rooms:** 10
**Credit Cards:** Most CCs Accepted
**Attractions**: Hot-air ballooning, mud baths, day spas, art galleries, restaurants, shopping, horseback riding, Napa Valley Wine Train, Napa Valley Opera House, Lincoln Theater, hiking, bicycling, walking tour, golf
**Services:** TV lounge, card/game area with movies, music room with grand piano, sun room, covered wrap-around veranda, fireplaces, private baths with showers and clawfoot tubs, radio, telephones, free WiFi, parking
**Restrictions:** No pets, 1 room accommodates disability, 2 night minimum for Saturday, Children by prior arrangement.
**Concierge:** Yes: available (daily) 9:00am–9:00pm
**Room Service:** No
**Restaurant:** The three course gourmet breakfast is served 8:30 to 10:00 a.m., and lunch or dinner for groups by prior arrangement.
**Bar:** No: Wine & Cheese reception (daily) from 5:30–7:30pm
**Business Facilities:** Limited: fax, copier, WiFi
**Conference Room:** 1 room / capacity: up to 45 people
**Sports Facilities:** Complimentary guest pass to nearby health club
**Spa Services:** We can arrange for Swedish or deep tissue massages to be given in the privacy of your guest room.
**Airport:** San Francisco, Oakland, Sacramento Airports
**Location:** Old Town Napa

# SEVEN GABLES INN

**Address:** 555 Ocean View Blvd
Pacific Grove CA 93950
**Phone:** 831-372-4341
**Fax:** 831-372-0150
**Email:** reservations@pginns.com
**Web:** www.thesevengablesinn.com
**Room Rates:** 209–369
**Suite Rates:** 499–729
**No. of Rooms:** 25
**No. of Suites:** 2
**Credit Cards:** Visa, MC, Amex
**Attractions**: 17-Mile Drive,
Cannery Row & the Monterey Bay
Aquarium, Carmel-by-the-Sea,
Point Lobos and Big Sur, World
Famous Golf Courses including
Pebble Beach, Old Fisherman's
Wharf, Whale Watching,
Lighthouse Tours, Wine Tasting &
Winery Tours, Historic Adob
**Services:** Rates include a
bountiful breakfast, afternoon
wine and cheese, evening turn
down service, evening milk and
cookies. Complimentary high-
speed wireless Internet included.
**Restrictions:** Non smoking, No
pets, 1 handicap accessible room
**Concierge:** 8am–10pm daily
**Room Service:** Yes—Wine and
champagne & Chocolates (no
food) 8- 10 pm
**Restaurant:** All Staff are happy
to assist with dinner suggestions
and/or reservation.
**Bar:** No
**Business Facilities:** Limited—
fax, copier, high-speed Internet
**Conference Room:** 1 room —
capacity: up to 30 people.
**Sports Facilities:** No
**Spa Services:** In-room massages
can be arranged with advance
notice. There are several full-
service day spas located within
minutes of the Seven Gables Inn.
**Airport:** Monterey Airport & San
Jose Int'l Airport
**Location:** On the very edge of
Monterey Bay

It's hard to imagine a more picturesque and romantic location than that of Seven Gables. The waves crashing along
the rocky shoreline, the sea otters frolicking just offshore,
the whales spouting, the surrounding mountains lit up by the
sunset ... these are the images seen from each guestroom of
this century old Inn.

Such natural beauty is complimented on the inside by a
wonderful collection of comfortable furnishings. A bountiful
breakfast, enjoyable afternoon wine and cheese, outstanding
guest service and the comfort of all private baths combine to
make Seven Gables truly one of the most outstanding inns in
California.

Seven Gables Inn is personally managed by the Flatley family. Open since 1982, the Seven Gables Inn has consistently
maintained a high level of customer service to ensure each
romantic holiday is one that will be remembered.

Relax, kick off your shoes, and smell the salty ocean air.
Walk along the beach and let the sound of crashing waves
cleanse your mind. Enter a timeless world as you bask in the
serenity of colorful, fragrant gardens surrounding our Pacific
Grove, California, luxury inn hotel. Let your senses reawaken
as you slow down and experience nature: joyful bird songs,
a gentle breeze in your hair, waves lapping against your bare
feet. Unlike many hotels, Seven Gables Inn boutique hotel
on the Monterey Bay Coast has the intimacy and slower pace
that you crave

# POSH PALM SPRINGS INN

**W**elcome to the desert's newest luxury boutique Inn, where the true meaning of POSH is experienced from the moment you arrive.

In days gone by affluent passengers of the most renowned steamships would often request a POSH suite onboard — POSH meaning "Portside Out and Starboard Home." The reason for the request was to be assured of following the sun for the entire voyage. Now you too can experience your own POSH vacation right here in the beautiful desert of Palm Springs, CA, where the sun shines 365 days a year.

Come and experience the ultimate in customer service, be it our 24/7 Concierge Service, to full gourmet breakfast, to complimentary lunch and hearty Hors d' Oeuvres served poolside every afternoon. And, don't forget the free parking, all the homemade Iced Tea and Lemonade you want all day long for free.

Relax in one of our Hollywood Regency decorated rooms with their beautiful 500 thread count linens and plush beds. All rooms are individually heated and air conditioned to fit your personal comfort needs. Luxuriate in your en-suite tub or shower with our wonderful Hydro Spa Bath Products. Wrap yourself in our monogrammed robes after your evening dip in our new Saltwater Spa. Every detail has been thought of to make your stay as special and memorable as possible.

You will find our decor is very different from most Bed and Breakfast or Inns you have stayed at. We are very modern with a flair of Art Deco and have the feeling of a serene spa. Come experience POSH for yourself.

Located within walking distance of the vibrant downtown area with its numerous dining, cultural and entertainment venues, POSH is nestled up against the gorgeous San Jacinto Mountains with breathtaking views and sunsets. Now, that's POSH!

**Address:** 530 E Mel Avenue
Palm Springs CA 92262
**Phone:** 760-992-5410
**Tollfree:** 877-672-6825
**Fax:** 760-992-5412
**Email:** info@poshpalmsprings.com
**Web:** www.poshpalmsprings.com
**Room Rates:** 154–225
**Suite Rates:** 174–259
**No. of Rooms:** 11
**No. of Suites:** 3
**Credit Cards:** Most CCs Accepted
**Attractions:** Car shows, craft fairs, world class music, art exhibits and gallery openings. Knotts Soak City, the Tramway, Palm Springs Follies
**Services:** Bed linens of 500 thread counts, elegant monogrammed Spa Robes, Hydro Bath Products, and cold bottled water, soda and fresh fruit.
**Restrictions:** No children under the age of 12, No pets, No smoking in rooms
**Concierge:** Yes: available (daily) from 7am–7pm
**Room Service:** No
**Restaurant:** Start Your Day with Suzy's special gourmet breakfasts. Relax by the pool and be served a light refreshing complimentary lunch, Join the other guests each evening for a POSH Martini and Hors' de Oeuvre.
**Bar:** No
**Business Facilities:** Front Desk assistance/computer/fax & copies
**Conference Room:** No
**Sports Facilities:** No: local "wellness" park located just blocks away
**Spa Services:** All rooms overlook our heated 20x40' pool and new 10 person Saltwater Spa. Enjoy an hour long massage with our On-Call Masseuse.
**Airport:** Palm Springs Int'l
**Location:** Palm Springs

# THE INN AT RANCHO SANTA FE

**Address:** 5951 Linea Del Cielo
Rancho Santa Fe CA 92067
**Phone:** 858-756-1131
**Tollfree:** 800-843-4661
**Fax:** 858-759-1604
**Email:** reservations@theinnatrsf.com
**Web:** www.theinnatrsf.com
**Room Rates:** 229–295
**Suite Rates:** 525–1,500
**No. of Rooms:** 87
**No. of Suites:** 10
**Credit Cards:** Most CCs Accepted
**Attractions:** Sea World, San
Diego Zoo, Wild Animal Park,
La Jolla Museum of Modern Art,
LegoLand, Del Mar Racetrack
beaches, shopping, museums, US
military base and tours
**Services:** Swimming pool,
Jacuzzi, Croquet, wireless High-
Speed Internet access.
**Restrictions:** Pets in designated
rooms only. Smoking outdoors.
**Concierge:** Yes: available 24/7
**Room Service:** Yes: 7:00am to
9:30pm daily
**Restaurant:** Infusing the
history and harvest of Southern
California traditional foods &
"East Meet's West" fine Asian
cuisine. This unique blending of
ethnic influences is prepared by
Executive Chef John Beriker
**Bar:** Yes:(daily) 10:30am-10:00 pm
**Business Facilities:** Full
Business: fax, copier, admin assist
**Conference Room:** 4 rooms /
capacity: up to 200 people
**Sports Facilities:** Exercise room
**Spa Services:** Spa and Salon
services on site including a
variety of massage treatments,
facials, manicures, pedicures
and hair cuts and styling. In
room treatments available upon
request.
**Airport:** San Diego Airport
**Location:** 25 miles from San
Diego

Nestled in the exclusive village of Rancho Santa Fe lies an historic inn that was the getaway of choice for the stars of a bygone era. Today, lush gardens, winding paths, and the recently renovated cottages, dining room and cozy bar create a new tradition of quiet elegance.

The 23-acres are lushly landscaped and bloom almost continuously, providing a verdant backdrop for The Inn's heated pool, Jacuzzi, Spa and tennis court. Discover signature cuisine, enjoy a round of golf in Rancho Santa Fe, play croquet or splash in the surf in nearby Del Mar.

Most accommodations are in cottages scattered about the property. Each cottage room has been individually decorated and nearly all have secluded porches or sun decks, and rooms with wood burning fireplaces. Kitchens are available, as well as interconnecting suites for larger groups.

The Inn is a perfect quiet getaway and a stunning location for weddings, conferences and executive retreats. San Diego North Country's premier resort destination offers romantic surroundings with personalized service. Come enjoy the relaxed charm of another era amidst the sunny splendor of Southern California.

# RANCHO CAYMUS

At Rancho Caymus, a Napa Valley inn, you'll experience the wonders of Napa Valley with all of your senses. This hotel in Napa Valley, CA is nestled among the wineries of the world-famous Rutherford Bench Wine Region, Rancho Caymus is a quaint, all-suites Napa Valley inn which offers a unique sense of rustic elegance conveniently located in the heart of the Napa Valley.

Smell the fragrances of this world famous wine growing region. Located in the very center of the Napa Valley, Rancho Caymus Inn is surrounded by the agricultural wonder of world famous vineyards and wineries.

Hear the tranquility of lodging in a petite, 26-room Napa Valley inn. Each of these suites is distinctively designed. The two story hacienda style inn surrounds an award-winning garden courtyard. These elements give Rancho Caymus, more of the feeling of an "escape" than just a hotel.

Feel the warmth of staying in a family owned and operated Inn. Over the course of nearly 20 years, four generations of the Komes family have worked and overseen hospitality at Rancho Caymus.

See the dedication to details. Built and maintained to honor the history of the Napa Valley; Rancho Caymus was created to be a Spanish Hacienda style Inn. The materials, architectural design, and furnishings are all part of that effort to recapture the spirit of Napa Valley's past.

Taste the bounty of the wine country. The Napa Valley is recognized as one of the world's foremost wine growing regions.

Join us in the "Heart of the Napa Valley" for a wine country experience unlike any other.

**Address:** 1140 Rutherford Road Rutherford CA 94573
**Phone:** 707-963-1777
**Tollfree:** 800-845-1777
**Fax:** 707-963-5387
**Email:** info@ranchocaymus.com
**Web:** www.ranchocaymus.com
**Room Rates:** 195 – 310
**Suite Rates:** 255 – 450
**No. of Rooms:** 26
**No. of Suites:** 5
**Credit Cards:** Most CCs Accepted
**Attractions:** Located in the center of the Napa Valley, within a five minute drive to dozens of world famous wineries, gourmet restaurants and health spas. Let us help you plan your perfect getaway, from golfing to culinary classes, Napa Valley offers everything.
**Services:** Complimentary continental breakfast, Some rooms with fireplaces, and balconies, All rooms have TV, Radio, Wet bar, Individual climate control, Refrigerators, Private baths with shower-tubs, Complimentary toiletries
**Restrictions:** No pets allowed, 2 rooms handicap equipped, 2 night minimum for weekends
**Concierge:** 10:00 am – 7:00 pm
**Room Service:** Check with front desk for available services.
**Restaurant:** Guests are invited to join us in our dining room for a complimentary continental breakfast every morning from 7:30 to 9:30 am. The dining room is also available for events and meetings by appointment
**Business Facilities:** 2 rooms – up to 80 people.
**Conference Room:** Full service dining parties of 80 — Mont St. John Room
**Spa Facilities:** No
**Sport Facilities:** None on site
**Airport:** San Francisco & Oakland
**Location:** Rural

# APPLE FARM INN

**Address:** 2015 Monterey Street
San Luis Obispo CA 93401
**Phone:** 805-544-2040
**Tollfree:** 800-255-2040
**Fax:** 805-544-2513
**Email:** kwykoff@applefarm.com
**Web:** www.applefarm.com
**Room Rates:** 179–349
**No. of Rooms:** 69
**Credit Cards:** Most CCs Accepted
Attractions: Nearby tennis, Golf,
Horseback riding and Sailing,
wineries, fishing village of Morro
Bay, Hearst Castle, Performing
Arts Center.
**Services:** Parking, Gift shop,
Fireplaces, Balconies (2 rooms),
Cable TV, Radio, Robes, toiletries,
newspaper, delicious homemade
snacks.
**Restrictions:** No pets allowed,
Non-smoking property
**Concierge:** Front desk available
24/7
**Room Service:** Breakfast only
**Restaurant:** Apple Farm
Restaurant, 7am–9:00pm Sun-
Thu, 7am–10pm Fri & Sat. A
favorite spot for decades for
locals as well as the traveler.
**Bar:** No
**Business Facilities:** Message
center, Copiers, Audio-visual,
Voice mail, Data ports on phones.
**Conference Room:** 2 rooms –
capacity up to 60 people
**Sports Facilities:** Outdoor
heated swimming pool, whirlpool
**Spa Services:** Experience the full
range of body treatments at Apple
Farm's Massage Center.
**Airport:** San Luis Obispo (SBP)
**Location:** Monterey Street near
Highway 101, Close to historic
downtown

The Apple Farm Inn is an experience in traditional hospitality. Guests enjoy what will be remembered as "good old
American" virtues: friendliness, cleanliness, honest value,
homemade food and cozy rooms. The inn conveys country
Victorian charm and provides modern conveniences and all
the comforts of a luxury hotel.

The sunny, spacious octagon-shaped lobby feels more
like a comfortable living room than a hotel lobby. It allows
spectacular views of both the giant sycamores that grace the
quiet banks of the San Luis Creek and the beautiful coastal
mountains. Each guestroom features a gas-log fireplace and
is uniquely appointed with canopy or enamel and brass beds,
love seats and wingback chairs. Service at the Apple Farm Inn
is based on the philosophy of warm hospitality. Fresh flowers
and plants in every room, three-sheet beds, remote control
TVs and breakfast in bed with a newspaper are just some of
the ways guests are pampered.

Take a strolling visit to the Old Millhouse. This is an operating gristmill with a 14-foot wheel, which harnesses water
to power a cider press, grind wheat and make ice cream. The
Apple Farm Gift Shop is an experience unto itself! Housed in
an exact replica of a two-story country Victorian house, it offers a wide variety of items. The Apple Farm Brand products
are the real draw of the shop—apple butter and spreads in
canning jars, pressed cider and mulled cider spices—are only
some of the items.

# INN OF THE SPANISH GARDEN

Experience the jewel of luxury boutique Santa Barbara hotels... Inn of the Spanish Garden offers a sophisticated Spanish-Mediterranean inspired design, quality amenities and close attention to personal service.

The hotel epitomizes the vitality of the City and honors its tradition by recreating the history, romance and intrigue of Spanish Colonial Santa Barbara. Located among the City's historic sites in its oldest neighborhood, it is just steps from fine shops, museums, theaters, corporate offices and downtown dining.

The Inn of the Spanish Garden is nestled in the heart of Santa Barbara's downtown Historic Presidio District. You are literally minutes from everything! Whether it is business or pleasure that brings you to our doors you will always find something new to do with each of your visits. So next time you come - bring a friend and experience us all over again.

**Address:** 915 Garden Street Santa Barbara CA 93101
**Phone:** 805-564-4700
**Tollfree:** 866-564-4700
**Fax:** 805-564-4701
**Email:** info@spanishgardeninn.com
**Web:** www.spanishgardeninn.com
**Room Rates:** 235–425
**Suite Rates:** 405–489
**No. of Rooms:** 23
**No. of Suites:** 1
**Credit Cards:** Most CCs Accepted
**Attractions**: The City's historic sites, fine shops, museums, theaters, zoo, local airport, and downtown dining.
**Services:** Our rooms feature a fireplace, private garden patio or balcony, French Press coffee makers free wireless, deep soaking tubs, DVD players & movies, Molton Brown product, covered parking.
**Restrictions:** Non-smoking property. Does not accept pets.
**Concierge:** From our front desk: 24/7
**Room Service:** Available: 24/7 special "Small Bites Menu"
**Restaurant:** Our complimentary deluxe continental breakfast is served each morning.
**Bar:** Featuring Local Wines and Beer by the Glass or Bottle.
**Business Facilities:** Secluded computer station for your use as needed.
**Conference Room:** 1 room, capacity up to 12 people
**Sports Facilities:** Lap pool and outdoor workout area; Day Pass to local gym
**Spa Services:** In-room spa services including massages, facials and beauty treatments.
**Airport:** Santa Barbara Airport
**Location:** 3 blocks from State St - 8 blocks from Ocean

# VINTNERS INN

**Address:** 4350 Barnes Road
Santa Rosa CA 95403
**Phone:** 707-575-7350
**Tollfree:** 800-421-2584
**Fax:** 707-575-1426
**Email:** info@vintnersinn.com
**Web:** www.vintnersinn.com
**Room Rates:** 195–375
**Suite Rates:** 295–495
**No. of Rooms:** 44
**No. of Suites:** 6
**Credit Cards:** Most CCs Accepted
**Attractions**: Wine tasting at
Ferrari-Carano Winery, Sonoma
County Wineries. Wells Fargo
Center for the Arts, Antique
shopping, Hot air ballooning with
pick-up at hotel, Golf, Tennis,
Hikin
**Services:** Valet service, Free
Parking, Gift shop, Fireplaces,
Balconies & Patios, wireless
Internet, Satellite TV with
HBO, DVD players, Radio/
CD player, local newspaper,
wine & continental breakfast.
**Restrictions:** No pets, No checks,
3 rooms handicap access.
**Concierge:** Yes: available 24/7
**Room Service:** Yes: available
(daily) Noon – 9:00pm
**Restaurant:** John Ash & Co., an
icon of gourmet dining.
**Bar:** Yes: our Front Room Bar/
open(daily) 4:00pm – 10:00pm
**Business Facilities:** Audio-
Visual, Teleconferencing,
Translators w/request
**Conference Room:** 4 rooms /
capacity: up to 50 people
**Sports Facilities:** Whirlpool,
Massage available on-site, fitness
equipment and weights on-site.
**Spa Services:** A short walk
from your room to our Courtyard
Spa Room designed for couples
massages and treatments.
**Airport:** San Francisco Int'l &
Oakland Airports
**Location:** 5 miles north of Santa
Rosa

Set in a 90-acre vineyard, the warm glow of terra-cotta walls and tile roofs evoke the mood of southern France, while the California mission detailing reminds you of the Sonoma County wine-making community, redwood forests, and Pacific beaches just minutes away.

The European-style Vintners Inn was patterned after a small village in Provence, with four guest buildings encircling the courtyard fountain plaza. The newly remodeled rooms are spacious, and have over-sized Provencal French furnishings and fluffy down comforters, feather beds and pillows to enhance your comfort. The main building leads to tile walkways, a trellis-covered sun deck Jacuzzi spa and fitness room. The Vintners Inn Event Center boasts 13,000 sq feet of indoor and outdoor meeting and event space. The friendly and well-trained staff is ready to assist in the success of your meetings or seminars.

Spend your day in the Russian River resort area and wind your way to the seal beaches at the coast. Start with an early morning hot-air balloon ride, go antiquing, or golf one of the local courses. Visit the sprawling orchards and fields by bike, hike the redwood forests, or go boating on Lake Sonoma.

Achieve business objectives in style and comfort. Our four-diamond inn features an exceptional range of facilities and amenities for business meetings, conferences, training sessions, seminars, and receptions. Our luxurious, fully equipped meeting rooms provide the quiet surroundings you need to get things accomplished and the additional services we offer will help your event run smoothly. John Ash & Co. is the award-winning and nationally acclaimed restaurant at the Inn, which epitomizes wine-country dining at its best.

Experience the magnificent wine country lifestyle at Vintners Inn — We Are Wine Country.

ESH 1549 25TH ED

# SANTA YNEZ INN

Our wine country getaway awaits you!
    The luxurious AAA-four diamond rated Santa Ynez Inn delivers a unique hotel experience with Victorian grace and warm hospitality nestled in the heart of Santa Barbara Wine Country. Enjoy a sumptuous full gourmet breakfast, evening wine and hors d'oeuvres, and nightly desserts all included with your stay.

In twenty individually decorated rooms, your accommodations will include unique antiques, queen or king-sized beds with Frette linens, remote-controlled gas fireplaces and whirlpool tubs/deluxe over sized air jetted tubs. Most rooms offer a private balcony or patio to savor the beauty and serenity of the Santa Ynez Valley.

Take advantage of all that Santa Barbara County has to offer. Visit over sixty wineries for wine tasting. Antique shops abound. Take a glider ride or Jeep tours. After a day of Southern California sightseeing adventures, you may wish to unwind with a massage or enjoy the outdoor hot tub or the tub in your room. Whatever your needs—whether you wish to arrange for wine tasting tours, shopping, dining, bicycle rentals or transportation—sit back and relax while the front desk staff makes all the arrangements.

Escape the frenetic pace of city life to our tranquil and serene surroundings. The Santa Ynez Inn is an ideal spot for a romantic getaway, honeymoon or a peaceful retreat.

**Address:** 3627 Sagunto Street Santa Ynez CA 93460
**Phone:** 805-688-5588
**Tollfree:** 800-643-5774
**Fax:** 805-686-4294
**Email:** info@santaynezinn.com
**Web:** www.santaynezinn.com
**Room Rates:** 285–475
**Suite Rates:** 475
**No. of Rooms:** 20
**No. of Suites:** 2
**Credit Cards:** Most CCs Accepted
**Attractions**: There are over 60 wineries in our area, also antique shopping, bicycle rentals, horseback riding, golf, art galleries.
**Services:** Vintage antiques and furnishings, plush beds with European linens, fireplaces, garden balconies, high-speed wireless Internet, flat-screen TVs, whirlpool tubs, steam showers.
**Restrictions**: No Pets
**Concierge:** Yes: available 24/7
**Room Service:** Yes: 7–9pm breakfast (limited) Dinner (full menu)
**Restaurant:** Start the morning with a gourmet breakfast. Wine country cuisine are at the adjacent Vineyard House Restaurant or order room service for a romantic dinner.
**Bar:** No: (daily) wine & cheese reception / 5–7:00pm. Join our festive happy hour with fine wines, hors d'oeuvres, and desserts every evening.
**Business Facilities:** Yes: computer, fax, copier, WiFi & high-speed Internet
**Conference Room:** 2 room / capacity: up to 120 people
**Sports Facilities:** Yes: on site fitness room
**Spa Services:** Enjoy health, wellness and pampering with a rejuvenating spa treatment or soothing massage in our spa.
**Airport:** Santa Barbara Airport
**Location:** Santa Ynez Valley

# DOLPHIN BAY RESORT & SPA

**Address:** 2727 Shell Beach Road
Shell Beach CA 93449
**Phone:** 805-773-4300
**Tollfree:** 800-516-0112
**Fax:** 805-773-5200
**Email:** info@thedolphinbay.com
**Web:** www.thedolphinbay.com
**Suite Rates:** 335 -1,000
**No. of Suites:** 62
**Credit Cards:** Most CCs Accepted
**Attractions**: Hearst Castle,
Wine Tasting, Kayaking, Jet
Skiing, ATV Riding, Hiking,
Museums, Shopping, Biking,
Golfing, Missions, Art Galleries,
Horseback Riding, Live Theatre
**Services:** Complimentary DVD
and board game libraries, Cruiser
bicycles for guest use, and beach
access is a short walk away, pool,
spa, yoga, Dolphin Bay Kid's Club
**Restrictions:** Pet Friendly!
**Concierge:** Yes—the front desk
is available 24/7
**Room Service:** Yes—during
restaurant hrs: 8am–9pm (wkdays)
& 8am–10pm (wkends)
**Restaurant:** Dolphin Bay's
signature restaurant, Lido,
features California Coastal
Cuisine
**Bar:** Yes—located in our
restaurant and open the same
hours
**Business Facilities:** Computer/
fax/copier—complimentary high-
speed & wireless
**Conference Room:** 4 rooms–
capacity/up to 150 people
**Sports Facilities:** State-of-the-
art cardiovascular and strength-
training machines
**Spa Services:** Spend a day at
La Bonne Vie Spa designed to
rejuvenate and replenish your
soul. Our luxurious spa features
an array of customized massages,
facials and body therapies.
**Airport:** San Luis Obispo Airport
**Location:** Central California
Coast

An elegant all-villa resort set along the rugged California Coast, just south of San Luis Obispo. Midway between San Francisco and Los Angeles on California's Scenic Highway 1, Dolphin Bay Resort & Spa is centrally located in Shell Beach and is ideal for romantic getaways or family vacations where guests stay as long as they would like. With 62 spacious 1 and 2 bedroom villas featuring full gourmet kitchens, Lido Restaurant, La Bonne Vie Spa and an array of activities, guests have all the comforts of home amidst the elegance of a resort.

Upon opening the solid-wood front door, guests are welcomed into a plush villa. A modern living room, dining room, and kitchen are handsomely furnished evoking a home-away-from home ambiance. Luxurious amenities such as signature appliances, custom-made wood cabinetry and granite counter tops are showcased. The spacious living areas feature travertine flooring and woven wool carpeting, custom furniture, plasma flat-panel televisions with surround sound systems, and DVD players. All villas offer private terraces or patios, laundry facilities, complimentary high-speed wired and wireless Internet access, personal incoming telephone and/or facsimiles lines and are serviced twice daily.

The 24-hour fitness center offers a full circuit of state-of-the-art cardiovascular and strength-training machines. Outdoors, guests can relax poolside at Dolphin Bay's infinity-edged saline pool. We invite all children, ages 5 to 12 years of age, to spend Saturday afternoons with us for a fun-filled day at Dolphin Bay's Kid's Club!

# INN AT OYSTER POINT

Located on the San Francisco Bay, Inn at Oyster Point offers a unique combination: convenient access to the city of San Francisco and the San Francisco Airport, as well as bay breezes and expansive views.

A unique haven for the business traveler, the Inn is the closest hotel to the Genentech campus, as well as, other major biotech and pharmaceutical companies. AT&T Park, home of the San Francisco Giants, is also conveniently accessible from the hotel via CalTrain.

Inn at Oyster Point, your intimate San Francisco Airport hotel, offers 30 oversized guestrooms featuring cozy fireplaces and featherbeds for an uniquely comfortable stay away from home. Enjoy panoramic views of the San Francisco Bay and Oyster Point Marina while relaxing in your room or dining in SouthHarbor Waterfront Restaurant and Bar.

Complimentary services such as continental breakfast are delivered to guestrooms daily, airport transportation 7am – 10pm, and high-speed wireless access are perfect for both business and leisure travelers. Flying out of SFO? Start your vacation with us.

We know your stay will delight your eye, soothe your mind and invigorate your palate. We look forward to your arrival.

**Address:** 425 Marina Blvd
South San Francisco CA 94080
**Phone:** 650-737-7633
**Tollfree:** 800-642-2720
**Fax:** 650-737-0795
**Email:** reservations@innatoysterpoint.com
**Web:** www.innatoysterpoint.com
**Room Rates:** 99 – 215
**No. of Rooms:** 30
**Credit Cards:** Most CCs Accepted
**Attractions**: Overlooking San Francisco Bay in the heart of Oyster Point's Marina, Fisherman's Wharf, China Town, Bay area cruises, Alcatraz Island, shopping, cable cars.
**Services:** Complimentary airport transportation from 7am–10 pm, Complimentary In-Room Continental Breakfast, 375-square-foot Executive Boardroom
**Restrictions:** Call for details
**Concierge:** Assistance available 24/7
**Room Service:** Yes—from 5:00pm – 9:30pm (Monday–Saturday)
**Restaurant:** Waterfront dining at its best! Open from 11 – 9:30pm (Mon-Fri); 4 – 9:30pm (Sat); and 10 – 3:00pm (Sun). Join us for a taste of California cuisine made from fresh local fare
**Bar:** Yes—in restaurant
**Business Facilities:** Available: 24/7 with free printing
**Conference Room:** 1 room: capacity for up to 12 people
**Sports Facilities:** No
**Spa Services:** Our staff will be able to assist you with appointments and directions to the Luminous Day Spa.
**Airport:** San Francisco Int'l
**Location:** Waterfront location on picturesque San Francisco Bay

# THE INN AT SOUTHBRIDGE

**Address:** 1020 Main Street
St Helena CA 94574
**Phone:** 707-967-9400
**Tollfree:** 800-520-6800
**Fax:** 707-967-9486
**Email:** info@innatsouthbridge.com
**Web:** www.innatsouthbridge.com
**Room Rates:** 245–600
**Suite Rates:** 425–700
**No. of Rooms:** 20
**No. of Suites:** 1
**Credit Cards:** Most CCs Accepted
**Attractions**: Walking distance to Tra Vigne, Martini House, Terra, Market, Go Fish, and Cindy's Backstreet Kitchen; downtown St Helena for boutique shopping, art galleries, antique shops, wine tasting
**Services:** Complimentary continental breakfast, in-room high-speed Internet, Fireplaces, Juliet balconies, Cable TV w/ DVD, Same day dry cleaning, Mini bar, Down comforter, and Complimentary parking.
**Restrictions:** No pets allowed, 2 rooms handicap equipped
**Concierge:** Yes: 24/7
**Room Service:** Yes: available (daily) from 11:30am til 8:30pm
**Restaurant:** The Tra Vigne for formal dining and Pizzeria Tra Vigne (a trattoria) serving casual Italian fare. Both within walking distance of the inn.
**Bar:** Yes: Pizzeria Tra Vigne is open 11:30am–8:30pm
**Business Facilities:** High-speed Internet, Fax, Copier, Audio-visual
**Conference Room:** 1 room / capacity: up to 45 people
**Sports Facilities:** Guest privileges at Meadowood Resort
**Spa Services:** Hotel guests have complimentary access to Health Spa Napa Valley.
**Airport:** San Francisco & Oakland Airports
**Location:** 1 block walk to downtown St. Helena

Just North of San Francisco, in the center of America's most famous wine growing region, lies the historic town of St. Helena and the charming Inn at Southbridge. Set in a stand of sycamore trees and wrapped around an inviting courtyard inspired by Europe's small town squares, this twenty-one room inn offers a unique destination where guests can savor the pulse and flavor of the Napa Valley.

Guests at The Inn at Southbridge are a short stroll from Merryvale vineyards with its award winning wines, and St. Helena with its shopping, galleries and Epicurean dining. Other local activities include wine tasting, balloon and glider rides, bicycling, boating and trail rides.

The first-floor lobby and living room, with hand-crafted furniture and limestone fireplace, are a congenial gathering place for friends and associates. The adjoining Courtyard Room is the perfect setting for celebrations or business meetings. Also on the ground floor is Pizzeria Tra Vigne. Pizzeria Tra Vigne offers Mediterranean dishes using superb local ingredients complemented by the wines for which the Napa Valley is world-famous.

French doors in the second-floor guestrooms reveal views from the balconies onto the courtyard or the rolling hills beyond. Rich ivory and sage fabrics, cherry wood finishes and white linens reflect the vibrant Napa Valley light. Further touches include fireplaces, down comforters, vaulted ceilings and communications systems for business needs.

We will be looking for you!

# INN ON SUMMER HILL & SPA

Upon arriving at the Inn on Summer Hill, a Santa Barbara bed and breakfast, you'll immediately recognize the "attention to detail" as its defining feature. The stunning Craftsman-style architecture creates the feel of home for guests traveling from all over. In addition, every room has ocean views.

A friendly, gracious staff member will escort you to your room and acquaint you with the many amenities you will enjoy during your stay. You will experience the delightful lobby and cozy dining room. Breakfast is available in the fireside dining room or on your patio or balcony. Afternoon hors d'oeuvres with wine, coffee, tea and cheese await you at three o'clock each day.

You can end the day with complimentary dessert before you retire to your fireside room. Don't forget to relax a while in the cozy outdoor spa before you settle in for the night.

We are here to accommodate you. Our concierge staff will assist you with information on things to do, see and experience. Upon request, we will make arrangements with one of our professional massage therapist for a massage or facial in the privacy of our massage/ spa room. We can make recommendations and reservations for dinner as you desire. Santa Barbara and Montecito have a large variety of delicious restaurants.

Our Santa Barbara inn is proud of its awards from several agencies, and is proud to be in the distinctive company of the top inns of the nation. Inn on Summer Hill has received the coveted AAA Four Diamond award every year since our opening in 1989.

**Address:** 2520 Lillie Avenue Summerland CA 93067
**Phone:** 805-969-9998
**Tollfree:** 800-845-5566
**Fax:** 805-565-9946
**Email:** info@innonsummerhill.com
**Web:** innonsummerhill.com
**Room Rates:** 229–289
**Suite Rates:** 389–429
**No. of Rooms:** 16
**No. of Suites:** 1
**Credit Cards:** Most CCs Accepted
**Attractions**: Active outdoors pursuits, antique shops, beaches, biking, botanical gardens, historic Santa Barbara, museums, Santa Barbara Mission Parks, Santa Ynez wineries, shopping, Stearns Wharf, whale watching.
**Services:** robes, TV/DVD, video library, hot teas/chocolate in rooms, soaps/lotions/shampoos, feather or regular pillows, high end sheets and down comforters, high-speed Internet, in-room telephones, surround sound stereos, ocean views.
**Restrictions:** No Pets, 1 room handicap accessible
**Concierge:** Yes—available from 7am till 11pm (daily)
**Room Service:** Limited— available from 7:30–11am; 3–5pm and (desserts only) 7:30-9pm
**Restaurant:** For our guests we provide a gourmet breakfast and fresh hors d'oeuvres and during the evening scrumptious baked desserts.
**Bar:** No
**Business Facilities:** Business Center available/computer, fax, copier, high-speed Internet
**Conference Room:** 1 room / capacity – up to 15 people
**Sports Facilities:** No
**Spa Services:** Couples massage, facials, aromatherapy, personal synergy massage, hot stone massage and more.
**Airport:** Santa Barbara (SBA)
**Location:** Edge of downtown

# TIMBER COVE INN

**Address:** 21780 North Coast Highway 1, Timber Cove CA 95450
**Phone:** 707-847-3231
**Tollfree:** 800-987-8319
**Fax:** 707-847-3704
**Email:** info@TimberCoveInn.com
**Web:** www.timbercoveinn.com/?chebs=esh_tci
**Room Rates:** 169–399
**Suite Rates:** 299–499
**No. of Rooms:** 45
**No. of Suites:** 5
**Credit Cards:** Most CCs Accepted
**Attractions**: Fort Ross, whale & seal watching, Sonoma's lush Wine Country, The Russian River, Armstrong Redwoods, stargaze, hike.
**Services:** Private hot tubs, fireplaces, ocean or forest views, flat screen TV, robes, wireless Internet.
**Restrictions:** Call for details
**Concierge:** Yes
**Room Service:** Yes
**Restaurant:** Alexander's cooks up mouth-watering meals made with local, organic ingredients. Match a locally brewed beer or Sonoma wine to your dish. And save room for delectable dessert while taking in the views!
**Bar:** Yes
**Business Facilities:** Complimentary Wireless
**Conference Room:** 2–5 rooms/ areas – capacity up to 260 people
**Sports Facilities:** Oceanfront Events Lawn
**Spa Services:** Enjoy a sip of wine and melt away the cares of the day in one of our hot tubs.
**Airport:** San Francisco & Oakland
**Location:** Timber Cove along Northern California coastline

Experience a relaxing retreat at Timber Cove Inn, a Northern California exclusive. Hidden in the coastal town of Jenner California where the Russian River joins the Pacific Ocean, the wild coast welcomes breathtaking Timber Cove Inn.

The stunning inn glows warmly inviting you in to its lively abode. Unwind in spacious suites complete with hot tubs, fireplaces and private decks. Savor Alexander's fine-dining and Sonoma County wines. Catch some Bay Area jazz or classical music in the Sequoia Lounge. Host a event with the Sonoma coast and waves as a beautiful backdrop. Find everything you need for a rejuvenating refuge by the sea.

The natural setting of Timber Cove Inn provides an abundance of Sonoma Coast activities. Explore your passions from whale watching to stargazing and from wine tasting to kayaking. Whether your passion is in salmon, rockfish and abalone fishing or wine, food and theatrical events, the eclectic nature of this beautiful area is alluring and satisfying for the leisure traveler. Whether you need outdoor adventures galore or non-stop peaceful relief, Timber Cove Inn caters to all! Check out the hotel's calendar of events and leisure guide to make the most of this incredible location.

Timber Cove Inn looks forward to welcoming you to its secluded Sonoma County hotel!

# POSTE MONTANE LODGE

With all the warmth and personality of a traditional European Inn, the Poste Montane Lodge has brought Old World charm to the heart of Beaver Creek, Colorado. Beaver Creek Resort is smaller, quieter and more refined than other local ski resorts. It is where you go when you want to get away from it all-but still have it all. The resort is known as a snow rider's paradise, and it keeps that reputation with the most advanced grooming equipment available.

Considered by many to be the jewel of Beaver Creek, the Poste Montane Lodge presides over the pedestrian village in a place of honor. Our lobby doors open onto the village plaza. No longer a winter destination only, visitors to Beaver Creek can stroll down quaint walkways that are conveniently linked by escalators to lead you through the village. Next door, the Vilar Center for the Performing Arts provides a world-class calendar of events to enrich your evenings. In the village, you will find a year-round outdoor ice-skating rink, sidewalk cafes and restaurants, colorful boutiques and galleries. The summer season also includes multiple festivals and weekly rodeo performances.

After a long day on the slopes or a full day of golf, it's comforting to know that a Jacuzzi, steam room and sauna await you at the Poste Montane Lodge. Or, as our guest you may schedule a luxurious treatment at the exclusive Allegria Spa where a full exercise facility and outdoor swimming pool are also available. Each of our 24 rooms and suites has been designer-decorated to suit the Old World ambiance of the Poste Montane Lodge. Thick terry robes, down comforters and pillows are just a few of the details.

The Poste Montane Lodge's European style of innkeeping offers a refreshing change of pace for those who prefer an intimate setting.

**Address:** 76 Avondale Lane Beaver Creek CO 81620
**Phone:** 970-845-7500
**Tollfree:** 800-497-9238
**Fax:** 970-845-5012
**Email:** pmlodge@eastwestresorts.com
**Web:** www.postemontane.com
**Room Rates:** 130–575
**Suite Rates:** 150–1,480
**No. of Rooms:** 7
**No. of Suites:** 17
**Credit Cards:** Most CCs Accepted
**Attractions**: Beaver Creek and Vail Ski Areas, Snowshoeing, Fly Fishing, Biking, Hiking, Golf, Horseback Riding, Rafting, Rock Climbing, Jeep Tours, The Vilar Center for the Arts, Ford Amphitheater, Glenwood Springs
**Services:** Complimentary Deluxe Continental Breakfast, Heated Underground Parking, Wireless Internet, Daily Housekeeping Service
**Restrictions:** No Pets Allowed, No Smoking in the Lodge
**Concierge:** Yes: available (daily) 7:00am–10:00am (seasonal)
**Room Service:** No
**Restaurant:** Beaver Creek village offers a number of world-class restaurants..
**Bar:** No: Complimentary reception (daily) 3:00pm–7:00pm
**Business Facilities:** Business Center with Internet access, Voicemail, Free WiFi, Copier, Fax
**Conference Room:** No
**Sports Facilities:** Complimentary guest passes for the Park Hyatt Allegria Spa Health Club, local ski & golf areas
**Spa Services:** The Park Hyatt Allegria Spa offers full spa services. In room massages are also available.
**Airport:** Eagle-Vail Airport (EGE)
**Location:** The Heart of Beaver Creek Village, Colorado

# CASTLE MARNE

**Address:** 1572 Race Street
Denver CO 80206
**Phone:** 303-331-0621
**Tollfree:** 800-926-2763
**Fax:** 303-331-0623
**Email:** info@CastleMarne.com
**Web:** www.castlemarne.com
**Room Rates:** 115–250
**Suite Rates:** 270
**No. of Rooms:** 9
**No. of Suites:** 1
**Credit Cards:** Most CCs Accepted
**Attractions**: Denver Zoo, Museum Nature and Science, Denver Botanic Gardens, Molly Brown's House, Denver Art Museum, US Mint, Colorado History Museum, Cherry Creek Shopping Ctr, Downtown 16th Street Mall, Aquarium, Colo. Rockies Baseball stadium, Den. Broncos stadium.
**Services:** Private baths, free WiFi, free parking, air conditioning, rose garden, whirlpool baths, hot tubs on private balconies, afternoon tea, full breakfast, late night cookies and tea, free bottled water
**Restrictions:** No pets allowed, Children over 10 welcome
**Concierge:** Daily
**Room Service:** Check with Front Desk for availability
**Restaurant:** Experience Denver's only Mansion dining. A private, romantic 6 or 4 course candlelight dinner served just for you in the original Formal Dining Room of our Castle.
**Business Facilities:** WiFi, FAX, computer/printer
**Conference Room:** 1 room, capacity 12
**Airport:** Denver Int'l Airport
**Location:** Downtown Denver, Wyman Historic District

Come fall under the spell of one of Denver's grandest historic mansions. Built in 1889, Castle Marne is considered by many to be the finest example of "America's most eclectic architect," William Lang (designer of Unsinkable Molly Brown's house). Its history glows through the hand-rubbed woods, the renowned circular stained glass "Peacock Window," and original ornate fireplaces. Historically accurate hand painted ceilings and frieze. "Castle Marne is truly one of Denver's great architectural legacies. Note the eclectic Richardsonian massing and detailing of the mansion—the heavily rusticated stonework juxtaposed with the refined, delicate elements of glass fenestration … Denver Chapter, American Institute of Architects."

Your stay at Castle Marne combines Old World elegance and Victorian charm with modern-day convenience and comfort. Each guestroom is a unique experience in pampered luxury. Carefully chosen furnishings bring together authentic period antiques, family heirlooms, and exacting reproductions to create the mood of long-ago charm and romance.

Awake to the spicy aroma of brewing Marne-blend coffee, homemade breads and muffins. Linger over a complete gourmet breakfast in the original cherry-paneled Formal Dining Room. Join other guests at from 4:30–6:00 p.m. for Afternoon Tea served in the Parlor. Work on the jigsaw puzzle or savor the beauty of a Colorado sunset. Relax your mind and spirit, soak up history—or just soak in a hot tub.

In the heart of one of Denver's most historic neighborhoods, the inn is just minutes from many fine restaurants, plus the city's finest cultural, shopping and sightseeing attractions.

# ROCHESTER HOTEL

In the tradition of the Old West, the Rochester Hotel will transport guests back to the days of gunslingers and railroad bandits amid Durango's scenic downtown setting. Built in 1892 and restored in 1994, the Rochester is a beautiful two-story brick Victorian hotel. The many antiques displayed throughout the hotel and its historical surroundings complement the Western motif.

Guests will delight in picturesque views of the mountains, courtyard, and downtown Durango. Each of the luxury guestrooms is uniquely decorated in a style true to the Old West and inspired by the many movies filmed in the Four Corners area. Rooms have high ceilings and a private bathroom.

Start your daily adventures with a delicious breakfast such as chive potato cakes, spinach-and-cheese-stuffed croissants, and scrumptious baked goods which can be enjoyed in the landscaped courtyard, the old-fashioned train car, or on the patio. Activities abound at the Rochester, where guests are within walking distance of the Durango and Silverton Narrow Gauge Railroad and many fine restaurants and shops. Nearby parks also offer hiking and biking trails and the Animas river offers exciting river rafting for all ages. In the courtyard or on the patio of the hotel guests will find a delightful spot to relax and enjoy the beauty of the area after a day in town.

At the Rochester Hotel, guests will leave behind their everyday lives and step into the historical world of the Old West where every moment is filled with adventure.

**Address:** 726 East 2nd Avenue Durango CO 81301
**Phone:** 970-385-1920
**Tollfree:** 800-664-1920
**Fax:** 970-385-1967
**Email:** stay@rochesterhotel.com
**Web:** www.rochesterhotel.com
**Room Rates:** 129–369
**Suite Rates:** 169–369
**No. of Rooms:** 25
**No. of Suites:** 7
**Credit Cards:** Most CCs Accepted
**Attractions**: Within walking distance to the Durango and Silverton Narrow Gauge Railroad, nearby are Soaring Tree Top Adventures, Mesa Verde, Durango Mountain Resort (skiing and boarding), fine restaurants, shops, parks, hiking and bike trails, river rafting.
**Services:** Off-street parking, gift shop, lounge area, card or game area, kitchens, fireplaces, patio/ gardens, cable TV, telephones, CD/Clock radios, individual climate controls, Aveda toiletries
**Restrictions:** Children welcome at $20 per night, Pets at $20 per night, 1 room handicap equipped
**Concierge:** Yes: available (daily) from 7:30am – 10:00pm
**Room Service:** No
**Restaurant:** A full gourmet breakfast served in the Rochester Lobby, 7:00–9:00am.
**Bar:** No
**Business Facilities:** Wireless Internet, Message center, E-mail, Copiers, Fax, Guest Computer
**Conference Room:** 3 rooms & courtyard / capacity: up to 20
**Sports Facilities:** No on-site gym or workout room
**Spa Services:** Our helpful staff would be pleased to assist you with recommendations, appointments and directions
**Airport:** Durango La Plata Airport
**Location:** Historic downtown district

# STRATER HOTEL

**Address:** 699 Main Avenue
Durango CO 81301
**Phone:** 970-247-4431
**Tollfree:** 800-247-4431
**Fax:** 970-259-2208
**Email:** reservations@strater.com
**Web:** www.strater.com
**Room Rates:** 109–289
**No. of Rooms:** 93
**No. of Suites:** N/A
**Credit Cards:** Most CCs Accepted
**Attractions**: The Durango &
Silverton Narrow Gauge Railroad,
the Great Durango Melodrama,
Mesa Verde National Park,historic
Main Avenue Shopping District.
River Rafting, Fishing, Hiking,
Biking, Railroading To Silverton,
Jeeping, Bar-D Wranglers, Sleigh
rides & Sk
**Services:** Fully modern
conveniences: cable television,
in-room hi-speed wireless
Internet, hot tub, free parking, 3
restaurants, melodrama theater,
activity packages, free continental
breakfast
**Restrictions:** Non-smoking
establishment. Limited
pet facilities. No handicap
accessiblity
**Concierge:** Yes: available 24/7
**Room Service:** Yes—available
(daily) from 7am–10:00pm
**Restaurant:** The Mahogany
Grille; The Office Spiritorium; The
Famous Diamond Belle Saloon;
And 1887 Catering Company.
**Bar:** Yes, two! The Office
Spiritorium & The Diamond Bell
Saloon/ open from 4:30pm–close
**Business Facilities:** Yes:
computer, fax, copies.
**Conference Room:** Yes: 3 rooms
**Sports Facilities:** Free pass to
local recreational center
**Spa Services:** Neighboring Salon
and Health Spas offer a complete
line of spa services.
**Airport:** Durango Airport
**Location:** Durango, Colorado

Welcome to Durango, Colorado!
Steeped in over 120 years of colorful history with 3 generations of Barker Family ownership, The Strater Hotel is Durango's most prominent downtown landmark. This historic hotel features 93 spectacular Victorian rooms, each filled with beautiful walnut antiques and period wallpapers. A beautiful lobby, A famous Ragtime Piano Bar, a spectacular Victorian "Spiritorium," Durango's Best Restaurant, a world class Melodrama, 5 professionally staffed elegant conference rooms, and much more await you in the heart of downtown Durango. We even have a 35 acre vacation rental just 12 minutes from the hotel if you are looking for a family reunion.

**Plenty to Do! Events for Everyone!** Durango is home to many events in both summer and winter and few, if any, of Durango's lodging options will put you so close to so many local attractions including the Durango and Silverton Narrow Gauge Railroad, the Henry Strater Theater and Melodrama, the historic Main Avenue Shopping District and a plethora of great restaurants. Great Music is no stranger to the Strater Hotel with several venues offering entertainment from local western performers to large touring national acts.

The hardest part about activities and events in Durango is picking and choosing which you'll need to save for your next visit! There's just so much to do, that you'll inevitably be forced to choose.

**We Can't Wait to See You!** Our friendly expert staff can help you plan your ideal Durango vacation, with insider tips about where to go, which services to use, and most of all, where to have a great time. We look forward to seeing you soon!

The Historic Strater Hotel has it all!

ESH 118 25TH ED

# HOMESTEAD INN

It is said the difference between real life and the movies is that real life has bad lighting and no score. All of that changes as one enters the grounds of Homestead Inn—Thomas Henkelmann in Greenwich, CT. The hotel and four star restaurant are nestled on a beautiful piece of land jutting into Long Island Sound aptly named Belle Haven. Grand Victorian homes and modern architectural achievements hug its stand like a sun kissed string of pearls. Purchased in 1997 by Theresa and Thomas Henkelmann as a showcase for Thomas Henkelmann's incredible cuisine, the existing hotel was a logical extension and a blank canvas for Theresa's design expertise.

Integrating the architecture that defers to the hotel's history and individuality, the Henkelmanns' purposeful and sensitive renovation is a salute to the past while resolutely embracing the new and the now. Art and artifacts from around the globe are seamlessly woven into each room and suite's décor. European in flavor, the hotel speaks to both the artist and the bon vivant. Each room differs in style and design and all have sumptuous amenities intended to coddle. A design thread throughout the hotel is the inspired use of color. Brave and bold, it effortlessly blends the old world with the new.

Critically acclaimed for his "flawless French food" Chef Thomas Henkelmann's contemporary French cuisine is inspired by his classical French training.

The charming gardens, exquisite individually designed and decorated guestrooms, knowledgeable and caring staff and the unparalleled cuisine of Master Chef Thomas Henkelmann creates an experience to treasure for a lifetime.

**Address:** 420 Field Point Road Greenwich CT 06830
**Phone:** 203-869-7500
**Fax:** 203-869-7502
**Email:** events@homesteadinn.com
**Web:** www.homesteadinn.com
**Room Rates:** 250–395
**Suite Rates:** 495
**No. of Rooms:** 18
**No. of Suites:** 7
**Credit Cards:** Visa, Most CCs Accepted
**Attractions**: New York City, Bruce Museum, Luxury Boutique Shopping, World renown restaurant Thomas Henkelmann, Long Island Sound, Financial Centers, Autobon Preserve
**Services:** Limousine service upon request, Fili d'oro linens, Exquisite robes, Hair dryers, Air conditioning, Cable TV & VCR, Wireless Internet & voicemail, AM/FM clock radio, Newspapers, Bulgari amenities.
**Restrictions:** No Pets, Children under 12 not recommended
**Concierge:** Yes—available 24/7
**Room Service:** Yes—available during restaurant hrs: 7am–9pm (daily)
**Restaurant:** Serving breakfast, lunch and dinner; offers French cuisine, seasonal specialties and classic signature dishes.
**Bar:** Yes—located in restaurant and open: 7am–9pm (daily)
**Business Facilities:** Audio-visual equipment available upon request, complete dining and catering facilities
**Conference Room:** 1 room / capacity 14–18
**Sports Facilities:** No
**Spa Services:** Supplied from one of our local spa establishments.
**Airport:** John F Kennedy, La Guardia & West Chester Airports
**Location:** Belle Haven on Long Island Sound

# SAYBROOK POINT INN & SPA

**Address:** 47 Falls River Drive
Ivoryton CT 06442
**Phone:** 860-395-2000
**Tollfree:** 800-243-0121
**Fax:** 860-388-1504
**Email:** info@saybrook.com
**Web:** www.saybrook.com
**Room Rates:** 199–449
**Suite Rates:** 409 -529
**No. of Rooms:** 82
**No. of Suites:** 6
**Credit Cards:** Most CCs Accepted
**Attractions**: Katherine Hepburn
Cultural Center, museums,
vineyards, casinos, river cruises,
½ from Mystic Seaport and
Aquarium, hiking, biking, Nordic
walks
**Services:** Bathrobes, iron and
ironing boards, fridge, in-room
coffee/tea, all amenities are made
in USA, balconies & fireplaces
**Restrictions:** No smoking. Pet
Friendly, Kid Friendly, 2 rooms
handicap accessible
**Concierge:** Yes: available 24/7
**Room Service:** Yes: from 9am to
11pm daily
**Restaurant:** Boasts waterfront
ambiance, delectable fare,
an extensive wine list, and
impeccable service. All dishes are
prepared "farm to chef."
**Bar:** Yes: in restaurant and in
summer—located in the Marina
**Business Facilities:** Yes:
Computer available, fax & copies,
wireless & High-speed Internet
**Conference Room:** 7 rooms /
capacity: up to 240
**Sports Facilities:** State of the art
health club. Two salt water pools
(indoor & outdoor).
**Spa Services:** From hot stone
treatments to European facials,
our services are the perfect
compliment to any New England
vacation.
**Airport:** Bradley Int'l Airport
**Location:** Connecticut river
meets Long Island sound

Nestled in historic Old Saybrook overlooking Long Island Sound. Only two hours from New York City, we offer gracious accommodations, world-class services, a luxurious spa, and a gorgeous shoreline that has enchanted guests for more than 130 years.

Enjoy classic intimacy in elegant rooms featuring balconies, water views, and glowing fireplaces. Stroll the planks of Saybrook Point Marina, taking in fresh, briny breezes and stunning vistas of broad marshlands dotted with villages and farmhouses. Savor sumptuous cuisine at Terra Mar Restaurant—our Four Diamond restaurant—then try your luck at nearby Foxwoods or Mohegan Sun casinos.

Each of our lodging options features dataports, wet bars, refrigerators, and European pillow-top mattresses. The spacious bathrooms are finished in Italian tile, with expansive vanities and a dressing area. For guests seeking the ultimate romantic getaway, we offer rooms with private balconies, water views, whirlpools, and working fireplaces. A union of historic elegance and contemporary luxury, our versatile, pet-friendly New England lodging choices offer amenities that include: Wireless Internet access, Iron and Ironing boards, Mini-refrigerator, Luxurious robes, DVD players, available on request.

ESH 1172 25TH ED

# WATER'S EDGE RESORT & SPA

Water's Edge Resort and Spa, a classic, turn-of-the-century New England shoreline estate offers all the amenities and conveniences of a full-service resort. Located on a bluff overlooking Connecticut's Long Island Sound, the grounds and buildings offer spectacular ocean views.

Fronted by a generous stretch of white-sand beach, the 20-acre property spreads over manicured lawns and is composed of finely-appointed guestrooms and suites, two-bedroom lofts, summer cottages, an award-winning restaurant, Sea View Bistro & Martini Bar, Sunset Bar & Grille, Cappuccio's Espresso Bar, indoor and outdoor pools, two tennis courts, fitness center, world-class luxury spa and specialty shops.

Green grass, deep blue waters and light blue sky frame your view of Water's Edge Resort & Spa. Take part in activities long associated with the shore: paddle boats, wind surfers, and a pool or private beach for swimming and lounging. Enjoy activities associated with contemporary fun, health and well-being in the new multi-million dollar health spa and fitness center. Follow up your workout with a swim in the heated indoor pool, or relax in the Jacuzzi or sauna. End with a massage or detoxifying body wrap.

Water's Edge Resort & Spa's central shoreline location is convenient to many attractions such as Essex Village, Gillette Castle, Goodspeed Opera House, Ivoryton Playhouse, Mystic Seaport, Foxwoods & Mohegan Sun Casinos, premium outlet shopping and so much more. Our private function facilities total 15,000 square feet making the resort a picture-perfect venue for weddings, social receptions and corporate business functions.

Located in the historic Bill Hahn Lodge, the multi-level Restaurant at Water's Edge offers panoramic ocean views and award-winning food. Guests always leave with the best in service and cuisine, and with a longing for their next visit.

Water's Edge Resort & Spa … A World All Your Own!

**Address:** 1525 Boston Post Road Westbrook CT 06498
**Phone:** 860-399-5901
**Tollfree:** 800-222-5901
**Fax:** 860-399-6172
**Email:** reservations@watersedge-resort.com
**Web:** www.watersedgeresortandspa.com
**Room Rates:** 145 – 315
**Suite Rates:** 165 – 385
**No. of Rooms:** 170
**No. of Suites:** 3
**Credit Cards:** Most CCs Accepted
**Attractions:** Essex Village, Gillette Castle, Goodspeed Opera House, Ivoryton Playhouse, Mystic Seaport, Mystic Aquarium, Foxwoods Casino, Mohegan Sun Casino, Tanger Outlets, Clinton Crossing Premium Outlets, Museums, Art Galleries, Antiques.
**Services:** Valet, Car hire, Laundry, Gift and Specialty Shops, Game Room, Cable TV, Telephones, DVD, Radio, high-speed Internet, Individual heating and air conditioning, toiletries.
**Restrictions:** 2-night min. stay —weekends in summer, No pets, Children stay free. 6 rooms handicap equipped.
**Concierge:** Yes: available 24/7
**Room Service:** Yes: available 7:30am – 10pm
**Restaurant:** Enjoy breakfast, lunch, dinner or Sunday brunch at The Restaurant at Water's Edge or Sunset Bar & Grill.
**Bar:** Sea View Bistro & Martini Bar open 11:30am – 2:00am
**Business Facilities:** High-speed Internet access, Copiers, Audio Visual, Fax
**Conference Room:** 5 rooms / capacity up to 650 people
**Sports Facilities:** Indoor & Outdoor Swimming Pools, Sauna, Fitness Center
**Spa Services:** Marine therapies that nurture body, mind and spirit.
**Airport:** Bradley Int'l
**Location:** Off I-95, exit 65

# THE INN AT MONTCHANIN VILLAGE & SPA

**Address:** Rt 100 & Kirk Road
Montchanin DE 19710
**Phone:** 302-888-2133
**Tollfree:** 800-COWBIRD
**Fax:** 302-888-0389
**Email:** inn@montchanin.com
**Web:** montchanin.com
**Room Rates:** 192–244
**Suite Rates:** 290–399
**No. of Rooms:** 28
**No. of Suites:** 6
**Credit Cards:** Most CCs Accepted
**Attractions**: Winterthur Museum
& Gardens, Hagley Museum &
Gardens, Longwood Gardens,
BrandyWine River Museum,
Delaware Art Museum, Nemours
Gardens & Museum, Delaware
Museum of Natural History,
Rockwood Museum
**Services:** All rooms have private
marble-baths, refrigerator with
ice-maker, coffee-maker and
microwave; complimentary coffee,
tea, bottled water and sodas; NY
*Times* (daily);in-room safes; daily
turn down; some rooms a gas
fireplace.
**Restrictions:** Non-smoking, No
pets.
**Concierge:** Yes: available 24/7
**Room Service:** Yes: 8:00am –
9:00pm / limited In-Room menu
**Restaurant:** Krazy Kat's.
Reservations appreciated. Dress
code: business casual.
**Bar:** Yes: "Honor Bar" open from
5pm till "closing"
**Business Facilities:** Message
Center, Copiers, Audio-visual, Fax,
Modems, Front desk assist.
**Conference Room:** 3 rooms /
capacity: up to 50 people
**Sports Facilities:** Full fitness
center
**Spa Services:** Feature the
Darphin skin care line.
**Airport:** Philadelphia Int'l
**Location:** Heart of Brandywine
Valley

The Inn at Montchanin Village, once a part of Winterthur Museum Estate, exists in a wonderful little world of its own. A world in which time has seemingly stood still. Into this rural vignette are cleverly woven twenty-eight guestrooms and suites appointed with period and reproduction furniture, marble baths and every modern convenience and amenities for the sophisticated traveler.

The unique walkways flow through the historic walled gardens, creating a sense of unity throughout the entire hamlet. The seasonal colors are complemented by the use of native plantings, capture the very essence of the Brandywine Valley and its surrounding world-class gardens.

Of the eleven carefully restored buildings dated from 1799 – 1910, nine were once houses for the workers of the Dupont black powder mills. The original blacksmith's shop is now Krazy Kat's Restaurant. The Dilwyne Barn houses Guest Services and a lounge with an honor bar.

A member of Historic Hotels of America, the Inn is listed on the National Register of Historic Places. Krazy Kats' Restaurant is described as "whimsical dining room with an eclectic menu and an award-winning wine list." Be sure to make a dinner reservation when booking your room.

# BOARDWALK PLAZA HOTEL

At the Boardwalk Plaza Hotel, we are proud of our history of superior service and the pampering amenities that make every guest feel like the only guest. From heavenly bedding and downy-soft bath towels to remarkable room service with a smile, our goal is to provide a comfortable respite from the world—where you can truly get away from it all.

There's no other beach experience like it. From the moment you step under the antique wrought-iron canopy and enter the lobby, the Boardwalk Plaza's staff stands ready to offer you exceptional service. Enjoy the view from the indoor glass elevator as you ride to the quiet interior corridor that leads to your room. Whether you choose a suite with a private balcony, a deluxe accommodation that adds a whirlpool bathtub-for-two, or something in between, you'll find an artful combination of Victorian-reproduction furnishings and state-of-the-art amenities like flat-screen TVs and wireless Internet access.

Add a generous helping of oceanfront to your meal. Victoria's offers fine dining in a charming setting. The Boardwalk Plaza Hotel and Victoria's Restaurant are open 365 days a year. Let us pamper you with a weeklong vacation or a romantic escape in any season—be it a summer beach holiday, an autumn festival, a cozy winter getaway or a springtime sojourn.

A long-term guest put it best—"the magic still happens here." Allow us to make the magic happen for you.

**Address:** 2 Olive Ave, Boardwalk Rehoboth Beach DE 19971
**Phone:** 302-227-7169
**Tollfree:** 800-33-BEACH
**Fax:** 302-227-0561
**Email:** bph@boardwalkplaza.com
**Web:** www.boardwalkplaza.com
**Room Rates:** 89–389
**Suite Rates:** 129–499
**No. of Rooms:** 33
**No. of Suites:** 51
**Credit Cards:** Most CCs Accepted
**Attractions**: Beautiful beach and mile-long boardwalk, tax-free shopping at in-town boutiques, antiques shoppes and over 140 outlet stores, walking distance to eateries galore, seashore state parks, golf, tennis and watersports nearby.
**Services:** Bellhops, DVD library, T1 and WiFi, heated spa-pool, beach towels(in season), complimentary parking. Adults-only concierge level: turn-down, robes.
**Restrictions:** Nonsmoking. No pets. Minimum stays may apply in season.
**Room Service:** Full Menu, 7am – 10pm
**Restaurant:** Victoria's Restaurant, 7:00 a.m.-10:00 p.m. and The Plaza Pub, 4 - 10 p.m. daily.
**Bar:** The Plaza Pub—serving drinks and light fare daily.
**Business Facilities:** State-of-the-art AV, Wireless T1 Internet, Copier, Fax, Teleconferencing
**Conference Room:** 4 rooms, capacity up to 110.
**Sports Facilities:** Fitness Room
**Spa Services:** Privately arranged, en-suite, or in the rooftop pavilion, or at guest's choice of local partner spas.
**Airport:** Philadelphia & BWI
**Location:** Oceanfront.

# HOTEL REHOBOTH

**Address:** 247 Rehoboth Avenue
Rehoboth Beach DE 19971
**Phone:** 302-227-4300
**Tollfree:** 800-247-7346
**Fax:** 302-227-1200
**Email:** info@hotelrehoboth.com
**Web:** www.hotelrehoboth.com
**Room Rates:** 119–399
**Suite Rates:** 149–429
**No. of Rooms:** 52
**No. of Suites:** 4
**Credit Cards:** Most CCs Accepted
**Attractions**: Ocean beach with
one mile long boardwalk, fine
dining, spas, golf, swimming &
boating & water sports, biking, tax
free boutique shopping as well as
140 outlet shops, nature trails, fun
land, Jungle Jim's Adventure Water
Park, play land and more.
**Services:** Complimentary
breakfast, shuttle service, beach
chairs & towels, heated pool &
sun deck, wine, cheese & crackers,
turn-down service, laundry &
parking.
**Restrictions:** No Pets & No
smoking
**Concierge:** Yes: available 24/7
**Room Service:** Yes: (daily)
6:00am – 10:00pm
**Restaurant:** Lupo di Mare
restaurant & bar, Italian style.
**Bar:** Yes: located in our Lupo di
Mare restaurant
**Business Facilities:** 24 hr access:
Internet, fax/scanner, printer. Free
high-speed WiFi & broadband
**Conference Room:** 1 room /
capacity: up to 60 people
**Sports Facilities:** Complimentary
guest pass at local facility
**Spa Services:** VIP Discounts at
Bad Hair Day Spa & Salon
**Airport:** Baltimore/Maryland &
Philadelphia Int'l Airports
**Location:** In the heart of
Rehoboth

Rehoboth's premier luxury hotel in the heart of Rehoboth Beach on the Avenue. Offering a wealth of complimentary amenities and services as well as comfort and space.

Park on-site and stroll Rehoboth Avenue and beach or hop on our open air beach shuttle for a little beach fun before heading back to relax in the comfort and privacy of your spacious guestroom or suite equipped with large granite bathrooms, luxurious bedding & linens, large flat screen HDTV's with DVD players, iPod clock radios, refrigerators, safes, sitting areas, coffee areas and more.

Enjoy breakfast and seasonal refreshments with cheese & crackers and wine reception nightly. Turn-down service with chocolates, WiFi & broadband Internet access as well as business center, shuttle with beach chairs & towels, outdoor heated pool with sun deck, grand piano lobby reception area with fireplace sitting area, evening room service, guest laundry, on-site restaurant & bar "Lupo do Mare," shops "Cleo's Boutique" and " Mod Cottage."

Our friendly attentive hotel staff looks forward to making your stay one worth repeating. Whether you are looking for a relaxing romantic stay, beach holiday, or fun-filled vacation, The Hotel Rehoboth is the ideal place to make magic memories to last a life time!

# THE BELLMOOR

We invite you to experience The Bellmoor Inn, offering the warmth and comfort of a friend's seaside home. Enjoy today's finest amenities amid yesterday's elegance in a warm, residential setting of Brazilian cherry floors, supple leather seating, libraries, game rooms, hearty country breakfasts, full service Day Spa, sun terrace, pools, gardens and much more.

The 78 room inn provides a wide range of extraordinary accommodations from garden rooms to suites in a warm, residential setting. The adults-only Club Level Suites offer unprecedented luxury and privacy, with exclusive elevator access, fireplaces, balconies, wet bar, marble baths and a private library.

The Garden Room is the perfect place to start the day with a complimentary hearty country breakfast overlooking the inn's gardens. Large windows and French doors allow the sun to stream in, bathing the room in a welcome glow. Afternoon refreshments daily. For Club Level Suites, there are drinks and snacks all day.

Our elegant Rehoboth Beach lodging is only a short walk to the fine boutiques and restaurants of downtown, beautiful Silver Lake or our ocean beach. Escape to The Bellmoor Inn and Spa, your oasis by the sea. After one visit, The Bellmoor Inn will become your favorite destination for celebration, re-laxation and rejuvenation.

**Address:** 6 Christian Street Rehoboth Beach DE 19971
**Phone:** 302-227-5800
**Tollfree:** 800-425-2355
**Fax:** 302-227-0323
**Email:** info@thebellmoor.com
**Web:** www.thebellmoor.com
**Room Rates:** 105–395
**Suite Rates:** 150–495
**No. of Rooms:** 55
**No. of Suites:** 23
**Credit Cards:** Most CCs Accepted
**Attractions:** Walk to fabulous boutique shopping, fine dining restaurants and the beach. Golf, tennis, fishing, sailing, birding, antiquing, seashore parks, and 160 outlet stores are nearby.
**Services:** On-site parking, bellman, gift shop, library, guest laundry, newspapers. All rooms have refrigerator, coffee maker, 2-line phone, cable TV & radio, high-speed Internet access.
**Restrictions:** Non-smoking, No pets, Children under 6 free, 4 rooms handicap equipped
**Concierge:** 8:00 a.m.-8:00 p.m.
**Room Service:** Check with front desk for available services.
**Restaurant:** Garden Room—serves a hearty country breakfast 7:30 a.m. - 10:30 am.
**Bar:** Located in restaurant
**Business Facilities:** Complete business and conference center, full time conference coordinator, 24 hour copy & fax
**Conference Room:** 5 rooms, capacity up to 110 people.
**Sports Facilities:** 2 outdoor pools, hot tub (adults only), Fitness room
**Spa Services:** Full service Day Spa (6 rooms), Massage, offering over 40 services.
**Airport:** Baltimore—Wash—Philly
**Location:** 2 blocks from the beach in South Rehoboth

# GREYFIELD INN - CUMBERLAND ISLAND

**Address:** 4 North Second Street
Fernandina Beach FL 32035
**Phone:** 904-261-6408
**Tollfree:** 866-401-8581
**Fax:** 904-321-0666
**Email:** seashore@greyfieldinn.com
**Web:** www.greyfieldinn.com
**Room Rates:** 395-525
**Suite Rates:** 575
**No. of Rooms:** 16
**No. of Suites:** 2
**Credit Cards:** Most CCs Accepted
**Attractions:** National Seashore
and Wilderness, 18 miles of
pristine white sand beach, native
wildlife, wilderness Jeep tours
**Services:** Airport pick up, Shuttle
service, Free parking, Gift shop,
Library, Robes, Complimentary
toiletries, All meals included in
room rate.
**Restrictions:** 2 night minimum
stay, No pets allowed, Children
5 and over welcome, 1 room
handicap equipped
**Room Service:** Yes
**Restaurant:** Greyfield Inn, open
to guests for breakfast, lunch
and dinner; dress code-jackets.
Complimentary non-alcoholic
beverages throughout the day, and
hors d'oeuvres in bar during
evening cocktail
**Bar:** Greyfield, open 24 hours
**Business Facilities:** Copiers and
Fax
**Conference Room:** 1 room,
capacity 22
**Sports Facilities:** Massage,
Croquet, Beach/Ocean,
Wilderness Jeep Excursions,
Fishing, Hiking, Biking, Boating
**Airport:** Jacksonville, FL
**Location:** Cumberland Island,
Georgia

Greyfield Inn is a grand and graceful mansion located on Georgia's largest and southernmost coastal island, Cumberland Island. Built in 1900, and opened as an inn in 1962, Greyfield is furnished today as it was at the turn of the century, with contemporary amenities blended in with the comfort of guests in mind.

Family portraits still hang in the living room; horsehair chairs flank a massive fireplace. Even the original books, including first editions are in place in the library. There is no check-in desk, no televisions or phones or ice machines or spa services. Just a rambling house with a spacious old verandah, dining rooms, bedrooms on this floor and that, large bathrooms with claw foot tubs and pedestal sinks. Bedroom windows face massive live oaks or the salt marshes along the Cumberland River.

In true southern fashion, they take great pride in their kitchen. Each morning, awaken to a full and satisfying breakfast which includes fresh-squeezed orange juice and fruit, homemade muffins and breakfast meats, as well as eggs, pancakes or one of the chef's specialties. Midday, enjoy the day's explorations with a satisfying picnic lunch. During cocktail hour each evening, Greyfield serves hors d'oeuvres in the Inn's well-stocked bar while sharing stories with fellow guests. Dinner is a casually elegant affair, served in the glow of candlelight. The nightly entrees feature fresh and creative cuisine, accompanied, if desired, by a selection from the wine cellar.

This grand Carnegie southern plantation is a step back in time. The dedicated staff is there to ensure that the stay on their idyllic, private island is the perfect retreat.

ESH 1694 25TH ED

# ISLAND COTTAGE OCEANFRONT INN CAFE & SPA

Island Cottage Oceanfront Inn is a quaint Key West style beach front bed & breakfast in Flagler Beach, Florida specializing in pampering & romance. This boutique style oceanfront bed and breakfast is ideal for anniversaries, romantic Florida honeymoons, spa retreats & spa getaways, Florida beachfront getaways & relaxing beachfront escapes.

Your hostess, Toni has an education in the field of advertising, marketing and design. An accomplished writer, poet, songwriter and artist as well, Toni's decorative touches and talents are evident throughout the villas and restaurant. While you visit Island Cottage, be sure to make a "Private" dinner reservation in the Tropical Breeze Cafe where Toni's culinary talents are also evident as she works in concert w/Mark to bring you a wonderful dining experience to be savored like fine wine.

Mark, your host, has hobbies that include antique car restoration, woodworking and boatbuilding. On occasion, guests have been invited in to Mark's private workshop where they have been able to watch the master as he worked on such projects as "Valentine," a 1969 Jaguar E-Type restoration completed in September, 2005. "Valentine" has since been entered in two Jaguar Concours events where she won "Best in her class" with scores of 98 and 99.8 respectively. "Miss Lola" is another of Mark's projects. She is a wooden Bahamian Dinghy designed, built and launched in the Island Cottage swimming pool during a fun filled Caribbean party with friends and guests.

Kissed by the sun, Island Cottage is warm, inviting, relaxing and luxurious offering the most romantic Florida beach front bed & breakfast getaway imaginable!

**Address:** 2316 S Oceanshore Blvd Flager Beach FL 32136
**Phone:** 386-439-0092
**Tollfree:** 877-662-6232
**Web:** www.islandcottagevillas.com
**Room Rates:** 269–369
**Suite Rates:** 329–399
**No. of Rooms:** 4
**No. of Suites:** 2
**Credit Cards:** Visa, MC
**Attractions**: Washington Oaks State Park, Bulow Ruins State Park, St. Augustine Historic District, Halifax Golf Course, Kayaking – Tomoka State Park, Flagler Beach Pier, Fishing, Swimming
**Services:** Whirlpool Tubs, Jacuzzis for Two, Fireplaces, Exquisite Gourmet Breakfasts, Solar Heated Pool, Private Secluded Beach, Free use of Bicycles, Great Ocean Views
**Restrictions:** Children over 15 only. Small dog acceptable in 1 room – $75 fee.
**Concierge:** Front desk assistance during regular hours
**Room Service:** Yes—available: 2–7pm from our "Wine, Sandwiches & Salads" menu
**Restaurant:** A gourmet breakfast is prepared and offered each morning to our guests.
**Bar:** No—however, fine wines & champagne are offered on our Room Service menu
**Business Facilities:** No
**Conference Room:** 1 room—Up to 14 persons
**Sports Facilities:** Not on site
**Spa Services:** Hot Stone & Swedish Massage, Facials, Wraps—Specializing in Couples services Side-by-Side.
**Airport:** Daytona, Sanford, & Jackson Airports
**Location:** Oceanfront

# THE PILLARS HOTEL - FORT LAUDERDALE

**Address:** 111 North Birch Road
Fort Lauderdale FL 33304
**Phone:** 954-467-9639
**Fax:** 954-763-2845
**Email:** guestservices@pillarshotel.com
**Web:** www.pillarshotel.com
**Room Rates:** 195–355
**Suite Rates:** 325 -579
**No. of Rooms:** 18
**No. of Suites:** 5
**Credit Cards:** Visa, MC, Amex
**Attractions**: Las Olas shops, restaurants and boutiques, Fort Lauderdale Beach, Boward Performing Art Center, Sawgrass Mills, Ft. Lauderdale Boat Show, The Everglades, The Bonnet House
**Services:** Complimentary Parking, Private Watertaxi stop, Library of books and DVDs, Newspapers, Cable TV and DVD players, Telephones, Individual air conditioning, Robes, Molton Browns toiletries.
**Restrictions:** No pets allowed, Children over 12 welcome, 1 room handicap equipped
**Concierge:** Yes: available 24/7
**Room Service:** Yes: available 24/7
**Restaurant:** The Secret Garden. Open 7 days a week in the winter and 5 days a week in the summer (closed on Sundays and Mondays)
**Bar:** Yes: Wine Bar (availability anytime)
**Business Facilities:** Fast Access and Wireless Internet, Fax and Copies
**Conference Room:** 1 room / capacity: up to 10 people
**Sports Facilities:** Outdoor Pool, Gym
**Spa Services:** Full spa services, manicures, pedicures, massages, facials.
**Airport:** Ft Lauderdale/ Hollywood
**Location:** Ft Lauderdale Central Beach

One block from Fort Lauderdale Beach on the Intercoastal Waterway are the lush tropical grounds of The Pillars at New River Sound.

The decor is inspired by an English plantation style, with a lovely mix of classic and cane and beautiful fabrics and colors. The twenty-three guestrooms and suites each contain a custom made bed with luxurious sheets, multiple pillows, and elegant bedspreads. The color schemes are tropical shades of green, gold and deep red.

The favorite suite is the Intracoastal Suite which is situated by the water. It has a Jacuzzi tub and magnificent views of the waterway from the well-appointed sitting area.

Should you wish to venture from the private paradise of The Pillars, Fort Lauderdale beach has a palm-lined promenade, lovely outdoor cafes and numerous shops overlooking the beach. Las Olas Boulevard beckons with world-class shopping, elegant dining and unforgettable nightlife.

The Pillars at New River Sound exudes the ambiance of a beautiful, comfortable home where guests experience a staff there to accommodate their every wish.

# CURRY MANSION INN

**B**e our guests at the Curry Mansion Inn, the moment you step inside, you begin to feel the unique ambiance of the Curry Mansion Inn, home of Florida's first millionaire. The house was named for William Curry, a penniless Bahamian immigrant who made his fortune reputedly as a salvager—those scurrilous fellows who preyed on shipwrecked travelers in Florida's pirate-infested waters. Curry attained status as Key West's first millionaire and began building the Mansion in 1869. The architectural details are common to wreckers, incorporating elements of many ports-of-call.

Rooms are beautifully appointed in wicker and antiques and offer private baths, phones, air conditioning, ceiling fans and cable television. Other amenities include off street parking, and a hot tub and swimming pool which can be enjoy 24 hours a day. Guests enjoy the finest amenities and full access to the 22-room mansion built by Florida's first millionaire family. Our Inn is barrier free.

Start your day with a complimentary full breakfast with made to order omelets and hash brown, fresh fruit, juice cereal, homemade rolls and pastries, coffee and tea—all served buffet style by the pool. In the afternoon enjoy an open bar cocktail party around the pool featuring live music and appetizers.

The temptations of Key West are just steps away. The easygoing life of Old Town Key West is within walking distance of the Inn. History abounds—visit Ernest Hemingway House Museum or collect a visitors pass and venture to the Zachary Taylor Start Park Beach (and Museum). Next explore the sophisticated shops, restaurants and sights of the local area or go snorkeling on North America's only living coral reef. Our staff can help you plan any special activities; dining, sports or fishing arrangements. The Inn is also equipped for corporate parties, conferences and receptions.

The Curry Mansion Inn ... where the elegance of Key West's past is equaled only by the elegance of its present.

**Address:** 511 Caroline Street Key West FL 33040
**Phone:** 305-294-5349
**Tollfree:** 800-253-3466
**Fax:** 305-294-4093
**Email:** frontdesk@currymansion.com
**Web:** www.currymansion.com
**Room Rates:** 145–325
**No. of Rooms:** 28
**No. of Suites:** 6
**Credit Cards:** Most CCs Accepted
**Attractions:** Historic Old Town, Ernest Hemingway House Museum, Audubon House, Maritime Heritage Society Museum, Fishing, Diving, Snorkeling in America's only living coral reef, Passes to Zachary Taylor State Park Beach & Museum
**Services:** Free parking, Laundry, Baby-sitting service, Card, billiards and game area, Balconies/decks, Cable TV, Telephones, Wet bar, Air-conditioning, full breakfast w/ made-to-order omelets
**Restrictions:** Pets under 25 lbs. only, 3 rooms handicap equipped
**Concierge:** Front Desk assist 24/7
**Room Service:** Delivery from local restaurants
**Restaurant:** Many fine restaurants within a short distance.
**Bar:** No—Cocktails served from 5:00–7:00pm w/live piano music
**Business Facilities:** Message center, Copier, Fax, Internet access via guest computer
**Conference Room:** 1 room, capacity 30 people
**Sports Facilities:** Swimming pool, Privileges at Zachary Taylor private beach
**Spa Services:** The front desk will make arrangements for a local masseuse or an appointment or directions to a local spa facility.
**Airport:** Key West Int'l Airport
**Location:** Historic downtown

# LA MER HOTEL AND DEWEY HOUSE

**Address:** 506 South Street
Key West FL 33040
**Phone:** 305-296-6577
**Tollfree:** 800-354-4455
**Fax:** 305-294-8272
**Email:** info@southernmostresorts.com
**Web:** www.southernmostresorts.com
**Room Rates:** 185–425
**No. of Rooms:** 19
**Attractions**: Swimming, snorkeling, sunbathing, shopping, historic sites, city tours, museums and galleries, sailing, glass bottom boat rides, sunset cruises, scuba diving, bike riding, plays and theater,
**Services:** Monogrammed bathrobes, Refrigerator, Umbrellas, Complimentary bottled water, Irons & boards, Coffee maker w/coffee, Kitchen/ Wet bars, Hair dryer, In room safes, "dipping pool on-site and access to three pools and Tiki Bars at our sister property.
**Restrictions:** Adult exclusive, Two night minimum on weekends.
**Concierge:** Yes: (daily) 8:00am to 5:00pm
**Room Service:** No
**Restaurant:** Charging privileges at Duval Beach Club. Open for breakfast, lunch and dinner.
**Bar:** Yes: our poolside Tiki Bar/ open from 10am–10pm
**Business Facilities:** Yes: Internet access from concierge and Tiki Bar
**Conference Room:** 1 room / capacity: up to 60 people
**Sports Facilities:** No: Swimming pool access at our sister property
**Spa Services:** The Oceanfront Cabana at our sister property.
**Airport:** Key West Airport
**Location:** Atlantic Ocean in Key West's Historic District

Key West's only luxury oceanfront bed and breakfast emanates island elegance against the backdrop of a white sand beach and lush, tropical flora and fauna. Lavishly renovated in 2003, this romantic island retreat with its distinctive turn-of-the-century architecture and gracious seaside setting, embraces sophisticated British Colonial style with an unexpected edge.

Dewey House, the original home of philosopher and educator John Dewey and its neighbor, the intimate La Mer Hotel are located in the heart of Key West's historic district on the Atlantic Ocean.

Indulge yourself in dramatically decorated garden and ocean view accommodations, exquisite bed linens, granite wet bars, private balconies and porches, spa tubs, sumptuous continental breakfasts, relaxing afternoon teas and weekday newspapers delivered right to your door. Unsurpassed quality and attention to every detail combine to assure you of the finest vacation experience Key West has to offer.

Unspoiled.

Uncomplicated.

Unforgettable … Come live the dream!

# CASA GRANDVIEW HISTORIC LUXURY INN COTTAGES & SUITES

1925 Mediterranean Revival Casa Grandview Luxury Historic Inn, Luxury Resort Vacation Cottages, & Art Deco Cabana Suites, offers all the modern conveniences of a downtown historic sophisticated city retreat, the privacy of a luxury vacation home or villa, state-of-the-art modern amenities and services of a luxury boutique hotel, and the unique character of an intimate charming bed and breakfast inn, nestled in a private tropical island luxurious resort setting, with a cozy Caribbean atmosphere and Mediterranean flair located in a prime "trendy" urban location near all WPB activities!

Unlike traditional hotels, Casa Grandview is a smaller boutique style resort property consisting of a collection of historic compound cottages available on weekly basis, offering private accommodations, with unique special touches, not found in larger West Palm Beach hotels, or typical vacation rentals.

Casa Grandview "compound" occupies half a city block from street to street within the Grandview Heights Historic District in Downtown West Palm Beach area. The well-lit grounds and exquisite pools are nestled among lush gardens and tropical landscaping. The stunning architecture evokes the best of historic South Florida charm, Miami Art Deco style, and modern amenities reminiscent of resort boutique style luxuries.

Casa Grandview is ideally located off I-95 East, South of Okeechobee Boulevard, and West of Intracoastal Waterway in the City's "trendy" Grandview Heights Historic District yet, within minutes of beaches, restaurants, cultural events, entertainment, and all the action Downtown venues, and nightlife.

**Address:** 1410 Georgia Avenue West Palm Beach FL 33401
**Phone:** 561-655-8932
**Tollfree:** 877-435-2786
**Fax:** 561-655-1795
**Email:** inquiries@casagrandview.com
**Web:** www.casagrandview.com
**Room Rates:** 150–350
**Suite Rates:** 150–400
**No. of Rooms:** 5
**No. of Suites:** 12
**Credit Cards:** Most CCs Accepted
**Attractions**: CityPlace, Worth Ave, Armory Art Center, Norton Museum, Kravis Center, Flagler Museum, Clematis Street, Lion Country Safari, Palm Beach, Palm Beach Atlantic University, Palm Beach, CVB, Intracoastal Waterway, Scenic Bike Trails, PBI Airport
**Services:** Tropical Pools with Jacuzzi, Spa Robes, Spacious Living Rooms, Fully Equipped Gourmet Kitchens, "Well Appointed" Luxurious Furnishings, King/Queen Beds with Fine Linens, Outdoor Grilling Lounging Area
**Restrictions:** Reservations guaranteed with 50% deposit of reservation total—balance at check-in.
**Concierge:** No
**Room Service:** No
**Restaurant**: Complimentary breakfast—designated guest rooms only. Several fine restaurants within walking distance.
**Bar:** Nearby
**Business Facilities:** No
**Conference Room:** No
**Sports Facilities:** Nearby
**Airport:** Palm Beach Int'l
**Location:** Downtown Area West Palm Beach—Grandview Heights Historic District

# REGENCY SUITES HOTEL ~ MIDTOWN ATLANTA

**Address:** 975 W Peachtree St
Atlanta GA 30309
**Phone:** 404-876-5003
**Tollfree:** 800-642-3629
**Fax:** 404-817-7511
**Email:** regenceysales@mindspring.com
**Web:** www.regencysuites.com
**Suite Rates:** 99–250
**No. of Suites:** 96
**Credit Cards:** Most CCs Accepted
**Attractions**: Six Flags,
Underground Atlanta, High
Museum of Art, Fox Theater,
Atlanta Symphony's home,
Woodruff Art Center, Carter
Center, Georgia Tech Campus,
Martin Luther King Jr. Center,
Atlanta Botanical Gardens, Center
Puppetry Arts, GA Aquarium
**Services:** Daily Complimentary
breakfast, Valet service, Garage
parking, Car hire, Cable TV,
newspapers, Hair dryers,
toiletries, Non-smoking suites,
Phones w/data ports, WiFi.
**Restrictions:** No pets allowed, 4
suites handicap equipped
**Concierge:** Yes
**Room Service:** Food Delivery
available from area restaurants
**Restaurant:** Steel Restaurant
w/wine list & signature dishes;
Marlow's Tavern w/open kitchen
to see the chefs at work; just a few
choices but steps away.
**Bar:** Directly across the
street — Marlows Tavern
**Business Facilities:** Open 24/7
wireless Internet.
**Conference Room:** 2 rooms,
capacity 50
**Sports Facilities:** State of the Art
Fitness Center open 24/7
**Spa Services:** Our concierge
will be more than happy to make
recommendations.
**Airport:** Hartsfield-Jackson
**Location:** Adjacent to MARTA
Midtown Station.

Luxury! Location! Elegance! Style! ~
This classic European Hotel in the center of Atlanta's Midtown brings guests quiet elegance along with friendly service in a homelike setting. With ninety-six well designed and carefully furnished suites that were newly renovated in 2006, it offers a welcome stay for the business or leisure visitor. All suites feature king, queen, or double/double beds and living rooms with queen-size convertible sofas. Kitchens are equipped with microwave ovens, refrigerators, coffee maker, small appliances, and table service for four people. Guests will also find valet service, covered parking, and on-site laundry. Choice microwavable food is available in the mini-convenience store.

Monday through Thursday evenings guests are offered a complimentary meal at Marlow's Tavern directly across the street. In addition, a complimentary breakfast is served daily in the Club Room.

Regency Suites Hotel is located in the center of Atlanta's cultural and business district, just 2 blocks from Interstates 75/85. Marta's Midtown Station, conveniently located a few steps away, offers a quick ride to Underground Atlanta, Downtown, the Georgia Dome, World Congress Convention Center, Woodruff Arts Center and Buckhead. Also located nearby are the Georgia Tech Campus and Piedmont Park.

# THE PRESIDENTS' QUARTERS INN

You've heard these words before; "General Robert E. Lee slept here."… when visiting his West Point classmate, General Alexander Lawton. Our parking lot was the residential site of Georgia's Royal Governor (ca. 1735) and we were a movie location for the television mini-series "Roots."

Voted "Best Savannah Bed and Breakfast B&B" (2008–2010), The Presidents' Quarters Inn epitomizes lodging with a legacy in the Landmark Savannah Historic District. The historic bed and breakfast inn differentiates with conservative rates, liberal amenities, overly spacious rooms and tranquil, on-the-square lodging that typifies historic Savannah's unique sense of place.

Overlooking Oglethorpe Square, the sixteen spacious Savannah hotel rooms feature elegant decor, all new private baths with retro black and white flooring, granite countertops, and amenities tailored for the most discerning of Savannah travelers. Four Savannah romantic suites feature a private balcony overlooking the courtyard gardens; two suites feature a private loft bedroom with full bath, plus a hospitality setting, wet bar and ½ bath for visitors; while our two premier suites provide private street-side access, plus private balcony.

The Savannah GA bed and breakfast epitomize the Old South, aristocratic southern style—living well and pampering guests. Carefree guests simply ease into exclusive Savannah experiences, coupled with executive mansion comforts of the 18th Century's ruling elite.

Contact The Presidents' Quarters Inn now for your unforgettable Savannah GA bed and breakfast stay in historic Savannah, Georgia—complete with top-tier introductions to the Best of Savannah!

**Address:** 225 E President Street Savannah GA 31401
**Phone:** 912-233-1600
**Tollfree:** 800-233-1776
**Fax:** 912-238-0849
**Email:** info@presidentsquarters.com
**Web:** www.presidentsquarters.com
**Room Rates:** 189–250
**Suite Rates:** 239–325
**No. of Rooms:** 16
**No. of Suites:** 4
**Credit Cards:** Most CCs Accepted
**Attractions**: Owens-Thomas House, Telfair Academy of Arts and Sciences, Mrs. Wilkes Dining Room, Savannah Music Festival, Forsyth Park.
**Services:** All inclusive amenities epitomize southern generosity. Small indulgences included in the rate are: daily chef's breakfast, on-site parking, nightly turn down, pillow top sweet, pre-dinner wine hour with hors d'oeuvres. Elevator to all floors.
**Restrictions:** No smoking inn. Pet and children friendly. Handicap accessible on first level.
**Concierge:** Yes: available 7am–10pm from our Front Desk
**Room Service:** No
**Restaurant:** Exclusive to lodging guests, a chef's breakfast is served in the parlor and courtyard.
**Bar:** No: Evening Wine & Hors d'oeuvres (included with rate)
**Business Facilities:** Secure WiFi, Copies/Fax and Front Desk Assistance
**Conference Room:** 3 meetings areas / capacity: up to 25 people
**Sports Facilities:** No on-site gym or workout room
**Spa Services:** Spas are within walking distance.
**Airport:** Savannah-Hilton Head Int'l Airport
**Location:** Historic District

# HOTEL HANA-MAUI AND HONUA SPA

**Address:** 5031 Hana Highway
Hana HI 96713
**Phone:** 808-248-8211
**Tollfree:** 800-321-HANA
**Fax:** 808-248-7264
**Email:** reservations@hotelmaui.com
**Web:** www.hotelhanamaui.com
**No. of Rooms:** 62
**No. of Suites:** 7
**Credit Cards:** Most CCs Accepted
**Attractions:** Hamoa Beach, all types of water sports, Hawaiiaan culture, museums, tours, golf, tennis, Kahanu Garden
**Services:** Robes, hair dryer, in-room safe, iron and board, organic cotton sheets/towels, welcome basket.
**Restaurant:** Located off the lobby is award-winning Ka'uiki with a full menu selection for breakfast and dinner and exquisite Maui dining. Connecting to the restaurant is the Paniolo Lounge offering lighter fare.
**Bar:** Cocktails from 11:30am – 10:00pm and music 6:30 – 8:30pm
**Business Facilities:** Limited
**Conference Room:** several areas/ up to 100 people
**Sport Facilities:** Yogo, weight training, aqua aerobics
**Spa Services:** At the Honua Spa, we magnify what Hana naturally offers by utilizing the abundant plants, minerals and water blended in our teas, baths, natural body and face products and treatments.
**Airport:** Hana Airport
**Location:** End of Hana Highway

On the lush eastern coast of Maui, Hawaii, at the end of the Hana Highway, is the legendary Hotel Hāna-Maui and luxury Honua Spa. Here, tranquility is a way of life and the blend of true Hawaii and leisurely amenities reflect the celebrated Hawaiian heritage and its natural beauty.

Find yourself at this enchanting Maui resort hotel and experience unspoiled serenity. Hotel Hāna-Maui is the perfect location for honeymoons and romantic getaways. Our resort guests who book their Maui accommodations at Hotel Hāna-Maui experience the ultimate in nurturing with massage, facials, and body treatments at the intimate Honua Spa, located on an acre of plush, landscaped grounds and overlooking the magnificent Hāna Bay.

Beyond our nurturing wellness services, the experience of Hāna is opened by the many on-grounds, Maui hotel & resort and surrounding local activities, including the awe-inspiring Seven Sacred Pools (O'heo Gulch). The Maui hotel & resort has long been a favorite Hawaii vacation retreat for generations seeking its healing and spiritual gifts. These celebrated freshwater pools and waterfalls are considered a sacred connection to life and serve as a reminder of how easy it is to savor every renewing moment at Hotel Hāna-Maui, a Maui hotel & resort. Experience natural tranquility, peace and serenity.

# THE NEW OTANI KAIMANA BEACH HOTEL

The New Otani Kaimana Beach Hotel is a jewel in a perfect setting. Nestled between a white sand beach and a 500-acre Kapiolani Park, with the famous Diamond Head Crater as its backdrop. This romantic boutique hotel presents stunning views, a fabulous open-air restaurant, and a casual and friendly ambiance, all at the preferred edge of Waikiki. Center of Waikiki Beach and famous International Marketplace is within 15 minutes of walking distance.

The hotel is located beachfront on Sans Souci Beach, across from Kapiolani Park; a beautiful park listed on the state's historic register as many of its exceptional trees date back over 100 years. Nearby sites are the Honolulu Zoo, Waikiki Shell—home to many outdoor concerts and shows, the Sunday art shows, tennis courts, soccer fields, archery range, and even a 3-mile jogger's course, which encompasses part of the Honolulu Marathon.

The Kaimana Beach Travel located in the hotel lobby is happy to assist you with all of your travel needs including shuttle service information, inter-airline ticketing, island tours, car rentals, dinner shows and cruise.

The New Otani Kaimana Beach Hotel is the perfect setting for small meetings or intimate receptions of up to 80 guests. We welcome any questions or special requests you may have.

**Address:** 2863 Kalakaua Ave Honolulu HI 96815
**Phone:** 808-923-1555
**Tollfree:** 888-524-6262
**Fax:** 808-921-7013
**Email:** rooms@kaimana.com
**Web:** www.kaimana.com
**Room Rates:** 180–440
**Suite Rates:** 530–1500
**No. of Rooms:** 120
**No. of Suites:** 5
**Credit Cards:** Most CCs Accepted
**Attractions:** Kapiolani Park, Diamond Head Crater, Sans Souci Beach, golf, all types of water sports, museums, tours, Waikiki Aquarium, Honolulu Zoo
**Services:** Airport transportation, ATM, baby sitting, baggage checkroom and storage, car rental, church services, fitness center, Internet access, and laundry service.
**Restrictions:** Registered guide dogs only
**Concierge:** Yes
**Room Service:** Limited 7am–9:30pm
**Restaurant:** The Hau Tree Lanai is the favorite beachfront restaurant for visitors and long-time residents alike. The Miyako Restaurant is cozy and Zen-like with its traditional Japanese decor.
**Bar:** Yes—Full Bar
**Business Facilities:** No—Kiosk
**Conference Room:** Yes
**Sports Facilities:** Gym—Nominal fee
**Airport:** Honolulu Int'l Airport
**Location:** Beachfront

# THE BUCKINGHAM ATHLETIC CLUB/EXECUTIVE HOTEL

**Address:** 440 S LaSalle Street
Chicago IL 60605
**Phone:** 312-663-8910
**Fax:** 312-663-8909
**Email:** bachotel@kempersports.com
**Web:** www.bac-chicago.com
**Room Rates:** 175–210
**Suite Rates:** 215–260
**No. of Rooms:** 21
**No. of Suites:** 3
**Credit Cards:** Most CCs Accepted
**Attractions**: Chicago Cultural
Center, Medieval Times
Dinner & Tournament, Sears
Tower Skydeck, The Hancock
Observatory.
**Services:** Each room has a
mini-bar and Internet access.
Complimentary continental
breakfast. Daily newspaper. Aveda
bath products.
**Restrictions:** Non smoking, No
Pets, No handicap accessible
**Concierge:** Yes: Mon–Fri 8:30am–
5:00pm
**Room Service:** No
**Restaurant:** One of the country's
premier dining rooms, Everest
shares the 40th floor. Open
Tu–Th 5:30–9pm, Fri 5:30–9:30,
Sat 5:00–10pm
**Bar:** Yes—located in the club
**Business Facilities:** Limited
access, fax copies, wireless &
high-speed
**Conference Room:** 2 rooms /
capacity: up to 75 people
**Sports Facilities:** Guest
privileges at the Athletic club
**Spa Services:** Massage
Therapy—full-body massage.
**Airport:** Midway Airport &
O'Hare Airport
**Location:** Downtown, located in
the business district

For intimate, business-friendly accommodations, the executive hotel at The Buckingham Athletic Club offers the luxury of a boutique hotel and the convenience of being located in the heart of Chicago's financial district. The executive hotel features 21 luxurious, over-sized hotel rooms (18 club rooms and three unique master suites) overlooking Chicago's skyline from a 40-story penthouse perspective.

Continue your penthouse perspective in our luxury rooms with such conveniences as a mini-bar and Internet access in each room. Enjoy a complimentary continental breakfast, a daily newspaper and Aveda bath products. Our guests enjoy access to our Corporate Concierge Services to fulfill special requests.

During a break from your meeting sample items from the Everest Restaurant In-Room Dining Service.

After a day of site seeing or planning mega financial mergers—our guests may enjoy a full-body massage from a relaxing touch to deep bodywork, our certified therapists can fulfill your needs. Perhaps a workout in the Buckingham Athletic Club will help you relax? Guests receive complimentary access to the elegant, state-of-the-art Buckingham Athletic Club, located on the third floor of the building.

Whether you are in Chicago for business or pleasure, The Buckingham Athletic Club/Executive Hotel is the place to stay.

# NEW HARMONY INN

A scenic two hour drive from Louisville Kentucky, St. Louis Missouri, under three hour drive from Nashville Tennessee, and Indianapolis Indiana.

The town of New Harmony preserves a past dating back to 1814, when German-speaking settlers homesteaded the community. A cluster of contemporary luxury lodgings, The New Harmony Inn was designed in the "traditional style" by Evans Woolen to harmonize with the architecture of one of American's most significant historic districts.

Eighteen of the ninety guestrooms have gas-burning fireplaces. A variety of guestrooms are available with a balcony, walk out patio, lake view, flat screen TV, yellow poplar floors, or spiral staircase leading to a sleeping loft. The Inn offers complimentary continental breakfast, wireless Internet, and parking. In addition, four guest houses are available ranging from the one bedroom 1840s Garden House to the gem of the property—the four bedroom Orchard House.

One of our many recreational opportunities is the indoor pool which is open year-round for your enjoyment. We also offer a fully-equipped fitness center, sauna, Jacuzzi, tennis courts, outdoor game area, putting green, complimentary bicycles, historic walking tours, walking trails, as well as abundant shopping. Enjoy dining at The Red Geranium Restaurant which features a daily selection of fresh seasonal American Cuisine. The New Harmony Inn Conference Center is a perfect setting for any type of meeting. The setting allows you to be very focused and creative.

Everything in New Harmony is within walking distance. Park your car when you arrive and you don't need to get back into it until you leave. Enjoy walking or taking a bicycle ride around town and along the nature trails by the Wabash River.

Visit New Harmony—relax and enjoy!!!

**Address:** 506 N Street
New Harmony IN 47631
**Phone:** 812-682-4491
**Tollfree:** 800-782-8605
**Fax:** 812-682-3423
**Email:** info@newharmonyinn.com
**Web:** www.newharmonyinn.com
**Room Rates:** 110–190
**Suite Rates:** 170–215
**No. of Rooms:** 90
**No. of Suites:** 2
**Credit Cards:** Most CCs Accepted
**Attractions**: Antique and Unique Shops, Art Galleries, Live Summer Theatre, Historic Tours, Granite Labyrinth, Roofless Church, Antique Show, Kunstfest Festival, Under the Beams Concerts, Gallery Stroll, Christmas in New Harmony, Paul Tillich Park
**Services:** Continental Breakfast, Outdoor Game Area, Walking Trails, Wireless Internet, Bicycles, Golf Car Rental, Tennis Courts.
**Restrictions:** Pet Friendly—Security Deposit Required
**Concierge:** Yes: available 24/7 from our front desk
**Room Service:** No
**Restaurant:** Red Geranium Restaurant.
**Bar:** Yes: Open (seasonal) from 11am–10pm / casual bar menu/ unique beers & extensive wine list
**Business Facilities:** Audio-visual, wireless Internet.
**Conference Room:** 5 rooms / capacity from 10-300 people
**Sports Facilities:** Indoor swimming pool, tennis courts
**Spa Services:** Full fitness center with pool, hot tub, sauna, etc.
**Airport:** Evansville Dress Regional Airport
**Location:** Historic small community

# THE CORNSTALK HOTEL

**Address:** 915 Royal Street
New Orleans LA 70116
**Phone:** 504-523-1515
**Tollfree:** 800-759-6112
**Fax:** 504-595-3196
**Email:** reservations@cornstalkhotel.com
**Web:** www.cornstalkhotel.com
**Room Rates:** 115–250
**No. of Rooms:** 13
**Credit Cards:** Most CCs Accepted
**Attractions:** French Quarter,
French Market, Art galleries and
museums. Buggy Rides, Aquarium
of the Americas, Bourbon Street,
Jackson Square, Imax Theatre,
Superdome, Tours and Harrah's
Casino. Many scheduled and non-
scheduled parades pass right in
front of proper
**Services:** All Rooms Include:
Private Baths, Cable T.V., Phone,
Wireless Internet. Available:
Hair dryers, Iron/Ironing Board,
Refridgerator/Microwave, Print
Services.
**Restrictions:** Pet & Smoking
restrictions
**Concierge:** Daily 8am to 12am
**Room Service:** No
**Restaurant:** No
**Bar:** No
**Business Facilities:** Fax, Wireless
Internet, Printing Services
**Conference Room:** Limited
**Sport Facilities:** No
**Spa Services:** No—will gladly
refer to local facilities
**Airport:** Louis Armstrong
National
**Location:** Central French Quarter
Location

The Cornstalk Hotel, once a private home, now welcomes visitors from around the world to step inside the famous Cornstalk Fence in the French Quarter and enjoy the hospitality of it's Victorian charm.

The historic Cornstalk Hotel, known throughout the years for its Victorian Charm, was built in 1816, with the Victorian façade having been added at a later date. This beautiful hotel with fourteen exquisite guestrooms, all with private bath, has been refurbished throughout with beautiful antiques and crystal chandeliers. It is the most unique and romantic boutique hotel in the French Quarter. The Cornstalk Hotel is perfect for your anniversary, engagement, honeymoon, or holiday vacation. On your visit to the Cornstalk Hotel you will enjoy the superb Southern Hospitality of our staff, who are happy and dedicated to help you make the most of your stay in the Big Easy.

The Cornstalk Hotel has an ideal location, right in the heart of the French Quarter, with the sights, the sounds, the gourmet foods and the night life of old New Orleans all within a short walk of the hotel. Our location offers you easy access to all of New Orleans' major attractions, as well as the closeness of antique and gift shops, art galleries and, riverboat and carriage tours and we are just minutes to the music and entertainment of Bourbon Street as well as the jazz of Frenchmen Street at night (without the noise).

The Cornstalk Hotel is also available for your exclusive use for private events such as weddings, receptions, family reunions, anniversary celebrations as well as office, birthday and holiday parties.

The Cornstalk Hotel, Your New Orleans Hotel!

# BELFAST BAY INN & LUXURY SUITES

When in the Belfast-Camden area . . .You are invited to Belfast's only AAA-Four Diamond award-winning and Select Registry boutique hotel where you will experience the intimacy of a bed and breakfast with the services and amenities of a luxury hotel.

Our eight luxuriously appointed two -person suites are located right in the heart of downtown Belfast on Main Street, nestled among quaint shops, art galleries and restaurants. Best of all, we're only steps to the waterfront at the town pier. Our beautiful seaside city is a short scenic drive to neighboring Camden and is perfectly located for a day trip at beautiful Acadia National Park.

Our romantic, premier boutique hotel offers elegant lodging and the finest in personalized accommodations for both leisure and business travelers. Perfect for getaways, wedding guests, retreats, family reunions, birthdays and anniversaries or just a night away.

**Address:** 72 Main Street Belfast ME 04915
**Phone:** 207-338-5600
**Fax:** 207-338-9100
**Email:** info@belfastbayinn.com
**Web:** belfastbayinn.com
**Room Rates:** 198–368
**Suite Rates:** 198–368
**No. of Rooms:** 8
**No. of Suites:** 6
**Credit Cards:** Visa, MC
**Attractions:** Seaside villages, eclectic collection of galleries, artists studios, shops, hiking in the local state parks, view maritime Maine history at the local museum, sailing/boating on the bay, explore various working lighthouses along the coast.
**Services:** Luxurious furnishings, harbor view/gas fireplaces/balconies in some rooms; private baths.
**Restrictions:** Call for details
**Concierge:** Front Desk
**Room Service:** Breakfast
**Restaurant:** There are several local area restaurants with wonderful smells/flavors to tantalize the taste buds. We will be happy to make recommendations and reservations
**Bar:** Nearby
**Business Facilities:** Limited
**Conference Room:** Limited
**Sports Facilities:** Nearby
**Spa Services:** In-Suite Therapeutic Massage available. After receiving massage therapy you will experience a feeling of well being, increased energy and overall balance. Let us recommend a treatment just for you!
**Airport:** Bangor Int'l Airport
**Location:** Heart of downtown Belfast

# BLAIR HILL INN

**Address:** 351 Lily Bay Road
Greenville ME 04441
**Phone:** 207-695-0224
**Fax:** 207-695-4324
**Email:** info@blairhill.com
**Web:** www.blairhill.com
**Room Rates:** 300–495
**Suite Rates:** 350–450
**No. of Rooms:** 8
**No. of Suites:** 1
**Credit Cards:** Visa, MC, Amex
**Attractions:** Enjoy Fly-fishing, Whitewater Rafting, Hiking, Kayaking, Boating, Seaplane Rides, Golf, Moose Safaris, Mountain Biking, Swimming and more. Don't forget about Moosehead Lake and the beautiful mountains surrounding us.
**Services:** Fine linens, Feather beds, Down comforters and pillows (non-allergenic available), Plush robes for winter & freshly pressed cotton robes for summer, All king/queen beds.
**Restrictions:** No Pets, No Smoking and Children Over 10 years of age Welcome
**Concierge:** Front Desk
**Restaurant:** Dine at one of Maine's most renowned restaurants. Five course, prix fixe menus combine with views that leave room for little response but awestruck silence. Life doesn't get much better.
**Bar:** The cocktail bar is a handsome and sumptuous place to unwind.
**Business Facilities:** Limited
**Conference Room:** Limited
**Sport Facilities:** No
**Spa Services:** Massage therapy enjoyed in the privacy of your guest room can be scheduled for you and your partner. Swedish, Neuromuscular and Hot Stone therapies are available.
**Airport:** Hancock County-bar Harbor Airport
**Location:** between Camden and Bar Harbor

Blair Hill Inn is a perfect place, a grand yet intimate country hotel sewn into the picturesque landscape overlooking Moosehead Lake. Sitting atop 20 foot high stone walls and drenched in natural light, its gardens and sweeping lawns seem literally to trickle down the hillside.

The interior of this 1891 mansion turned Maine Inn draws an extraordinary landscape inwards. Transformed from a private estate into one of the country's premiere luxury inns, proprietors Dan and Ruth McLaughlin have created a masterpiece.

Each space has been individually designed and decorated with taste and imagination that reflects a 'fresh air' style. Beautiful private baths with high-end materials such as slate, marble, stone & cedar and current features like rain showers, vessel sinks and custom vanities … and MORE!

Maine's most beautiful inn is distinguished as much for its exquisite architecture and vast lake views as for its luxurious accommodations, award winning restaurant and summer evening concerts. Refined and elegant but oh so easy and comfortable, Blair Hill Inn is the choice for the discriminating traveler who enjoys genuine luxury, nature's magnificence and sumptuous dining.

ESH I 592 25TH ED

# KENNEBUNKPORT INN

The Kennebunkport Inn—Kennebunkport, Maine's quintessential classic New England inn—has been a renowned and timeless landmark Kennebunkport hotel in Kennebunkport since 1899. Once a tea merchant's expansive mansion, the Kennebunkport Inn captures the classic appeal of that era with a sophisticated modern blend of service and attention to detail. The warm and welcoming staff provides a rare blend of personal attention and knowledge to ensure an exceptional stay.

With a superb location in Kennebunkport's Dock Square, the Kennebunkport Inn is within steps of world-class shopping and dining and a myriad of activities: art galleries, museums, golf, fishing, sailing, whale watching, swimming and biking.

The Kennebunkport Inn offers 49 casually sophisticated lodging accommodations. On-site dining options include "One Dock" the Kennebunkport Inn's award-winning restaurant, the lively piano bar featuring some of the finest local talent, and dining under the stars on Artemesia's outdoor patio. Spa services, in-room fitness equipment, morning coffee service, complimentary continental breakfast, beach passes & chairs, and a guest computer area complete the array of offerings at the Kennebunkport Inn.

Casual elegance, timeless architecture, a superb location, and outstanding staff make this Kennebunkport hotel the ideal choice for a romantic getaway, active vacation, family celebration or business retreat.

**Address:** One Dock Square Kennebunkport ME 04046
**Phone:** 207-967-2621
**Tollfree:** 800-248-2621
**Fax:** 207-967-3705
**Email:** kportinn@roadrunner.com
**Web:** www.kennebunkportinn.com
**Room Rates:** 99–399
**Suite Rates:** 279–439
**No. of Rooms:** 46
**No. of Suites:** 3
**Credit Cards:** Visa, MC, Amex
**Attractions**: Historic District and harbor, Day sailing, Sightseeing, Deep-sea fishing excursions, Boat charters, 1 mile to beach; Antique shops, art galleries, 5 golf courses, tennis.
**Services:** Parking, Cable TV, Telephones, Private bath, Complimentary toiletries, Views of village and river, Kitchen and fireplaces available. Pool. Wireless Internet, Massage shower heads, CD Players.
**Restrictions:** No pets, No smoking
**Concierge:** Yes: 7:00am–11:00pm (daily)
**Room Service:** No
**Restaurant:** One Dock offers creative, contemporary New England cuisine and traditional Maine favorites.
**Bar:** The Bar At One Dock: open from 5-12:00pm (seasonal)
**Business Facilities:** Fax, Copier, Wireless Internet, Guest Computer
**Conference Room:** 2 rooms / capacity: up to 50
**Sports Facilities:** Outdoor swimming pool
**Spa Services:** Including Therapeutic Massage and Spa Body Treatments.
**Airport:** Portland Int'l Airport
**Location:** Center of Kennebunkport.

# THE WHITE BARN INN & SPA

**Address:** 37 Beach Avenue
Kennebunkport ME 04046
**Phone:** 207-967-2321
**Fax:** 207-967-1100
**Email:** innkeeper@whitebarninn.com
**Web:** www.whitebarninn.com
**Room Rates:** 310–685
**Suite Rates:** 585–1,600
**No. of Rooms:** 26
**No. of Suites:** 9
**Credit Cards:** Visa, MC, Amex
**Attractions**: The village of
Kennebunkport offers a multitude
of fine shops and art galleries.
Beach walks, biking, swimming,
horseback riding, deep sea
fishing, whale watching, sailing,
and antiquing.
**Services:** Parking, Laundry
service, TV Lounge, Fireplaces,
Cable TV, whirlpool baths,
Twice daily maid service, Robes,
Toiletries and newspaper,
breakfast and afternoon tea
**Restrictions:** Call for details
**Concierge:** Yes: available (daily)
8:00am–9:00pm
**Room Service:** No
**Restaurant:** Encompassing two
restored barns and with a menu
that is refreshed every week.
**Bar:** Yes: our Piano Bar/ open
from 6:30pm till Midnight
**Business Facilities:** Message
center, Admin assist, Copier,
Audio-Visual
**Conference Room:** 4 rooms (on
& off site) / capacity: up to 160
people
**Sports Facilities:** Outdoor
heated pool & off site fitness
**Spa Services:** Launched in the
summer of 2006 and created
exclusively for guests of the inn,
the White Barn Spa assures spot-
on relaxation in the privacy of the
inn without the bothers of visiting
a remote spa.
**Airport:** Portland Airport &
Logan Airport
**Location:** Lower Village

Constructed in the 1860s, the White Barn Inn has offered superb hospitality and an excellent table for boarders since the days of the civil war. It has operated as the White Barn Inn since 1973.

The White Barn Inn is a charming country inn offering luxurious accommodations year-round and award-winning gourmet dining. The Inn features several room types, a pool, gardens and a prime location in the heart of Kennebunkport, Maine where there is a variety of shopping, dining and sights.

The 26 guest accommodations enjoy a careful selection of coordinated fabrics and wall coverings throughout. Features vary by room type. Several have fireplaces. Every guestroom is appointed with fresh flowers and fruit, plush terry cloth robes, TV & CD system, voice mail, and Molton Brown toiletries. Guests enjoy complimentary country continental breakfast and newspapers, afternoon tea, port and brandy, turndown service, use of a heated pool, public-area fireplaces, lending library, touring bicycles, canoes and beach chairs.

Launched in the summer of 2006, the White Barn Inn is now home to a luxurious full service spa.

The White Barn Inn Restaurant is New England's premiere AAA Five Diamond dining establishment. Located adjacent to the Inn.

# ANTRIM 1844 COUNTRY HOUSE HOTEL

Nestled in the rolling Catoctin Mountains in central Maryland, The Antrim 1844 is a restored country inn resort, which is acclaimed both regionally and nationally.

The mansion, outbuildings, and grounds of Antrim 1844 create an ambiance of Antebellum grace with European style. Surrounded by 24 acres of countryside, Antrim 1884 is a true respite from the cares of urban life. Guests may choose to leisurely stroll the magnificent grounds, or for those interested in more active recreation, there is croquet, tennis, a golf green, horseshoes, and a swimming pool with a gazebo. Antique shops are a short walk from the Inn. Gettysburg battlefields are only 12 miles away.

Antrim 1844 is truly the Country Hotel wedding experience you have always dreamed off. Our experienced event planners will guide you through every step. Antrim offers an extraordinary variety of facilities for your business gathering

Antrim 1844 is renowned for its superb cuisine. Start your day with continental wake up tray delivered right to your guestroom. At Antrim 1844 rediscover a time long lost, a time when grace, elegance, and hospitality were the domain of the Great American hotels.

**Address:** 30 Trevanion Road Taneytown MD 21787
**Phone:** 410-756-6812
**Tollfree:** 800-858-1844
**Fax:** 410-756-2744
**Email:** info@antrim1844.com
**Web:** www.antrim1844.com
**Room Rates:** 160–300
**Suite Rates:** 260–400
**No. of Rooms:** 40
**No. of Suites:** 15
**Credit Cards:** Most CCs Accepted
**Attractions**: Gettysburg Battlefield, Antiquing, Hiking, Waterfalls, Fine Dining, Baltimore Inner Harbor, Hershey Park, Horseback Riding
**Services:** Gift shop, TV in the pub, library, fireplaces, balconies, newspaper, radio, Robes, hair dryer, whirlpool baths, breakfast, afternoon tea, turn down service, CD players, high-speed Internet.
**Restrictions:** No pets allowed, 2 rooms are handicap equipped
**Concierge:** Assistance available 24/7 at the front desk
**Room Service:** No
**Restaurant:** Experience world class dining at it's best the Smokehouse Restaurant.
**Bar:** Pickwick Pub, 3:00pm-12:30am, Weekend pianist, Hors d'oeuvres 6:30 – 7:30pm
**Business Facilities:** Message center, Copiers, Fax, High-speed Internet
**Conference Room:** 3 rooms, capacity 8-250
**Sports Facilities:** Outdoor swimming pool, Croquet, Putting green, 1 Nova Grass tennis court, Volleyball
**Spa Services:** Massages, Jacuzzi bath tub, spa products
**Airport:** BWI; Reagan; Dulles
**Location:** Catoctin Mountains of Central Maryland

# HAWTHORNE INN BED AND BREAKFAST

**Address:** 462 Lexington Road Concord MA 01742
**Phone:** 978-369-5610
**Fax:** 978-287-4949
**Email:** Inn@ConcordMass.com
**Web:** www.ConcordMass.com
**Room Rates:** 159 -329
**No. of Rooms:** 7
**Credit Cards:** Most CCs Accepted
**Attractions**: Walk to homes of authors Hawthorne, Alcott (Little Women), Emerson, explore the pathways about Walden Pond to visit Thoreau's cabin site, Near Old North Bridge, "Shot Heard Round the World," Concord Museum and Great Meadows National Wildlife
**Services:** Wireless Internet service, telephone, bottled water, snacks, bathrobes, toiletries, hair drier, Stearns & Foster mattress, iron and board.
**Restrictions:** Smoke-free facility, Minimum stay on holidays
**Concierge:** (daily) 9am—9pm
**Room Service:** Small trays can be provided—see concierge
**Restaurant:** Complimentary multi-course breakfast served each morning around a common table on hand-painted Dedham pottery. For evening meal we will make reservations for you at one of our many local restaurants.
**Bar:** No—receive complimentary wine with room up-grade
**Business Facilities:** Wireless Internet, In-room Telephones, Fax
**Conference Room:** Small Meetings
**Sports Facilities:** No
**Spa Facilities:** We will assist with recommendations
**Airport:** Logan- Boston, Hanscom-Be Airports
**Location:** Historic Village

Relaxed Elegance. Just 19 miles from Boston is your intimate bed & breakfast sanctuary where history, literature and artistic whimsy entwine.

Three Rivers wind through a Colonial landscape of Minutemen's fields where moss-covered stonewalls embrace the homes of Hawthorne, Alcott, Emerson and Thoreau. As you amble in the footsteps of Patriots and Poets you will savor the Inn's unique location near the Author's homes, the Village Shops, Walden Pond, Minuteman National Park and the Old North Bridge, where was fired, "the shot heard 'round the world."

Solicitous for the well being of our guests we have filled the Inn with much to delight your eyes and sensibility. Original artworks, archaic artifacts and natural curiosities are a wonder to behold and burnished antiques speak of home and security. Displayed throughout the Inn are fascinating collections of Japanese Ukiyo-e prints, Pre-Colombian artifacts, modern paintings, bas-relief sculptures and a varied library that will satisfy all tastes. Our seven vibrant Guestrooms, inspired by a refreshing mix of tradition and artistic expression, offer you abundant comforts and amenities.

Many choose the Hawthorne as a base for day-trips; to explore Boston, Cambridge, Old Sturbridge Village, Salem, Plymouth Plantation, Lowell Textile Museum, Ocean Beaches and the many nearby College Campuses. Pass your time leisurely basking near the whispering fire with a book in hand, be led by the resident cat to a seat in the bountiful floral gardens for a spot of tea, seek your inner Muse on forest pathways and explore the many treasures of Concord's layered history.

We look forward to introducing you to the Hawthorne Inn and our historic 17th century village.

# CARPE DIEM GUESTHOUSE & SPA

**S**EIZE THE DAY—make your Provincetown stay extraordinary! The Carpe Diem is an intimate Cape Cod Guesthouse & Spa and a romantic hideaway combined with luxurious amenities and personal service.

Quietly located in the center of town each room is named after a renowned writer, decorated with European antiques and ambience and offers private bath, queen size bed, down bedding, bathrobes and luxury products. Some feature fireplaces, whirlpool tubs, private entrance and/or private patios.

Enjoy our homemade gourmet breakfast and join us for our daily Wine & Cheese hour. The common rooms are a great place to relax, read a good book, or chat with new friends. There is a fireplace, video library, complimentary sherry and port, a 24-hour coffee station, as well as a guest office and WiFi for those that need to stay connected to the "real" world.

Our Namaste Spa offers a wonderful array of spa experiences that allow you to feel the benefits of heat and cold, light and darkness, touch and aromas. Our atmosphere is soothing and enjoyable.

And for those who like the excitements of shopping and nightlife, Commercial Street, the pulsating lifeline of Provincetown, is only steps away.

Carpe Diem—a magical place on the edge of the continent!

**Address:** 12 Johnson Street Provincetown MA 02657
**Phone:** 508-487-4242
**Tollfree:** 800-487-0132
**Fax:** 508-487-0138
**Email:** info@carpediemguesthouse.com
**Web:** www.carpediemguesthouse.com
**Room Rates:** 115–445
**No. of Rooms:** 19
**Credit Cards:** Most CCs Accepted
**Attractions**: Miles of unspoiled beaches, bike trails and organized dune tours,whale watching tours, unique shops, art galleries, marvelous restaurants, fishing, boating & kayaking, golf, tennis courts
**Services:** DVD library, laundry service (fee), floral/champagne (fee), off street parking, robes & slippers, CD/Stereo, fireplaces, IPod docking
**Restrictions:** No pets allowed, No smoking inside! We are an adults only resort.
**Concierge:** Yes: available (daily) 9:00am–9:00pm
**Room Service:** No
**Restaurant:** Mornings enjoy a complimentary breakfast in our homemade German-style. Dinner? – Walking distance to all Provincetown has to offer.
**Bar:** No— wine/cheese served daily
**Business Facilities:** WiFi Computer, Fax
**Conference Room:** 1 - non private lounge area / capacity: up to 10 people
**Sports Facilities:** No
**Spa Services:** Featuring a Turkish Bath (Steam Room), Finnish Dry Sauna and Hydrojet Spa Tub. Thai Massage and stress reducing Energy Work.
**Airport:** Boston Logan Int'l
**Location:** Quiet, center of town

# THE RAPHAEL HOTEL

**Address:** 325 Ward Parkway
Kansas City MO 64112
**Phone:** 816-756-3800
**Tollfree:** 800-821-5343
**Fax:** 816-802-2131
**Email:** information@raphaelkc.com
**Web:** www.raphaelkc.com
**Room Rates:** 169–259
**Suite Rates:** 259–459
**No. of Rooms:** 126
**No. of Suites:** 85
**Credit Cards:** Most CCs Accepted
**Attractions**: Country Club
Plaza, premier shopping, dining,
entertainment and cultural center;
Nelson-Atkins Museum of Art.
Sprint Center.
**Services:** Telephones with
voicemail and high-speed
Internet access, iron and board,
gourmet coffee brewing system,
refrigerator, hair dryer, plush
cotton robes, iHome clock radio,
digital climate controls, VCR and
CD player rental
**Restrictions:** Not pets allowed,
Children under 18 free with
parents, Non-smoking rooms
**Concierge:** Yes: 24/7
**Room Service:** Yes: 24/7
**Restaurant:** Menus feature
creative, regional American
cuisine energized by ethnic and
geographic influences.
**Bar:** Yes: Chaz Lounge /open
11:00 am – midnight w/ live music
**Business Facilities:** Audio-visual
equipment, Copiers, Message
center
**Conference Room:** 2 rooms /
capacity: up to 55 people
**Sports Facilities:** Workout room
**Spa Services:** Our hotel
concierge will be happy to assist
you with recommendations.
**Airport:** Kansas City
**Location:** Situated on a tree-lined
neighborhood boulevard.

For travelers who appreciate what makes a city unique, the Country Club Plaza is the place to see and The Raphael is the place to stay.

Originally constructed in the 1920s, the restored hotel is one of Kansas City's enduring architecturally significant buildings. Its landmark features include hand-made wrought iron gates and canopied entrances. The intimate lobby, with its mahogany-paneled ceiling, ornate woodwork, intricately detailed chandeliers, fine art and richly textured fabrics, is reminiscent of a small European hotel.

Guest accommodations are generously sized rooms and suites. Amenities include many of the modern comforts today's traveler expects, including communications system with voice mail and complimentary high-speed Internet access, flat screen TV, plus French terry robes, personal refrigerator with refreshment center and Keurig gourmet coffee maker. Same day laundry service is available if needed, as is 24-hour room service.

Chaz on the Plaza, The Raphael's signature restaurant, is noted for capturing the city's unique culture, history and spirit. The room's intimacy lends itself to business breakfast, lunch or dinner. It features creative American cuisine with a heartland flavor. Chaz Lounge hosts a popular Happy Hour weekdays and features a variety of classical, jazz, blues and pop music performed by local artists Tuesdays – Saturdays.

# TRIPLE CREEK RANCH - RELAIS & CHATEAUX

Triple Creek Ranch is a wondrous place of serenity, beauty and comfort nestled in a secluded, unspoiled mountain wilderness. The resort offers luxurious accommodations, world class cuisine, outstanding service, exhilarating activities, spectacular scenery and wildlife.

The main lodges three-story log and cedar structure tiered with balconies provide panoramic views of the surrounding mountainous landscape. Western genre original artwork can be found throughout the lodges interior which demonstrates Triple Creek Ranch's affinity for the art and culture of the American West. Here is the focal point for social activity on the ranch, where an exquisite dining experience can be found or football game and cocktails in the Rooftop Lounge.

Twenty-three individual Western style log cabins take luxury to a new height and feature king log beds, woodburning fireplaces, fully stocked wet-bar, air conditioning, private or nearby hot tubs, in-cabin service, nightly turn-down, daily fruit with fresh-baked cookies and trail mix, satellite TV and blu-ray player, in-cabin safe, stocked refrigerator and more. All to provide you a cozy, romantic home-away-from-home!

The endless array of activities, at any time of year, will satisfy any adventurous spirit from horseback riding, hiking, fishing, horseback riding, birding and nature tours and casting clinics to downhill and cross-country skiing, ORVIS endorsed guided fly fishing, cattle drives, mountain biking, ATV rides, snowmobiling and much more! Whatever your pleasure, all activities are designed to enhance the experience of this wondrous landscape, to inspire and to invigorate the weary traveler. Of course, you may choose to relax among the towering pines with a good book near a crackling fire or lounge in an outdoor hammock with a refreshing drink. . . also, highly recommended.

**Address:** 5551 West Fork Road Darby MT 59829
**Phone:** 406-821-4600
**Tollfree:** 800-654-2943
**Fax:** 406-821-4666
**Email:** Info@TripleCreekRanch.com
**Web:** www.triplecreekranch.com
**Room Rates:** 750–2,495
**Suite Rates:** 950
**No. of Rooms:** 30
**No. of Suites:** 2
**Credit Cards:** Most CCs Accepted
**Attractions:** Lost Trail Powder Mountain Ski Resort, Lewis & Clark Trail, Bitterroot River, Salmon River, Trapper Peak, golf, art galleries, shops, Chief Joseph Pass, Big Hole Battlefield National Monument, rafting.
**Services:** Airport pick up, parking, gift shop, fireplace, hot tub, stocked wet bar, voice mail, satellite TV and blue-ray player, wireless Internet, refrigerator, A/C, in-room safe, daily housekeeping & turndowns
**Restrictions:** Children age 16 and over are welcome. No pets.
**Concierge:** Yes: available (daily) 7:30am – 11:00pm
**Room Service:** Yes: available (daily) 7:30am – 9:00pm
**Restaurant:** Offerings range from traditional French, Southwestern, West Indies and Central American. Hours: 7:30am to 9:00pm
**Bar:** Yes—Rooftop Lounge open (daily) 7:30am – 10:00pm
**Business Facilities:** Computer, copiers, fax, modems
**Conference Room:** 3 rooms / capacity: up to 180 people
**Sports Facilities:** Fitness center, outdoor heated pool, tennis court
**Spa Services:** Private in-cabin massages upon request (fee).
**Airport:** Missoula Int'l Airport
**Location:** Ranch setting

# THE BALSAMS GRAND RESORT HOTEL

**Address:** 1000 Cold Spring Road Dixville Notch NH 03576
**Phone:** 603-255-3400
**Tollfree:** 800-255-0600
**Email:** jmciver@thebalsams.com
**Web:** www.thebalsams.com
**Room Rates:** 99-750
**No. of Rooms:** 202
**Credit Cards:** Most CCs Accepted
**Attractions:** Canoeing, kayaking, fly-fishing, heated swimming pool, golf, tennis, ice skating, dog sledding, horsebacking riding, hiking, alpine & Nordic skiing, mountain biking — on 8,000 acres of fun!
**Services:** The BALSAMS offers a great variety of amenities & resort services to our guests, from outdoor adventures to conveniences inside the Resort.
**Restrictions:** No pets allowed.
**Concierge:** Available 24/7
**Room Service:** Limited menu
**Restaurant:** From the elegance and true ambiance of the Grand Dining Room to more casual offerings such as The Tavern or The PANORAMA Country Club, The BALSAMS has an abundance of choices.
**Bar:** The Tavern and LaCave are located off the main lobby. Pool bar in summer.
**Business Facilities:** Faxing, copies, Admin assist, Internet
**Spa Services:** The finest in personal care, from facials and manicures to full body treatments.
**Airport:** Portland Airport or Manchester Airport
**Location:** Mountain resort

Realize The BALSAMS full experience, offering guests fine dining, inviting accommodations, a Donald Ross golf course and unlimited access to our 8,000 acre property. The BALSAMS, always at one simple rate, with everything added in and nothing added on! Come create lasting traditions in a setting surrounded by the tranquility and natural beauty of the rugged New Hampshire mountains. Enjoy exquisite dining and live entertainment. Play another round of golf, or start a game of tennis. Paddle a kayak into the sunset, or explore miles of trails on a mountain bike. The BALSAMS experience gives guests freedom to enjoy it all.

Revel in the history of a New Hampshire grand hotel. Highly regarded for its tradition of culinary artistry, The BALSAMS provides a world-class table d'hôte dining experience wrought with elegance and careful service.

Extend to employees and clients the hospitality of a Grand Resort. Our Conference Center offers a memorable location to host summit meetings, weddings, quiet retreats, large-scale family reunions and special events. The BALSAMS offers lovely surroundings with spacious accommodations and meeting areas, complemented by an attentive staff and excellent service. The BALSAMS full experience awaits each guest.

# THE INNS & SPA AT MILL FALLS

Discover The Inns and Spa at Mill Falls located along the shore of Lake Winnipesaukee in the quaint town of Meredith and step back in time while experiencing the luxuries of today.

With four Inns, the Cascade Spa, five restaurants, numerous shops and eateries along Main Street and fourteen stores in the Mill Falls Marketplace, there is something here for everyone. Choose from one of four fine Inns, Bay Point and Church Landing located right on the water, and Mill Falls and Chase House just across the street, all sharing many of the same spectacular views of the lake and surrounding mountains. Combined, the four Inns offer 159 designer decorated rooms, most feature a fireplace and lake view balcony. Specialty rooms with whirlpools baths and suites are available as well.

When you're not taking advantage of the many amenities provided by the Inns, venture down historic Main Street, and take in the local color. Through a perfect blend of historic renovation and preservation Meredith has been transformed into a quintessential New England destination.

The common thread that you will find throughout all of the Inns is the superior attention to detail and renowned customer service.

**Address:** 312 Daniel Webster Hwy Meredith NH 03253
**Phone:** 603-279-7006
**Tollfree:** 800-622-6455
**Fax:** 603-677-8695
**Email:** info@millfalls.com
**Web:** www.millfalls.com
**Room Rates:** 119–359
**Suite Rates:** 249–499
**No. of Rooms:** 159
**No. of Suites:** 10
**Credit Cards:** Most CCs Accepted
**Attractions**: Lake Winnipesaukee, Swimming, Kayaking, Boating, Fishing, Golf, Cruise Aboard the M/S Mt. Washington, Keepsake Quilting, Gunstock Ski Area, Ice Skating, Shopping, Antiquing.
**Services:** WiFi, Beach, In-Room Fireplaces and Whirlpool Tubs, Hair Salon, Cable TV, Telephone, Radio, Individual Climate Controls.
**Restrictions:** 6 rooms handicap equipped, Smoke Free rooms, Children 12 and under free in parent's room
**Room Service:** 6:30 am – 2pm, 5 – 9pm (limited menu).
**Restaurant:** Lago Costa Cucina, Camp, Waterfall Cafe, Giuseppe's Pizzeria and Ristorante, Town Docks (seasonal), & The Lakehouse Grille.
**Bar:** 6 bars
**Business Facilities:** WiFi, Copiers, Audio-visual, Fax
**Conference Room:** 15 rooms, capacity 300
**Sports Facilities:** Indoor Swimming Pool, Whirlpool, & Deluxe Fitness Room
**Spa Services:** Cascade Spa offers exclusive treatments including massages, facials, body wraps.
**Airport:** Manchester, NH
**Location:** Downtown Historic Village

# ANGEL OF THE SEA
# BED & BREAKFAST

**Address:** 5 Trenton Avenue
Cape May NJ 08204
**Phone:** 609-884-3369
**Tollfree:** 800-848-3369
**Fax:** 609-884-3331
**Email:** info@angelofthesea.com
**Web:** www.angelofthesea.com
**Room Rates:** 95 – 315
**No. of Rooms:** 27
**Credit Cards:** Most CCs Accepted
**Attractions**: Museums, Zoo,
Atlantic City Casinos, Historic
District, Atlantic Ocean,
Complimentary bicycles available
for riding around town, swimming
and other water sports in Atlantic,
whale & dolphin watching
**Services:** Off-street parking,
bicycles, beach equipment (in
season), lobby gift shop, Cable TV,
CD/Radio alarm clock, AC, WiFi,
fax, complimentary toiletries,
blow-dryers, afternoon tea &
sweets.
**Restrictions:** No pets allowed,
Children 8 years old and above
are welcome
**Concierge:** 8:00am – 11:00pm
7 day per week
**Room Service:** No
**Restaurant:** Full gourmet
breakfast. Our concierge will be
happy to assist you with local
suggestions and appointments
with the local area restaurants
and eateries.
**Bar:** No – evening wine & cheese
**Business Facilities:** No
**Conference Room:** No
**Sports Facilities:** No
**Spa Services:** Our concierge will
be happy to assist you with local
suggestions and appointments.
**Airport:** Atlantic City Airport
**Location:** Historic District

Built in 1850, the inn is an airy, Victorian "painted lady." Completely renovated in 1988, the Angel is one of the premier B&Bs in the country. She has been featured on NBC, CBS, ABC, QVC, Public TV, the Learning Channel, Discovery, Good Morning America, and Oprah Winfrey's "Best Vacations in the World."

There are twenty-seven guestrooms, all with private baths, and many with ocean views. All rooms are decorated in Grand Victorian style and each has its own unique personality. One of the most sought after rooms is furnished in white wicker accented with a charming, purple floral pattern. It boasts ten windows with views of the ocean, a pleasant sitting area, and a claw foot tub and shower where one can relax in total luxury.

Memories begin with a buffet of fresh fruits, just-baked muffins, cakes and a variety of juices and cereals. Unwind while enjoying the exquisite views from one of the many verandas, or take a refreshing dip in the Atlantic Ocean. In fine weather, ride into town using on of the inn's complimentary bicycles.

So whether guests arrive in the summer to enjoy the sand and surf, or prefer to visit in the off-season to relax and savor the charm of Cape May, their stay at the Angel of the Sea will be an unforgettable experience.

# CHIMNEY HILL ESTATE
# & OL' BARN INN

Enjoy New Jersey lodging at its finest at the historic Chimney Hill Estate Inn. Chimney Hill Estate was built in 1820. The original two-story farmhouse was expanded in 1927. The grounds occupy the site very near to where George Washington surveyed the Delaware during the bitter winter of 1776. The expansion was done to create a summer retreat for international attorney, Edgar Hunt. Hiring Margaret Spencer, one of MIT's first female architecture graduates, to design an addition featuring two stone wings, the inn's distinct elegance sets it apart. With numerous gables and fireplaces the verandahs overlook rolling hills and formal gardens.

**Address:** 207 Goat Hill Road Lambertville NJ 08530
**Phone:** 609-397-1516
**Tollfree:** 800-211-4667
**Fax:** 609-397-9353
**Email:** info@chimneyhillinn.com
**Web:** www.chimneyhillinn.com
**Room Rates:** 169–305
**Suite Rates:** 360–419
**No. of Rooms:** 13
**No. of Suites:** 5
**Credit Cards:** Visa, MC, Amex
**Attractions**: Shopping, Dining, Bowman's Hill Wildflower Preserve, Canal Rides, Biking, Hot Air-Ballooning, Historical Sites, Walking Tours, Covered Bridge Tour, Trenton Thunder ball team, kayaking, river tubing, canoeing, fishing, mule barge rides, theaters
**Services:** Private baths, canopied beds, fireplaces, Jacuzzis, jetted tubs, Phones, Data ports, TV or TV/VCR, Butler's Pantry: microwave, fridge, coffee maker
**Restrictions:** No smoking, Children over 12 welcome.
**Concierge:** Yes: available 8:00–5:00pm
**Room Service:** No
**Restaurant:** Awake to a delicious homemade breakfast served in our 1820 colonial dining room. Delicious cookies in the afternoon with ice tea or lemonade.
**Bar:** No: Weekend wine & cheese reception 4–6pm
**Business Facilities:** Limited: fax, copies, WiFi and high-speed Internet
**Conference Room:** 2 rooms / capacity: up to 50 people
**Sports Facilities:** No
**Spa Services:** Our front desk will be happy to arrange appointments at the local spa.
**Airport:** Philadelphia & New York Int'l Airport
**Location**: Historic district

The house is accented with hand-stenciled trim, raised paneling and wide-plank floors. There are plenty of nooks and crannies throughout the home that reflect architectural elements from the 19th century.

Thirteen distinct guestrooms offering a quiet respite from the world. Each suite is tastefully decorated with period furnishings, and many have canopied beds and fireplaces, or even Jacuzzis.

# CHATEAU INN & SUITES

**Address:** 500 Warren Avenue
Spring Lake NJ 07762
**Phone:** 732-974-2000
**Tollfree:** 877-974-5253
**Fax:** 732-974-0007
**Email:** info@chateauinn.com
**Web:** www.chateauinn.com
**Room Rates:** 89–329
**Suite Rates:** 119–359
**No. of Rooms:** 37
**No. of Suites:** 10
**Credit Cards:** Most CCs Accepted
**Attractions**: The seaside resort
of Spring Lake offers its visitors
stretches of pristine beaches
and New Jersey's largest non-
commercial, two mile boardwalk.
Spring Lake Five Mile Run, Big
Sea Day, the New Jersey Lifeguard
Tournament.
**Services:** Bicycles, DVD Movie
Rentals, high-speed Internet
access, Premium Cable Channels,
Wall Mounted Sony LCD TV's,
WiFi
**Restrictions:** No pets allowed,
1 room handicap equipped, all
non-smoking rooms
**Concierge:** Yes: available 24/7
**Room Service:** No
**Restaurant:** Within walking
distance: Whispers, The Black
Trumpet and The Mill.
**Bar:** No
**Business Facilities:** Message
center, Copiers, Audio-Visual, Fax,
Data Ports, high-speed Internet
**Conference Room:** 3 rooms /
capacity: up to 60 people
**Sports Facilities:** Complimentary
guest pass to: The Atlantic Club
Fitness Center
**Spa Services:** Milagro Spa.
Complimentary membership
privileges.
**Airport:** Newark Int'l Airport
**Location:** Historic Spring Lake

Understated elegance. Historic charm. A quiet dedication to the good life. For over a century, these hallmarks have defined the idyllic seaside resort of Spring Lake. These too, are the qualities you'll discover at its most refined choice for luxurious accommodations: The Chateau Inn & Suites.

Nestled between Divine and Potter Parks and overlooking "The Lake," The Chateau offers upscale ambience and sophisticated amenities of a boutique hotel married with the personalized service and signature touches of a small luxury hotel.

The Chateau's thirty-seven richly appointed guestrooms and one bedroom suites embody the essence of tasteful living. A newly updated palette of warm mocha, gold, buff and cream provides a soothing backdrop to deep mahogany furniture, plush leather sofas, exquisite Italian fabrics and imported marble bathrooms. Wood burning fireplaces, Jacuzzis, 42 inch plasma TV's, deep soaking tubs for two, refrigerated wet bars, high-speed Internet access and furnished balconies are just some of the Inn's distinctions.

Just a short stroll along "The Lake" on tree lined streets flanked by ancient sycamores, you'll find a pristine stretch of coastline awaits with beaches, ocean pavilions and two miles of boardwalk. An eclectic array of specialty shops, boutiques, art galleries and award winning restaurants are steps away.

Whether you're looking for a romantic weekend escape, midweek getaway or the finest business accommodations, the Chateau affords a host of packages and services to suit your needs. And if you can't find what you want, just ask. Our gracious and professional staff will do their utmost to ensure that your stay at the Chateau will exceed your expectations.

# LA FONDA

An historic landmark on the Plaza, La Fonda is known for its award-winning pueblo style Spanish architecture and decor, including thick wooden beams, carved corbels and a myriad of other details created by local artisans. The lobby, hallways and meeting rooms are filled with colorful artwork and memorabilia. Fonda is Spanish for "inn" and there has been a Fonda on the Plaza since the town was founded in 1607. Today's La Fonda was built in 1922.

The interesting and busy lobby features part of La Fonda's eclectic art collection as well as a newsstand, several interesting shops and galleries and a highly professional concierge desk. Each of its 167 colorful rooms and suites is uniquely decorated with hand-painted wooden furniture and other distinctive touches created by the hotel's staff artist. Although it is historic, La Fonda has thoroughly modern amenities—including a brand new spa which opened in the spring of 2002. A special attraction is the La Terraza rooftop garden featuring 14 private and secluded luxury rooms and suites that offer special amenities.

At the heart of La Fonda is La Plazuela, a beautiful enclosed courtyard restaurant featuring an award-winning culinary team and interesting, contemporary Nuevo Latino cuisine as well as New Mexican favorites. La Fiesta Lounge features light fare, a special lunch buffet and live entertainment nightly. The hotel's Bell Tower Bar is open from late spring through early fall for cocktails and the best sunset views in town.

**Address:** 100 E San Francisco St Santa Fe NM 87501
**Phone:** 505-982-5511
**Tollfree:** 800-523-5002
**Fax:** 505-988-2952
**Email:** reservations@lafondasantafe.com
**Web:** www.lafondasantafe.com
**Room Rates:** 219–389
**Suite Rates:** 349–529
**No. of Rooms:** 167
**No. of Suites:** 36
**Credit Cards:** Most CCs Accepted
**Attractions:** Only hotel on the historic Plaza, Galleries, Shopping, Historic churches, Museums, Restaurants
**Services:** Covered parking, Newsstand, Shops, Lounge, Laundry service, Fireplaces, Balconies, Cable TV, Clock radio, Individual heat & air-conditioning control, Hair dryers, Irons & ironing boards, Data port phones, high-speed Wireless Internet access.
**Restrictions:** 5 rooms with handicapped access, No pets allowed, Children under 12 no extra charge in room
**Concierge:** (daily) 9am–10pm
**Room Service:** (daily) 7am–10pm
**Restaurant:** La Plazuela — 7am–10pm
**Bar:** La Fiesta Lounge, 11am–Midnight, Live entertainment
**Business Facilities:** Copiers, Fax, high-speed Internet access
**Conference Room:** 8 rooms, capacity up to 600
**Sports Facilities:** Outdoor swimming pool, Exercise Room
**Spa Services:** Whirlpool, massage
**Airport:** Albuquerque Airport
**Location:** Downtown Historic Plaza

# THE BAKER HOUSE 1650

**Address:** 181 Main Street
East Hampton NY 11937
**Phone:** 631-324-4081
**Fax:** 631-329-5931
**Email:** info@bakerhouse1650.com
**Web:** www.bakerhouse1650.com
**Room Rates:** 275 – 1,200
**Suite Rates:** 1,450
**No. of Rooms:** 6
**No. of Suites:** 1
**Credit Cards:** Most CCs Accepted
**Attractions**: Ocean and bay beaches, nature walks, historic tours, horseback riding, bicycling, boating, fishing, tennis, golf, Boutiques, antique stores, art galleries, museums, farmer's markets, craft and antique fairs, outlet stores.
**Services:** robes/slippers, Internet wireless, mini bars, flat screen/cable TV service, Ipod docking, sheets by Frette, fireplaces, Jacuzzi or claw footed bathtub.
**Restrictions:** No pets allowed, Smoking outside only, Children over 10 welcomed.
**Concierge:** Yes—7am until 11pm (daily)
**Room Service:** Breakfast hours (only) from 8:30 – 10:30am
**Restaurant:** Complimentary breakfasts.
**Bar:** Yes—open from Noon until 11:00pm (daily)
**Business Facilities:** Wireless Internet, Computer, Fax
**Conference Room:** 2 rooms—capacity/up to 20
**Sports Facilities:** Access to nearby Gym
**Spa Services:** Guests can reserve the state-of-the-art spa (lap pool, spa tub, sauna, steam shower) privately for massage and purification.
**Airport:** East Hampton Airport
**Location:** Main Street in East Hampton Village

The Baker House 1650 (formerly the J. Harper Poor Cottage) in East Hampton has been recognized as one of the finest luxury inns in the United States. The sweeping lawn and beautiful English gardens have been featured in many books and magazines. Outdoor terraces, a 200 year old wisteria, and vine-covered garden walls transport guests to a manor house in France or the English countryside.

Each bedroom is beautifully decorated with linens by Frette, individually controlled central air conditioning and heat, Bartech minibar, in-room security safe, flat screen television with full cable services and DVD, top-of-the-line Bose radios, CD players and iPod connect kits, multiple telephone lines, and wireless Internet access. Most of the rooms have wood-burning fireplaces and whirlpools. Bathrooms are lavish, with amenities by L'Occitane and bathrobes by Frette.

Each morning begins with a sumptuous breakfast in the garden-side breakfast room, in the garden itself, or continental breakfast in your own room, delivered with your choice of morning paper. Local organic produce and farm products are used wherever possible. For business meetings or family gatherings, the inn has a luxurious living room with a large fireplace. There is also a dining room with a fireplace and a well-stocked library with books, magazines and DVDs, which can be borrowed for in-room viewing.

The last thing one would expect in a historic 1648 house is a state-of-the-art spa facility, but this is what one finds on the lower level. A lap pool, spa tub, sauna, steam shower, and change room comprise the spa. Guests can enjoy massages and facials in this beautiful room.

The Baker House is available for special events including weddings, private parties and photo shoots.

ESH 1434 25TH ED

# THE MILL HOUSE INN

The Mill House Inn is a luxury Bed & Breakfast Inn providing fine lodging in the historic oceanfront village of East Hampton, NY. Our beautiful rooms, spectacular dog & child-friendly suites, "the best breakfast in the Hamptons" and our dedicated professional staff receive rave reviews.

Situated in the heart of one of America's most beautiful villages, surrounded by endless beaches, pristine bays and picturesque country roads, our intimate B&B is just steps from world-class restaurants, shops, galleries & theatres. We are within walking distance of the ocean and a short drive to the Hamptons' myriad attractions—fishing and surfing in Montauk, farm stands in Amagansett, antiques in Sag Harbor, wineries in Bridgehampton and the mansions of Southampton!

Enjoy quality amenities, fine linens, featherbeds, fireplaces, soaking tubs, steam showers, lush gardens and a leisurely breakfast our guests proclaim "simply the best." Let our Concierge help you plan your day's adventure—experience a massage in your spacious suite or a run on the beach with your dog, a tour of the Long Island Wine Region or a family outing at the Children's Museum, golf at Montauk Downs, horseback riding on the beach or just curling up with a good book by the fireplace in the comfort of your room.

Whether you travel to East Hampton for a honeymoon or family vacation, business conference or romantic getaway our attention to detail, comprehensive concierge service, old fashioned hospitality and a wonderful relaxed atmosphere assure your visit will remain a treasured memory.

**Address:** 31 North Main Street East Hampton NY 11937
**Phone:** 631-324-9766
**Fax:** 631-324-9793
**Email:** innkeeper@millhouseinn.com
**Web:** www.millhouseinn.com
**Room Rates:** 225–895
**Suite Rates:** 325–1395
**No. of Rooms:** 4
**No. of Suites:** 6
**Credit Cards:** Most CCs Accepted
**Attractions:** A fisherman's playground, a vintner's paradise and an artist's inspiration, the East End of Long Island is home to some of the world's most spectacular ocean beaches, pristine bays, foggy mornings, lazy sunny days, blazing sunsets and star-filled nights.
**Services:** Kids eat free, ice machine, safety deposit box, porter/bellman, daily housekeeping, dry cleaning/laundry, parking (fee)
**Restrictions:** No Smoking, No Pets
**Concierge:** Full Service
**Room Service:** For availability inquire at front desk
**Restaurant:** "The Breakfast" guests proclaim Gary's menu the best in America—30 signature items redefine how to begin the day!
**Bar:** BYOB (Liquor License circa May 2011)
**Business Facilities:** High-speed Wireless Internet access
**Conference Room:** Small Meetings – up to 20 people
**Sports Facilities:** Complimentary gym passes
**Spa Services:** The Mill House Inn is within walking distance of excellent spas, yoga and gym facilities.
**Airport:** ISP, JFK, LGA
**Location:** In the heart of the historic ocean-front village of East Hampton NY

# INN AT GREAT NECK

**Address:** 30 Cutter Mill Road
Great Neck NY 11021
**Phone:** 516-773-2000
**Fax:** 516-773-2020
**Email:** rowenburg@innatgreatneck.com
**Web:** www.innatgreatneck.com
**Room Rates:** 219–279
**Suite Rates:** 339–389
**No. of Rooms:** 85
**No. of Suites:** 10
**Credit Cards:** Most CCs Accepted
**Attractions**: Village of Great
Neck Plaza, over 300 shops,
restaurants, and entertainment
spots. Downtown Manhattan,
Citi Field (home of the NY Mets),
Belmont Race Track, National
Tennis Center (Site of US Tennis
Open).
**Services:** Valet, twice daily maid
service, spacious vanities, multi-
phase lighting, marble bathrooms
w/oversize bathtubs/Jacuzzi, mini-
bars, cable LCD TV & DVD, video
rentals, 2 line speaker phones,
data port & WiFi.
**Restrictions:** Pet friendly, 4
rooms handicap accessible
**Concierge:** Front Desk assistance
available 24/7
**Room Service:** Available (daily):
7:00am–11:00 p.m. Special menus
available
**Restaurant:** The Giraffe Room,
open daily 7:00 a.m. - 11:00 p.m.
**Bar:** Lounge is open daily from:
12 noon - 11:00pm
**Business Facilities:** Business
center/2 computers, fax, copier,
Internet
**Conference Room:** 4 rooms—
capacity: up to 350 people
**Sports Facilities:** Exercise Room
**Spa Services:** Our concierge
will be able to assist you with
appointments and directions to
the local area facilities
**Airport:** La Guardia Airport
**Location:** 20 minutes from
Manhattan

Located in the heart of the Village of Great Neck Plaza, on picturesque Long Island, just minutes from Manhattan, surrounded by 300 shops, restaurants and entertainment spots, the Inn at Great Neck offers a combination of luxurious guestrooms and suites.

Every guestroom is furnished and appointed in an Art Deco style reminiscent of the golden era of the 1920s. All rooms have separate reading and work areas and feature multi-phase lighting, two line speaker phones with facsimile and personal computer capabilities, video players, minibars and marble bathrooms with oversized bathtubs or Jacuzzis. A complimentary high-speed Internet connection is available in all guestrooms.

For your dining pleasure the luxurious restaurant serves breakfast, lunch, dinner and a Sunday brunch featuring the best in American Continental Cuisine. The Giraffe Room offers an exquisite ambiance suitable for a romantic dinner, a group celebration, or a gathering of friends and business associates. The Inn at Great Neck is Long Island's premier banquet and meeting destination specializing in innovative cuisine and complete event and menu planning.

The Inn at Great Neck offers the perfect stopping off location for the business or leisure traveler visiting New York City and points east on Long Island as well as the perfect atmosphere for a relaxing escape.

If you are looking for a Long Island or New York hotel, we are confident your stay at the Inn at Great Neck will be memorable and most enjoyable. If there is anything more we can do for you, just let us know. It is always our pleasure to serve you.

# THE ANDREW

Welcome to The Andrew Hotel in Great Neck, a luxury boutique hotel with a superb Long Island location convenient to Manhattan.

Centered in the heart of the Village of Great Neck, The Andrew is the first designer boutique hotel in Long Island. Its modern design, sensibility and unique approach to luxurious minimalism and restrained elegance makes it a must for business or vacation getaways.

And, if business brings you to Great Neck, a complete conference and business center can provide anything from a small boardroom meeting to full catering services. In addition, each guestroom features technological amenities such as high-speed wireless Internet access, 32" flat screen LCD TVs, DVD player, and cordless phones. Additional highlights are custom-designed cherry and limed oak furniture and decadent fabrics such as ostrich skin, mohair and raw silk in the guestrooms. A lobby features rosewood wall panels, limestone floors and a front desk surrounded by purple glass while the The Andrew boasts a fresh white stucco and gray limestone exterior.

Nestled among 300 restaurants and designer retailers, close to baseball, tennis, golf and the seashore, this location is a perfect fit for almost anyone. And, since The Andrew is a mere twenty-five minutes from New York City, it's a perfect getaway for those who might want a little break from the hustle and bustle of the city while still getting "that hip energy."

However, there is much more to The Andrew than exquisite design. Unprecedented service and high attention to detail is second nature to the staff who quietly and inconspicuously provide for your needs.

**Address:** 75 North Station Plaza Great Neck NY 11021
**Phone:** 516-482-2900
**Tollfree:** 866-843-2637
**Fax:** 516-482-4643
**Email:** guestservices@andrewhotel.com
**Web:** www.andrewhotel.com
**Room Rates:** 179–249
**Suite Rates:** 319–399
**No. of Rooms:** 62
**No. of Suites:** 5
**Credit Cards:** Most CCs Accepted
**Attractions**: Miracle Mile shopping, Shea Stadium, Arthur Ashe Tennis Stadium, Jones Beach, US Golf Open. Tennis and golf. North Shore University Hospitals, US Merchant Marine Academy, State Park, CW Post University.
**Services:** Garage/parking, Valet parking, Car hire, Laundry, Comp. newspaper, Cable TV/VCR, CD player, Phone, Radio, Wet bar, Climate controls, Robes, Deluxe continental breakfast, high-speed Wireless.
**Restrictions:** Pets welcome with $150 deposit, Children welcome and free with parents, 1 room handicap equipped
**Concierge:** Yes: available 24/7
**Room Service:** Yes: available from 12:00pm–11:00pm (except Friday)
**Restaurant:** Colbeh Restaurant, open daily.
**Bar:** Yes: located in restaurant 12 noon till close (except Fridays)
**Business Facilities:** Fax, copies
**Conference Room:** 1 room / capacity: up to 12 people
**Sports Facilities:** Guest privileges at NY Sports Club
**Spa Services:** In-room massage therapy by appointment and guest privileges at a nearby fitness center and spa.
**Airport:** JFK Int'l & La Guardia Airports
**Location:** Village Center

# HOTEL PLAZA ATHENEE

**Address:** 37 East 64th Street
New York City NY 10065
**Phone:** 212-734-9100
**Tollfree:** 800-447-8800
**Fax:** 212-772-0958
**Email:** res@plaza-athenee.com
**Web:** www.plaza-athenee.com
**Room Rates:** 875–1,190
**Suite Rates:** 1,800–8,000
**No. of Rooms:** 114
**No. of Suites:** 28
**Credit Cards:** Most CCs Accepted
**Attractions**: Madison Avenue
offering some of the best
shopping in New York City!
Museums and restaurants
surround the hotel, Central Park.
**Services:** CD players, High-
speed Internet, iPod docking
stations, In-room movies, Two-
lined speaker phone, writing
desks, Italian linens, Deluxe
toiletries, Bathrobes and hair
dryers, Valet parking, Twice-daily
Housekeeping, In-room safe.
**Restrictions:** Small pets allowed,
Some rooms equipped for
physically challenged.
**Concierge:** Yes—available 24/7
**Room Service:** Yes—available
24/7 – full menu
**Restaurant:** Arabelle Restaurant
serves breakfast, lunch & dinner
from 6:30am–9:15pm (daily).
**Bar:** Bar Seine Lounge is open
from 11am–1:30am (Thur–Sat) and
from 11am–12:30 (Sun-Wed)
**Business Facilities:** Full business
center
**Conference Room:** 2 rooms /
capacity—up to 150 people
**Sports Facilities:** Complimentary
access to Fitness Center
**Spa Services:** The new Plaza
Athenee Spa is exclusive to hotel
guests and features four Asian
themed, private treatment suites
offering therapies and treatments
**Airport:** John F Kennedy & La
Guardia Airports
**Location:** Upper East Side

Nestled among the residences of the fashionable Upper East Side of Manhattan, this charming boutique hotel is located on a quiet tree-lined street, just one block to Central Park. Nearby museums include the Museum of Modern Art (MOMA), The Whitney Museum and the Frick Collection. This prime location on East 64th Street and Madison Avenue is close to bustling midtown making the location perfect for the business or leisure traveler, for a romantic get-away or family vacation with children.

Guestrooms and suites offer a variety of style, giving each room an individual look and feel. The color palettes, ranging from vibrant cinnamon and yellow, to a soothing gray, beige and mint green, and have been accented with traditional Beaux-Arts furnishing, reflecting a contemporary European townhouse ambiance. Additional items to enhance the new decor include luxurious Italian bed linens, Asian inspired silks, Plasma TV's, sitting areas, writing desks and wireless Internet service.

Arabelle Restaurant offers diners an elegant atmosphere in a gorgeous gold-domed room and serves breakfast, lunch and dinner daily. Arabelle is also a perfect venue for an intimate function.

The hotel's complimentary Fitness Center is accessible by guestroom key on a 24-hour basis. Located on the first floor, featuring Techno-gym equipment & cardio-theater, with windows that overlook the beautiful townhouses on tree-lined 64th Street. For guests' comfort headsets, fresh fruit, water, and chilled towels are provided.

# SMYTH - A THOMPSON HOTEL

Smyth, Thompson Hotels' fifth Manhattan property celebrates TriBeCa's rich history and contemporary lifestyle. Conceived by architects Brennan Beer Gorman with interiors by Yabu Pushelberg, Smith mixes sleek and modern design with rich and vintage accents to create a truly bespoke hotel.

Smyth features 100 hotel rooms and amenities galore, providing a chic and unique experience. Guests can retreat to the lobby lounge and cocktail bar for food and drink from afternoon to late in the evening, and experience the first-in-class, concierge services Thompson Hotels are known for.

Smyth Tribeca represents a modern vision of sophisticated elegance mixing sleek design with vintage accents to create a truly bespoke hotel. Guest rooms include rich, walnut paneling, chrome accented furniture, and hallways textured with maroon, ostrich-embossed leather walls. Signature suites boast striking Manhattan views with floor to ceiling windows and private terraces. Marble bathrooms, amenities galore, and first class concierge services provide a unique experience for an eclectic and savvy clientele. Guests can enjoy specialty cocktails in the lobby's Smyth Bar, retreat to Toro, the cellar lounge, or dine at Plein Sud by famed restaurateur Frederick Lesort.

**Address:** 85 W Broadway New York City NY 10007
**Phone:** 212-587-7000
**Tollfree:** 888-58SMYTH
**Fax:** 212-587-7077
**Email:** infoSmyth@thompsonhotels.com
**Web:** www.thompsonhotels.com
**Room Rates:** 229–850
**Suite Rates:** 450–5,000
**No. of Rooms:** 100
**No. of Suites:** 16
**Credit Cards:** Most CCs Accepted
**Attractions:** Financial district – Wall street/World Trade site, Statue of Liberty, museums, Stock Exchange SoHo – downtown shopping, sightseeing, local art galleries, Tribeca film festival, restaurants and eateries
**Services:** Mobile Phones & Laptop computers available; Domestic & international newspapers; Multi-lingual staff.
**Restrictions:** No Pets; 10 rooms handicap accessible
**Concierge:** Yes: available 24/7
**Room Service:** Yes: open from 6:30am–12:00am /special In-Room Menu
**Restaurant:** French Brasserie "Plein Sud" is located in our lobby and open for breakfast, lunch and dinner 7 days a week.
**Bar:** Lobby Bar: open from 2pm-12am; TORO Lounge open 5pm-2am
**Business Facilities:** Limited facilites—computer, fax, copies
**Conference Room:** 2 rooms / capacity up to 30 people
**Sports Facilities:** Fitness Center —accessible 24/7
**Spa Services:** Our concierge will be happy to assist you with an appointment for an in-room massage or directions to a nearby spa facility.
**Airport:** La Guardia & John F Kennedy Int'l Airports
**Location:** Tribeca, NYC

# THE BLAKELY ~ NEW YORK

**Address:** 136 West 55th Street
New York City NY 10019
**Phone:** 212-245-1800
**Tollfree:** 800-735-0710
**Fax:** 212-582-8332
**Email:** reservations@blakelynewyork.com
**Web:** www.blakelynewyork.com
**Room Rates:** 325–395
**Suite Rates:** 425–525
**No. of Rooms:** 118
**No. of Suites:** 54
**Credit Cards:** Most CCs Accepted
**Attractions**: 5th Avenue Shops,
Central Park West, Broadway
theaters, Rockefeller Center and
Radio Music Hall, Times Square,
MoMa Museum of Modern Art
**Services:** Full kitchenette w/
mini-fridge, microwave, and
coffeemaker. Flat-screen TV,
DVD/CD player, in-room movies.
Voicemail and two phones
per room (one cordless), work
desk. Feather mattress topper,
down pillows, luxurious duvet &
Egyptian li
**Restrictions:** No Pets; 2
Handicap accessible, Smoking
areas available
**Concierge:** Yes: available 24/7 —
at the Front Desk
**Room Service:** Yes: from
7:30am – 11:00pm / special menu
**Restaurant:** Since opening the
Abboccato has brought true
Italian cuisine to Manhattan!
**Bar:** Yes: restaurant — 1st floor
**Business Facilities:** Yes:
Computer room, admin assist
available
**Conference Room:** 1 room /
capacity: up to 14 people
**Sports Facilities:** 24-hour access
to on-site fitness facilities
**Spa Services:** Nearby services.
Our concierge can assist with
appointments.
**Airport:** La Guardia & John F
Kennedy Airports
**Location:** Midtown West
Manhattan

I n contrast to recent trends of modern boutique hotels, where comfort takes a back seat to style, The Blakely New York has been created in a traditional design with the emphasis on service and comfort.

Our Deluxe Rooms measure 310 square feet and are elegantly appointed in the fashion of an English library with cherry furnishings, rich oak baseboards and trimmings, flat screen TV, CD/DVD player, wireless Internet access, work desk, full kitchenette with sink, microwave, mini-fridge, dishes and flatware, luxurious down bedding with linen duvet and pillow-top mattresses, marble bathroom with tub and shower and Penhaligon's amenities. All rooms include complimentary use of Frette robes, in-room safe, iron and ironing board.

Our Deluxe Studio Suites feature all of the deluxe room amenities at 425 square feet, which includes a sitting area. Our Deluxe One Bedroom Suites measure 525 square feet and feature Deluxe room accommodations and include a separate living room area with dark hardwood floors, an extra long daybed/couch, and a second flat screen TV.

Need something for business? Or a wedding reception? Try the Penthouse Boardroom Located on the 17th floor. The Penthouse Boardroom is the perfect venue for small meetings and presentations, intimate dinner parties, or showroom use. The boardroom's private garden terrace can also be used as an excellent breakout space or for outdoor luncheons overlooking the city.

# THE KIMBERLY HOTEL

Offering European-style elegance and service, this 187-room hotel is conveniently located in the heart of midtown Manhattan's fashionable east side, steps away from the world-renowned shops on Madison, Fifth, and Park Avenues, and from Rockefeller Center. The Kimberly guests enjoy the luxury of over-sized one- and two-bedroom suites, which feature a separate living room with dining area, marble bathrooms, an executive kitchenette, and most offer a private balcony. They offer a warm home away from home ambiance.

A wraparound veranda that offers panoramic views of Manhattan's Upper East Side surrounds the hotel's only meeting room, the Penthouse Suite. It extends the entire length of the hotel's 31st floor, making an opulent backdrop for festive receptions, intimate weddings and executive board meetings. Sunset cruises during the spring and summer weekends allow hotel guests to luxuriate on a 75-foot yacht while discovering Manhattan during the evening.

The hotel has two excellent dining options: Ferro's offers fine American eclectic cuisine, from pizza to steaks and serves a tempting buffet breakfast, complete with someone making your eggs to order. Nikki Midtown is the hip restaurant lounge. It provides a visually stunning venue, bringing the Nikki Beach concept to the heart of midtown Manhattan. Open for dinner only, Nikki Midtown offers the perfect atmosphere to dine or party with your friends.

**Address:** 145 E 50th Street New York City NY 10022
**Phone:** 212-702-1600
**Tollfree:** 800-683-0400
**Fax:** 212-486-6915
**Email:** info@kimberlyhotel.com
**Web:** www.kimberlyhotel.com
**Room Rates:** 199–619
**Suite Rates:** 229–1,209
**No. of Rooms:** 188
**No. of Suites:** 158
**Credit Cards:** Most CCs Accepted
**Attractions**: Park Avenue, Madison Avenue, Fifth Avenue shops, Rockefeller Center, UN Headquarters, Radio City Music Hall, Museum of Modern Art, New York Public Library and St. Patrick's Cathedral.
**Services:** Same-day valet, turn down on request, in-room safe, 2-line phones w/data port, wired/wireless Internet, bath robe, honor bar, daily newspaper, seasonal sunset cruises.
**Restrictions:** Pet Friendly, 1 hotel "floor"designated for smoking, 4 rooms handicap accessible
**Concierge:** Yes: available (daily) 8:00am–11:00pm
**Room Service:** Yes: open (daily) 6:00am–11:00pm
**Restaurant:** New restaurant "Alfred" Coming soon.
**Bar:** Yes: "Upstairs"—our hip rooftop lounge (open year round)
**Business Facilities:** Voice mail, high-speed wired & wireless access
**Conference Room:** Meeting & reception rooms, capacity 30–50
**Sports Facilities:** On site fitness center. Guest pass to NY Health & Racquet Club.
**Spa Services:** Our staff can book treatments for you at a nearby spa or in the comfort of your suite.
**Airport:** John F Kennedy, La Guardia, and Newark Airports
**Location:** Midtown Manhattan's East Side

# DANFORDS HOTEL & MARINA

**Address:** 25 East Broadway
Port Jefferson NY 11777
**Phone:** 631-928-5200
**Tollfree:** 800-332-6367
**Fax:** 631-928-9082
**Email:** info@danfords.com
**Web:** www.danfords.com
**Room Rates:** 169–549
**Suite Rates:** 359–549
**No. of Rooms:** 86
**No. of Suites:** 12
**Credit Cards:** Most CCs Accepted
**Attractions**: Museums, wineries,
beaches, quaint villages, parks,
shopping, boating, hiking, ice
skating (seasonal), fine dining all
within walking distance or a short
scenic drive. Come explore the
North Shore!
**Services:** Comfortable
overstuffed chairs & plush
bedding, 32-inch flat-screen TV w/
premium channels, IPOD home
docks & personal work spaces.
Kinu body products. In-room
Wolfgang Puck gourmet coffee.
**Restrictions:** No pets allowed, 2
rooms handicap equipped
**Concierge:** Yes—please inquire
**Room Service:** Yes—from 7am
until 11pm
**Restaurant:** Wave Restaurant
& Lounge is a unique blend of
old world charm and culinary
innovation. Wave features a
contemporary nautical theme and
unique dining experience.
**Bar:** Wave Lounge
**Business Facilities:** 24-hour
business services
**Conference Room:** 8 Rooms/
capacity up to 150 people.
**Sports Facilities:** 24-hour fitness
center.
**Spa Services:** Our newly
renovated Spa and Salon is open
7 days a week.
**Airport:** Long Island MacArthur
Airport.

Situated 50 miles from New York City at Port Jefferson on Long Island Sound, Danfords Hotel & Marina is the perfect location for a relaxing getaway and virtually any event, from an intimate dinner celebration or grand wedding reception, to a first-class business conference.

Each of our 86 guestrooms and suites with spa-inspired, glass enclosed showers is unique, for a personal retreat as individual as you are. Infused with nautical elegance and signature design elements—many with balconies with panoramic views, fireplaces, pillow top bedding, 32-inch flat screen televisions, iPod docking station, and personal work spaces with wireless Internet—each is an airy, cozy and inviting environment. Surrounded by spectacular views of Long Island Sound—and nestled in the heart of historic Port Jefferson Village—Danfords Hotel & Marina offers the finest in contemporary comfort and elegance. Rich mahogany woods reminiscent of fine yacht furniture and beautifully textured, vibrantly colored fabrics, offset by muted yellows, are paired with nautically-inspired accents and artwork.

Dining at Danfords is an experience like no other: one that delights your palate as you soak in the sights of spectacular Long Island Sound. Offering the eclectic flavors of New American cuisine in our new waterfront restaurant, WAVE, and tapas menu in our "hip" lounge, there's something for everyone at Danfords.

# THE ADELPHI HOTEL

It was called the Queen of the Spas, and no wonder......
The legendary Adelphi Hotel was built in the high
Victorian style that prevailed just before the turn of the cen-
tury, with 12-foot ceilings and window treatments to match.
Today it remains replete with classic Victorian furnishings,
and reflects all of the opulence of that era.

**Address:** 365 Broadway
Saratoga Springs NY 12866
**Phone:** 518-587-4688
**Fax:** 518-587-0851
**Email:** info@adelphihotel.com
**Web:** www.adelphihotel.com
**Room Rates:** 130–350
**Suite Rates:** 170–550
**No. of Rooms:** 39
**No. of Suites:** 16
**Credit Cards:** Visa
**Attractions**: Near Saratoga
Performing Arts Center, Saratoga
Raceway, Museums, Antique
Shops, Restaurants and eateries,
shopping, sightseeing,
**Services:** Cable TV, air-
conditioning, telephone,
toiletries, breakfast, custom
pillow and handmade
bedspreads, antique & elegant
furnishings, bath robes, room
safe, full cable TV service
**Concierge:** Front Desk assistance
**Room Service:** Limited
**Restrictions:** No pets allowed,
Children welcome
**Restaurant:** Complimentary
breakfast provided. Cafe
Adelphi—serves specially
blended drinks(like espressos,
etc.) unique wines and desserts.
**Bar:** Cafe Adelphi, 5:00 p.m.–
midnight
**Business Facilities:** Limited
**Conference Room:** Special
rm rates/& catering from local
eateries
**Sports Facilities:** Outdoor
swimming pool
**Spa Services:** Saratoga reigned
as America's "Queen of the
Spa's" area for many years. There
are still local facilities that we
will be happy to assist you with
in making appointments and
offering directions.
**Airport:** Albany Airport
**Location:** Broadway

Guestrooms are unusually large, and each is uniquely
decorated with a variety of wall coverings and color schemes.
Suites are furnished in a variety of styles including English
Country, French Provencal, Adirondack, and High Victorian.
The lodgings have also been updated to provide guests with
modern conveniences. Still, the original facade of ornamental
brickwork and three-story Victorian columns with elaborate
fretwork at the top remain, retaining the aura of the era.

Saratoga Springs is a charming town in which to stroll, and
find interesting antique shops and restaurants. Also of interest are the Saratoga Performing Arts Center, the Saratoga
Raceway, and several large and small museums. The hotel's
Cafe Adelphi consists of several rooms, one featuring a wrap-
around mural, and another, an enclosed patio overlooking
the flower-laden courtyard. The Cafe offers specially blended
drinks, unique wines, desserts, espresso, and cappucinos.

Come join us! The Adelphi Hotel is a popular gathering
place after—the track, a ballet, or performance at the performing arts center.

# THE INN AT FOX HOLLOW

**Address:** 7755 Jericho Turnpike
Woodbury NY 11797
**Phone:** 516-224-8100
**Tollfree:** 800-291-8090
**Fax:** 516-224-8200
**Email:** info@theinnatfoxhollow.com
**Web:** www.theinnatfoxhollow.com
**Suite Rates:** 169–389
**No. of Suites:** 145
**Credit Cards:** Most CCs Accepted
**Attractions**: Enjoy the many Arts
& Entertainment venues on Long
Island such as Nassau Coliseum
and the Tilles Arts Center at
CW Post College. Mansions,
Museums, Wineries, Beaches,
Golf, Shopping, Adventureland
Park & Splish Splash water park
are also nearby.
**Services:** Full American breakfast
buffet served daily, extensive hot
and cold dinner buffet served
Sunday -Thursday, with wine
and beer. Missed meal-service
Sun–Thurs, 37 inch Flat Screen
TVs, In-suite safes, Wireless
Internet.
**Restrictions:** Rates are based on
single or double occupancy, Add'l
Adults 12 & older are $20.00. Max
4 per room.
**Concierge:** For availability,
inquire at front desk
**Room Service:** Yes for Dinner
**Restaurant:** The Rose Hunt
Restaurant and Lounge at Fox
Hollow.
**Bar:** On premise restaurant and
bar
**Business Facilities:** Fax, copies
**Conference Room:** 5 rooms /
capacity up to 65 people.
**Sports Facilities:** 24 hour Fitness
Center
**Spa Services:** In-room Massages.
**Airport:** JFK, LGA, ISP
**Location:** Long Island, New York-
Nassau County

The Inn At Fox Hollow, Long Island's most luxurious life-style hotel offering 145 all suite accommodations. Located in Woodbury, Long Island (New York) in the heart of the Gold Coast, The Inn offers unparalleled comfort, superior amenities, complimentary services and dynamic hospitality.

The Fox Hollow's 134 classic suites include a complete kitchen with a full-size refrigerator and freezer, microwave, stovetop range, dishwasher, cooking and dining utensils and dining table, brand new 37"; Toshiba HD LCD Flat Screen TVs in 134 Classic Suites. 42" screen Flat Screen TV in Royal Suites. 11 Exclusive VIP Royal Suites are also available.

The Inn is the ideal venue for executive travel and meetings on Long Island. The Inn At Fox Hollow's exceptional attention to detail, fine cuisine and tasteful décor lend itself perfectly to your next special event.

Whether staying for business or a weekend getaway, an extended stay or on their wedding day, The Inn at Fox Hollow redefines luxury and has truly earned its place in the hearts and minds of those with discriminating taste.

Amenities and services that are"Above and Beyond" the ordinary. A leader in the Long Island Hotel industry with a customer service philosophy that believes in Everyday Rewards with Caring Comfort; that's The Inn At Fox Hollow.

# THE AUGUSTUS T ZEVELY INN

The only lodging in the Old Salem Historic District, the Augustus T. Zevely Inn, on the National Historic Register, has been meticulously and accurately restored to its mid-19th century appearance. Attention to authenticity has been carried out in the furnishings and use of the rooms. The warm and inviting Moravian atmosphere found in Old Salem continues as one enters the Zevely Inn—through the use of only Old Salem Collection furniture, fixtures, accessories, tiles, floor coverings, and window treatments. Some were made especially for the Zevely Inn; others are high-quality reproductions from originals found in the homes and museums in Old Salem. Many rooms have been closely returned to their original appearance and use, or sensitively adapted as guestrooms. Electrified beeswax window candles warmly welcome guests.

Inside, a corner fireplace, characteristic of Moravian architecture, graces the parlor where in winter, a wood fire burns and complimentary wine and cheese is served. Throughout the year, the parlor is a gathering place for guests; its comfortable surroundings encouraging conversation and kindling new friendships.

A formal dining room, off the parlor, also has a corner, wood-burning fireplace. It can be used as a private meeting room or by guests who prefer this setting to the parlor. The rear wall has a historically accurate mural that presents a view of Old Salem in 1844 from this perspective; several buildings in the mural exist today.

Our guests are not just visitors; they are part of a living 18th century restored Moravian town, which maintains the spirit, character and ambiance of its Moravian founders.

**Address:** 803 South Main Street Winston-Salem NC 27101
**Phone:** 336-748-9299
**Tollfree:** 800-928-9299
**Fax:** 336-721-2211
**Email:** reservations@winston-salem-inn.com
**Web:** www.winston-salem-inn.com
**Room Rates:** 95 -240
**Suite Rates:** 240
**No. of Rooms:** 12
**No. of Suites:** 1
**Credit Cards:** Most CCs Accepted
**Attractions**: Old Salem is surrounded by the City of Winston-Salem, North Carolina, formed by merger in 1913 of Salem and the new town of Winston. The city forms, with Greensboro and High Point, the "Triad," which has become a center of industry, education.
**Services:** All rooms have outstanding views of Old Salem and/or our period landscaped yard, a color television, radio alarm clock, telephone.
**Restrictions:** Children 12 and older welcome, 1 room Pet Friendly ($15.00 per day), Limited handicap accessiblity
**Concierge:** Yes: available (daily) 7:00am–8:00pm
**Room Service:** No
**Restaurant:** Complimentary continental breakfast on the weekdays and full breakfast on weekends.
**Bar:** No: Complimentary wine & cheese reception 5:30–6:30pm
**Business Facilities:** Limited: WiFi, fax and copies
**Conference Room:** 1 room / capacity: up to 10 people
**Sports Facilities:** No
**Spa Services:** We would be happy to offer you suggestions and assist you with reservations and directions.
**Airport:** Greensboro Int'l Airport
**Location:** Old Salem historic district

# THE ALLISON INN & SPA

**Address:** 2525 Allison Lane
Newberg OR 97132
**Phone:** 503-554-2525
**Tollfree:** 877-294-2525
**Fax:** 503-476-0680
**Email:** reservations@theallison.com
**Web:** www.theallison.com
**Room Rates:** 295–355
**Suite Rates:** 450–1100
**No. of Rooms:** 77
**No. of Suites:** 8
**Credit Cards:** Most CCs Accepted
**Attractions**: The Willamette
Valley features over 200 wineries
within 20 minutes from the
resort. Nature Hikes, golf &
tennis nearby. Visit wineries on
horseback, by hot air balloon,
helicopter or limousine. Art
galleries, farmers markets,
numerous dining options.
**Services:** Valet parking, twice
daily maid service, WiFi Internet
service, estate gardens, half acre
chef's garden. Hair & nail salon.
**Restrictions:** Pet friendly
(fee), children 12 & under -
complimentary
**Concierge:** Services available.
**Room Service:** 24 hours
**Restaurant:** JORY, a 100 seat
signature restaurant, showcases
Oregon Wine Country Cuisine.
**Bar:** JORY Bar
**Business Facilities:** Available on
request
**Conference Room:** 6 rooms /
capacity: up to 850 people
**Sports Facilities:** Swimming
pool & fitness studio
**Spa Services:** 15,000 sq. ft. &
12 treatment rooms, whirlpool,
sauna, steam. Pinotherapy
treatments.
**Airport:** Portland PDX
**Location:** Willamette Valley wine
country

Experience Oregon's premier luxury destination resort on 35 hillside acres, 5 of which are vineyards. LEED Gold certification, The Allison is the quintessential wine country property for sophisticated travelers.

Just an hour's drive from downtown Portland & less than 2 hours from the coast, it is an ideal choice for leisure guests as a romantic getaway, executive meetings, celebrations, weddings or a spa retreat.

Spacious, deluxe accommodations, all with fireplaces, views, a terrace or balcony, spa-like bathrooms and inviting window seats. The earth toned interior design palette utilized for the accommodations pays tribute to the rich colors of the countryside; *lichen*, *bark*, *berry*, *pear*, *beet* and *squash*, inspired by the neighboring vineyards and nearby farmlands. The furnishings are custom-crafted complemented by original artwork featuring local artisans. Large windows ensure you will enjoy either hillside or vineyard views.

Embracing thoughtful service and being well educated, our highly trained service staff at our JORY restaurant will graciously offer to customize your wine pairing to complement the cuisine ordered. In-room dining menus, private dining and catered affairs will also be created under a similar focus. The Allison's spa services are designed to provide the ultimate in comfort and relaxation for men and women alike. With 15,000 square feet dedicated to health, wellness, pampering and a touch of indulgence, neither stress nor worry can survive our spa environment.

Unwind, indulge and enjoy the charm and unspoiled natural beauty of the award-winning Willamette Valley, world famous for Pinot Noir.

# GOLDEN PLOUGH INN AT PEDDLER'S VILLAGE

Set in scenic central Bucks County countryside, The Golden Plough Inn is part of Peddler's Village, an 18th-century style shopping, dining, lodging and family entertainment attraction. The property features over 70 unique specialty shops and restaurants, the Giggleberry Fair Family Entertainment Center with a beautifully restored antique carousel, year-round festivals and events, waterwheel and gazebo, all set on 42 acres of award-winning landscaped grounds and winding brick pathways. The buildings are reproduction Bucks County stone-and-wood architecture.

Each room is spacious and individually decorated for comfort and convenience. Most are 18th-century American Country style, plus some newer English-Country style, each appointed with fine fabrics and rich colors. Designer fabric treatments on windows, bedding and crown canopies help create a warm, elegant ambiance.

The Golden Plough excels at pampering. Upon arrival, guests will find a complimentary split of wine, snacks and beverages. Complimentary toiletries are presented in attractive baskets. The Inn is an ideal location for business meetings, reunions and wedding that require overnight accommodations. An overnight stay at the Inn includes a hearty continental breakfast at the Sweet Lorraine's Restaurant, which also serves lunch, dinner and late-night snacks.

Your special key to this idyllic getaway is waiting … at the Golden Plough Inn at Peddler's Village.

**Address:** Route 202 and Street Road, Lahaska PA 18931
**Phone:** 215-794-4004
**Fax:** 215-794-4008
**Email:** lodging@peddlersvillage.com
**Web:** www.goldenploughinn.com
**Room Rates:** 149–285
**Suite Rates:** 285–550
**No. of Rooms:** 70
**No. of Suites:** 10
**Credit Cards:** Most CCs Accepted
**Attractions**: Giggleberry Fair Family Entertainment Center, Shopping village on-site, Wineries, Antiques, Museums, Historic sites, Covered bridges, Hiking.
**Services:** Gift shop, Library, Cable TV, Phone, Radio, Individual climate controls, In-room coffee/tea service, Hair dryer, Iron, Complimentary wine, snacks, toiletries, Continental plus breakfast included in room rate.
**Restrictions:** No pets allowed, Children welcome, under 2 free with parents, 3 rooms handicap
**Concierge:** Yes—available 24/7
**Room Service:** No
**Restaurant:** Enjoy breakfast, lunch, or dinner in our own Sweet Lorraine's restaurant.
**Bar:** Yes—located in Sweet Lorraine's restaurant, hrs 7am–12pm
**Business Facilities:** Message center, Admin. assistance, Copiers, Audio-visual, Fax.
**Conference Room:** 8 rooms, capacity 250 people
**Sports Facilities:** Privileges to nearby gym and golf course
**Spa Services:** Choose the ultimate relaxation with The Spa Getaway Package.
**Airport:** Philadelphia or Newark Int'l Airports
**Location:** Peddler's Village

# MORRIS HOUSE HOTEL

**Address:** 225 South 8th Street
Philadelphia PA 19106
**Phone:** 215-922-2446
**Fax:** 215-922-2466
**Email:** info@morrishousehotel.com
**Web:** www.morrishousehotel.com
**Room Rates:** 159–219
**Suite Rates:** 189–349
**No. of Rooms:** 15
**No. of Suites:** 9
**Credit Cards:** Most CCs Accepted
**Attractions**: The Morris House
Hotel is located in America's most
historic square mile, the place
where history comes alive. Two
of the most treasured moments
celebrating America's freedom—
Independence Hall and Liberty
Bell—are located just blocks
away.
**Services:** Private bathrooms
with a shower and/or bath, air
conditioning, phones, hair dryers,
CD AM/FM clock radio, TV/
DVD and smoke alarms. Irons,
ironing boards are available upon
request.
**Restrictions:** No pets allowed
**Concierge:** Yes: available 24/7
**Room Service:** Yes: open
(Tues–Sat) from 5–10:00pm
**Restaurant:** We are proud to
inform you that our on-site M
Restaurant has recently opened
for dinners.
**Bar:** Yes: open (Tues–Sat) from
5-10:00pm
**Business Facilities:** Full business
center/computer/fax/copier
**Conference Room:** 1 room /
capacity: up to 15 people
**Sports Facilities:** No on site gym
or workout room
**Spa Services:** Our helpful staff
will be able to assist you with
recommendations.
**Airport:** Philadelphia Airport
**Location:** Historical center city
district

We cordially invite you and your clients to experience Center City's most unique and intimate new hotel, located in the heart of beautiful Washington Square West. The historic Morris House Hotel offers fifteen exquisitely appointed rooms, equipped with today's indispensable amenities, such as cable entertainment, high-speed Internet access, and luxury baths. In addition, the city's finest restaurants and shopping, and renowned historic sites are just steps from the hotel's doors.

Distinguished by its personalized service, unique surroundings and a warm, cordial staff not often found in large chain hotels, the Morris House also offers an excellent value. Our room rates for a minimum one-night stay will pleasantly surprise you, and are well below what other top tier hotels charge. Complimentary continental breakfast is included the room rate, as well.

Discover Philadelphia's newest and loveliest gem, the Morris House Hotel' give us a call to arrange a tour of the grounds and guestrooms, or, make a lasting impression, and send your clients over for an unforgettable stay.

# THOMAS BOND HOUSE
# BED AND BREAKFAST

Thomas Bond was a doctor best known, along with Benjamin Franklin, for helping to establish the first public hospital in the United States. His house, built in 1769, is an important example of classic Georgian style architecture. Today it stands as a carefully restored townhouse with an ambiance of quiet luxury, and is listed on the National Register of Historic Places.

The refurbished guestrooms and suites have private baths and are furnished with period furniture and authentic accessories. In keeping with the custom of the Federal Period, the most luxurious accommodations are those closest to the first floor. During the week guests are served a continental breakfast featuring freshly squeezed orange juice and freshly baked muffins, and, on weekends, a sumptuous full breakfast is served. The charming parlor serves as a gathering place where guests relax and enjoy a game of chess or bridge and start their evening with complimentary wine and cheese. Evenings end with freshly baked cookies.

In the heart of Philadelphia's Old City with easy access to downtown, The Thomas Bond House is walking distance to many historic sites, including Independence Hall. It is on the doorstep of fine restaurants, theaters, museums, world-class shopping and the internationally acclaimed Kimmel Center for the Performing Arts, the Academy of Music and the Philadelphia Orchestra. It is the only inn located in Independence National Historical Park and is owned by the National Park Service.

**Address:** 129 South 2nd Street Philadelphia PA 19106
**Phone:** 215-923-8523
**Tollfree:** 800-845-2663
**Fax:** 215-923-8504
**Email:** info@thomasbondhousebandb.com
**Web:** www.ThomasBondHouseBAndB.com
**Room Rates:** 115–165
**Suite Rates:** 190
**No. of Rooms:** 12
**No. of Suites:** 2
**Credit Cards:** Most CCs Accepted
**Attractions**: Philadelphia Museum of Art, University of Pennsylvania, Barnes Foundation, Independence National Historical Park, Constitution Center, Antiques Row, Philadelphia Zoo, Please Touch Museum for Children, Reading Terminal Market, Philadelphia Flower Show
**Services:** Parking, library, cable TV, telephone, radio, in-room climate control, hair dryer, desk, some fireplaces & whirlpool tubs, free local calls.
**Restrictions:** Children welcome under supervision, No pets, Non-smoking facility
**Concierge:** Yes: (daily) 9:00am–9:00pm
**Room Service:** No
**Restaurant:** A complimentary continental breakfast on weekdays, and full breakfast on weekends.
**Bar:** No: Complimentary Wine & Cheese reception (daily) 5:30–6:30pm
**Business Facilities:** Limited: Copier, fax, WiFi
**Conference Room:** 1 room / capacity: up to 20 people
**Sports Facilities:** No on site gym or workout room
**Spa Services**: Will refer to local facilities
**Airport:** Philadelphia Int'l Airport
**Location:** Old City Area

# THE PRIORY

**Address:** 614 Pressley Street
Pittsburgh PA 15212
**Phone:** 412-231-3338
**Fax:** 412-231-4838
**Email:** info@thepriory.com
**Web:** www.thepriory.com
**Room Rates:** 119–125
**Suite Rates:** 134–195
**No. of Rooms:** 24
**No. of Suites:** 3
**Credit Cards:** Most CCs Accepted
**Attractions**: Galleries, theaters, and restaurants, Warhol Museum, PNC Park, Heinz Field, the Children's Museum, National Aviary, the Carnegie Science Center, Mattress Factory, the Photo Antiquities Museum.
**Services:** Shuttle to downtown Pittsburgh on weekdays, Parking, Library, Car hire, Game area, Cable TV, newspaper, Telephone, Radio, Internet access, Individual climate control, toiletries, continental breakfast.
**Restrictions:** No pets allowed, Children under 13 free with parents, 2 rooms handicap equipped
**Concierge:** Yes: available 24/7
**Room Service:** No
**Restaurant:** Our staff will be happy to offer suggestions and assist with reservations and directions.
**Bar:** Yes—full bar in Library, available from 5–10:00pm
**Business Facilities:** Fax, DSL line, copier, workspace
**Conference Room:** 2 rooms / capacity: up to 350 people
**Sports Facilities:** Full fitness center
**Spa Services:** We will be happy to assist you with a local suggestion.
**Airport:** Pittsburgh Int'l Airport
**Location:** North Shore

The only European-style hotel in the city of Pittsburgh, The Priory's twenty-four guestrooms have been carefully restored to Victorian elegance, while nevertheless maintaining the modern amenities of a larger establishment.

The Priory offers a hearty continental breakfast including meats, cheeses and hard-cooked eggs every morning in its cheerful dining room.

The Priory is within walking distance of downtown Pittsburgh, with its galleries, theaters, and restaurants, as well as many North Side attractions, such as the Warhol Museum, PNC Park, Heinz Field, the Children's Museum, the National Aviary, the Carnegie Science Center, the Mattress Factory, and the Photo Antiquities Museum.

Guests can relax in the lush courtyard in the spring or utilize the well-equipped fitness room in summer or sip wine by the fire in the sitting room in the winter, or enjoy a book in the library at anytime of year. Whatever the season, whatever your business or pleasure—come to The Priory.

# THE FRENCH MANOR INN AND SPA

A luxurious and intimate country inn modeled after an actual French Manor on 45 private acres that command a sweeping view of the Pocono Mountains. Let the whimsical nature of The French Manor entrance you. This stone chateau is an attraction in itself with imported Spanish slate roofs, cypress interior, a Romanesque-arched entryway and impressive stone fireplaces. Find respite in the shade of its lush grounds or inside its beautiful guestrooms and suites. Honored with AAA four-diamond ratings in both accommodations and restaurant, its gourmet cuisine, uncompromising hospitality and amazing views ensure your every wish will be fulfilled!

Romance comes to mind first when thinking of The French Manor. Each of its 5 spacious rooms and 14 private suites is the epitome of refined elegance and intimate luxury.

Each Suite, named after various cities in France such as Nice, Bordeaux, Marseilles and Calais, are decorated to provide the ultimate sense of comfort and luxury while providing all the amenities that today's travelers require.

The newest addition to the French Manor is the Spa building which houses the five Spa Suites each with a fireplace, whirlpool tub, and private balcony view, as well as a green spa facility in the lower level. The suites are very similar to the La Maisonneuve Suites, only with a more contemporary decor and "Green" in design. The Logan family took great care in using only sustainable materials and modern technology to build this newest addition. In the lower level of the spa building is a green spa—Le Spa Foret, offering a complete array of Green spa treatments. The calming and eco-friendly environment of Le Spa Foret is sure to eliminate any stresses of everyday life.

**Address:** 50 Huntingdon Road South Sterling PA 18460
**Phone:** 570-676-3244
**Tollfree:** 877-720-6090
**Fax:** 570-676-8573
**Email:** info@thefrenchmanor.com
**Web:** www.thefrenchmanor.com
**Room Rates:** 175–275
**Suite Rates:** 250–375
**No. of Rooms:** 5
**No. of Suites:** 14
**Credit Cards:** Most CCs Accepted
**Attractions:** The French Manor is centrally located in the Pocono Mountains – convenient to many recreational facilities such as Bushkill Falls, Horseback Riding, Promised Land and Tobyhanna State Parks, wonderful antiquing and many outlet stores.
**Services:** Pianist on the weekends, automatic turn-down service with Godiva chocolates.
**Restrictions:** Sorry, no pets. Not suitable for children under 12 years.
**Concierge:** Yes
**Room Service:** Available for breakfast, dinner, and afternoon tea.
**Restaurant:** Classical and Nouvelle French Cuisine, Proper attire required (Jackets for gentlemen)
**Bar:** Full bar available. Fine wine list.
**Business Facilities:** Free high-speed wireless Internet, fax, copier, computer, voice mail, AV equipment
**Conference Room:** Yes.
**Sports Facilities:** Indoor Pool, Hot Tub, Fitness Room.
**Spa Services:** Le Spa Foret.
**Airport:** Scranton/Wilkes Barre
**Location:** Pocono Mountains

# 1843 BATTERY CARRIAGE HOUSE INN

**Address:** 20 South Battery
Charleston SC 29401
**Phone:** 843-727-3100
**Tollfree:** 800-775-5575
**Fax:** 843-727-3130
**Email:** batterych@bellsouth.net
**Web:** www.batterycarriagehouse.com
**Room Rates:** 149–309
**Suite Rates:** 259–309
**No. of Rooms:** 11
**No. of Suites:** 1
**Credit Cards:** Most CCs Accepted
**Attractions**: The Battery Carriage House Inn is located within easy walking distance to most of the historic sites in the downtown area including shopping and dining--not far from the beach, golf courses, tours to Ft. Sumter and other fun activities.
**Services:** Elegant Silver Tray Continental breakfast, free WiFi in lobby area, Cable TV (& HBO), Robes, Telephone, Radio, Whirlpools (in some rooms), Robes, newspaper.
**Restrictions:** No children under 12 years. No pets allowed, No smoking in rooms, 2 night minimum stay on weekends,
**Concierge:** 8:30am–10:00pm
**Room Service:** No
**Restaurant:** Our concierge will be happy to recommend and assist with appointments.
**Bar:** No
**Business Facilities:** No
**Conference Room:** No
**Sports Facilities:** No
**Spa Services:** Our concierge will be happy to recommend and assist with appointments.
**Airport:** Charleston Int'l
**Location:** Quiet historic waterfront residential district

The Battery Carriage House Inn is "No. 20 on the Battery," built in 1843, and the childhood summer home of the owner's grandmother. Beyond the wrought iron gates lies beautiful White Point Gardens in Charleston's Historic Residential District at the quiet end of the Battery overlooking Charleston Harbor.

The atmosphere is European, garden-centered, history-laden, romantic and intimate. Eight guestrooms are located in the old carriage house in the garden of the antebellum mansion, and another three rooms are on the ground floor in what was once the kitchen area of the mansion. Each room has a private entrance and each is individually decorated. The most unusual room is a small suite, which was the old cistern of the house! This extremely private lodging has its own sitting area under the porch. Of course, all conveniences are provided, including private steam bath shower units in some rooms, whirlpool tubs in others, staff to assist you with reservations and tours, and a private phone line with answering machine in each room.

Guests begin their day with the deluxe continental breakfast served with the morning newspaper, either in-room or under the Lady Bankshire rose arbor. For dinner, it's just a 10- to 15-minute walk up High Battery to Charleston's celebrated selection of fine restaurants.

This is definitely the right spot for a gracious, relaxing, European-style getaway south of the Mason-Dixon Line.

# ANSONBOROUGH INN

Originally a three-story stationer's warehouse (circa 1901), the building was designed for individual condominium units. As a result our suites are larger than most hotel rooms. They range from 450 to 750 square feet, which is unlike the typical 288 sq. ft. hotel room. Following the original renovation, the Ansonborough Inn has been transformed into this charming all-suite inn rivaling any in the South. Exposed heart pine beams and local fire red brick were commonly used in buildings of the period and these elements were incorporated in the décor throughout the Inn.

The Ansonborough Inn, for those familiar with maritime history, the very name speaks to its nautical heritage. The Inn is located within the historic district of downtown Charleston, so named when Lord Anson of England won the property in a spirited poker game with famous Charlestonian Thomas Gadsden. Lord Anson was sent to Charleston in 1724 to protect the coast of South Carolina from pirates. Admiral Anson was by no means a mere gentleman with a title—he was an exceptional sailor by any standard. He was the third Englishman to circumnavigate the globe. On his many voyages he captured Spanish ships filled with treasures. The most celebrated being in the mid-1740s when he abducted a Spanish vessel carrying booty worth a million and a quarter pounds of sterling. The Ansonborough district stretches from King Street to the edge of the Cooper River, between Society and Calhoun streets. These farmlands were divided into a borough of 25 lots in 1746.

**Address:** 21 Hassel Street Charleston SC 29401
**Phone:** 843-723-1655
**Tollfree:** 800-522-2073
**Fax:** 843-577-6888
**Email:** info@ansoboroughinn.com
**Web:** www.ansoboroughinn.com
**Suite Rates:** 159–359
**No. of Suites:** 45
**Credit Cards:** Most CCs Accepted
**Attractions**: SC Aquarium, USS Yorktown, The Battery, downtown shops, restaurants, museums, tours. The Ansonborough district stretches from King Street to the edge of the Cooper River, between Society and Calhoun streets. Enjoy the unique environment the historic district offers guests!
**Services:** Coffee, iced tea and lemonade served all day long.
**Restrictions:** Call for details
**Concierge:** available 24/7
**Room Service:** No
**Restaurant:** Step inside our authentic British Pub for a pint, spirits, or a glass of wine.
**Bar:** Yes—Admiral Anson's Pub
**Business Facilities:** Yes—full computer networking capabilities and A/V necessities
**Conference Room:** Yes
**Sports Facilities:** Small fitness center
**Spa Facilities:** We will refer you to the local establishments
**Airport:** Charleston International
**Location:** Center of city

# TWO MEETING STREET INN

**Address:** 2 Meeting Street
Charleston SC 29401
**Phone:** 843-723-7322
**Tollfree:** 888-723-7322
**Fax:** 843-723-7802
**Email:** innkeeper2meetst@bellsouth.net
**Web:** www.twomeetingstreet.com
**Room Rates:** 225-479
**No. of Rooms:** 9
**Credit Cards:** Most CCs Accepted
**Attractions:** Located in the heart
of historic Charleston, on the
famous Battery, the Inn is within
a few blocks from the best the
city has to offer: Colonial museum
houses, carriage rides from the
Old Market, antique stores, art
galleries, Fort Sumter.
**Services:** A hot Southern
breakfast, Lowcountry afternoon
tea, evening sherry, Gilchrist &
Soames toiletries, waffle-weave
bathrobes, WiFi, newspapers,
iPod docks and free parking.
**Restrictions:** Please inquire
about our policy regarding
children. Smoking no. No pets.
**Concierge:** Availability 24/7
**Room Service:** Limited menu/
from 7:00am–11:00pm
**Restaurant:** The Inn is within
just a few blocks of many
wonderful eateries and fine dining
experiences.
**Bar:** No
**Business Facilities:** Computer/
fax/copier accessible from front
desk area
**Conference Room:** No
**Sports Facilities:** No
**Spa Services:** Staff will be happy
to assist you with arrangements
for an in-house massage or for an
appointment and directions to
the local spa facilities.
**Airport:** Charleston Int'l
**Location:** At The Battery.

No other place is like Charleston, and in Charleston, no place is quite like Two Meeting Street Inn- the jewel in the crown of the city's historic inns. From Two Meeting Street Inn's gracious southern veranda- one of the most photographed porches in the South- guests enjoy layer upon layer of natural beauty while perusing literature or indulging in afternoon tea with an enticing array of lemon squares, rum cakes and dark chocolate plantation brownies. Surrounded by century-old live oaks amid lush gardens with a finely manicured lawn and cherry red azaleas, the inn overlooks Charleston's historic harbor, The Battery and White Point Gardens. A few blocks away, world-class dining, modern boutiques, antique shops, art galleries, historic museum houses and cultural festivals wait.

Two Meeting Street Inn's nine distinctive guestrooms provide the perfect setting for a romantic celebration or a tranquil retreat from everyday life. Whether you choose a magnificent honeymoon suite or an inviting third floor room, your experience will be memorable. The Inn offers you the amenities of a luxury Charleston hotel along with the special, personal touches one expects from a congenial Southern host. On the piazza overlooking the courtyard, guests enjoy a plentiful Southern breakfast. In the late afternoon, one is rejuvenated with a gracious afternoon tea. At the end of the day, evening sherry awaits you.

At Two Meeting Street Inn the pace slows and the mind rests. The Inn invites you to discard your stress and relish the exquisite civility and romance of Charleston. We await your arrival.

# VENDUE INN

The luxurious Vendue Inn is located in the heart of the Historic District at the beautiful Waterfront Park on Charleston Harbor. This in-town gem, famous for comfort, excellent staff, service and convenience, was lovingly restored from French Quarter warehouses (ca. 1860).

From indulgent suites with fireplaces and whirlpool tubs to charming historic quarters in the inn's original style, the accommodations at the Vendue Inn reflect the history of Charleston. All sixty-six rooms and suites, many with poster, canopy or sleigh beds, are individually decorated with 18th century style English or French period furnishings, and antiques. Fireplaces and marble bathrooms with Jacuzzis and separate showers are available in Junior and Deluxe Suites. Soft bathrobes, Egyptian cotton linens, and other fine amenities add to the comfort. In the evening, enjoy a special turn down service.

The Library, an intimate restaurant, exemplifies the Inn's standards of excellence, offering progressive American cuisine prepared with a uniquely Charleston flare. Mornings begin with a delicious complimentary Southern breakfast. Wine and hors d'oeuvres are served each afternoon in the Music Room. Don't miss the Roof Top Bar & Restaurant, a favorite spot to savor the colorful sunsets over the picturesque steeples and rooftops of historic Charleston.

Walk cobblestone streets to historic homes and churches, art galleries, antique shops, the old City Market, or stroll through parks and along the Battery. You'll agree you've found a very special place at Charleston's Vendue Inn where exquisite comfort, attentive service and Southern hospitality are a way of life!

**Address:** 19 Vendue Range Charleston SC 29401
**Phone:** 843-577-7970
**Tollfree:** 800-845-7900
**Fax:** 843-577-2913
**Email:** info@vendueinn.com
**Web:** www.vendueinn.com
**Room Rates:** 179–339
**Suite Rates:** 269–459
**No. of Rooms:** 66
**No. of Suites:** 22
**Credit Cards:** Most CCs Accepted
**Attractions**: Heart of the Historic District, local Restaurants, Antique Shops, Boutiques, Art Galleries, Museums, City Market and Aquarium, sightseeing, Gardens and Historic Forts, golf, walking tours, carriage rides
**Services:** Southern Breakfast, Dry cleaning, Free newspapers in lobby, Free wireless Internet access in public areas, Valet parking, Wake-up calls, doorman, parking garage, Express check-in/out.
**Restrictions:** Non-smoking, ADA Handicap Room, Pets by special permission
**Concierge:** Yes: available 24/7
**Room Service:** Yes: available (daily) 7:00am–9:30pm w/limited menu
**Restaurant:** The Vendue Inn provides an extraordinary breakfast experience.
**Bar:** Yes: the Roof Top Bar & Restaurant w/live entertainment
**Business Facilities:** Computer, Fax, Copier, Audio-Video
**Conference Room:** 4 rooms / capacity: up to 50 people
**Sports Facilities:** No on-site gym or workout room
**Spa Services:** Our helpful staff will be happy to assist you with suggestions.
**Airport:** Charleston Int'l Airport
**Location:** Historic District at Waterfront Park

# THE SANCTUARY HOTEL - AT KIAWAH ISLAND GOLF RESORT

**Address:** One Sanctuary Beach Dr
Kiawah Island SC 29455
**Phone:** 843-768-6000
**Tollfree:** 800-654-2924
**Fax:** 843-768-2736
**Email:** reservations@kiawahresort.com
**Web:** www.kiawahresort.com/
accommodations/the-sanctuary
**Room Rates:** 1,015 – 14,070
**No. of Rooms:** 255
**Credit Cards:** Most CCs Accepted
**Attractions**: In Charleston there
are museums, theater, the City
Market, South Carolina Aquarium,
Comedy Festival & the Oyster
Festival.
**Services:** Preferred golf and
tee times, preferred tennis and
court times, nature programs and
Kids Kamp, door-to-door resort
transport, trash/towel service
**Restrictions:** Call for details
**Concierge:** Yes—7am–11pm
(daily).
**Room Service:** Yes: available
24/7 – full menu
**Restaurant:** The Ocean Room
and Kiawath's steakhouse. For
a warm, low country, traditional
dining tradition—try the Jasmine
Porch.
**Bar:** Lobby Lounge 1pm –
Midnight; Ocean Rm Lounge
6 – 10pm (Tues-Sat)
**Business Facilities:** Full Center
with Admin Assist upon request
**Conference Room:** 8 rooms /
capacity: up to 600 people
**Sports Facilities:** Full fitness
room / 2 pools (indoor & outdoor)
**Spa Services:** Kiawah's vast
coastline and lush greenery were
the inspiration behind several of
our signature treatments.
**Airport:** Charleston Int'l
**Location:** Island just off the coast

Whether you are looking for a family beach vacation spot, a relaxing private vacation rental home, or an island family villa, Kiawah Island Golf Resort has an extraordinary property waiting for you.

The Sanctuary offers 255 spacious rooms and suites, including the 3000 square foot Presidential Suite. Our king rooms are among the largest on the East Coast with the smallest measuring 520 square feet. All hotel rooms are uniquely designed to include such exquisite amenities as a handcrafted desk and armoire, an elegantly appointed sofa and chair, and custom made beds. You'll enjoy full maid service each day, newspaper delivery and complimentary use of four bicycles to explore the island. Fine Italian-woven, Egyptian cotton bed linens, spa-quality bath amenities and plush bathrobes provide luxurious comforts. You'll also receive full access to The Sanctuary at Kiawah Island Golf Resort's fitness center.

Whether you are looking for a family beach vacation spot, a relaxing private vacation rental home, or an island family villa, Kiawah Island Golf Resort has an extraordinary property waiting for you.

# HOTEL ST GERMAIN

A Relais & Chateaus property, the boutique Hotel St. Germain offers seven luxury suites, two parlors, two dining rooms and a New Orleans-style courtyard. The Hotel and Restaurant are both winners of the prestigious Zagat Award and both have received the Four Diamond designation from AAA.

All of the suites are decorated with turn-of-the-century antiques from France and New Orleans and each has a working fireplace. Feather beds are canopied with luxurious fabrics from fourteen-foot ceilings. Amenities include cable television, VCR and CD/cassette players plus Jacuzzis or soaking tubs, European toiletries and signature terry cloth robes.

The convenience of a 24-hour concierge, a butler, room service, valet parking and business services are available. The Hotel specializes in catering, banquets, weddings and special events.

At Hotel St. Germain, guests dine by candlelight in the dramatic Old-World ambiance of the romantic grand Dining Room overlooking the ivy-covered garden courtyard. Wines from the extensive cellar are served in imported cut crystal and meals are presented on the proprietor's collection of antique Limoges china. The sumptuous seven-course, gourmet dinner changes monthly. Dinner is prix fixe and is available Tuesday through Saturday evenings by advance reservation.

**Address:** 2516 Maple Avenue Dallas TX 75201
**Phone:** 214-871-2516
**Tollfree:** 800-683-2516
**Fax:** 214-871-0740
**Email:** genmgrstgermain@aol.com
**Web:** www.hotelstgermain.com
**Suite Rates:** 290–650
**No. of Suites:** 7
**Credit Cards:** Most CCs Accepted
**Attractions**: Boutique shopping across the street, 30 restaurants, 25 art galleries, 20 antique shops
**Services:** Valet, Beauty/Barber shop, Laundry service, Lounges, Shoe shine, Fireplaces, Balconies, Cable TV/VCR, Radio, CD/Cassette players, Mini-bar, Robes, Whirlpools, Toiletries & newspaper, Deluxe European breakfast included
**Restrictions:** 7 day cancellation policy, small pets (under 20 lbs) $50 per night
**Concierge:** Available assistance—24/7
**Room Service:** 24/7
**Restaurant:** Enjoy dinner in our Hotel St Germain Restaurant. Dinner served Tues–Saturday. Advance reservations required.
**Bar:** Parisian Style with extensive Champagne List.
**Business Facilities:** Message center, Admin. assistance through concierge, Staff speaks several languages
**Conference Room:** 3 rooms / capacity up to 175 people
**Sports Facilities:** No—however, nearby full health facilities (fee)
**Spa Services:** There are local spas within walking distance.
**Airport:** Love Field & Dallas/Fort Worth Airports
**Location:** Oak Lawn, Near downtown

# SORREL RIVER RANCH RESORT & SPA

**Address:** Mile 17 Hwy 128
Moab UT 84532
**Phone:** 435-259-4642
**Fax:** 435-259-3016
**Email:** stay@sorrelriver.com
**Web:** www.sorrelriver.com
**Room Rates:** 399–539
**Suite Rates:** 539–699
**No. of Rooms:** 55
**No. of Suites:** 8
**Credit Cards:** Most CCs Accepted
**Attractions**: Whether you choose to bike Moab's many roads or famous mountain biking trails, to hike in Utah's National Parks, to get your feet wet with a lazy float trip or some wild whitewater rafting, you will treasure these new memories and adventures.
**Services:** Yoga Fitness Room. 160 acres, horseback riding, wireless Internet, large selection of hotel amenities AND LOCATION!
**Restrictions:** Yes—Pet Friendly, no smoking, 2 handicap accessible
**Concierge:** Yes: available (daily) 8am till 8pm
**Room Service:** Yes—available (daily) 8am till 10pm / Special In Room menu
**Restaurant:** Yes
**Bar:** Yes—open 12 noon – 10:00pm (daily)
**Business Facilities:** Full business facilities
**Conference Room:** 6 rooms / capacity: up to 150 people
**Sports Facilities:** Fitness Room – open 24/7
**Spa Services:** The Spa at Sorrel River provides rejuvenation after a tough day on the trail.
**Airport:** Moab Airport & Grand Junction Airport
**Location:** 17 miles from Moab, UT

Set amongst some of the most spectacular scenery in the American Southwest, Sorrel River Ranch Hotel & Spa Resort elevates the expectation of luxury lodging in Moab Utah. In addition to all the amenities of a small luxury hotel, our resort offers 160 acres of sprawling green pastures alongside the Colorado River surrounded by southern Utah's famous arches, towering red rock cliffs, mountain buttes and dramatic mesas, all beneath a vast, flawless desert sky.

Our expansive resort grounds are meticulously groomed and landscaped to the highest standard, with attention to sustainable consciousness and eco-friendly practices. Our main lodge offers guests a central place to congregate in the riverside lounge or relax in solitude on the outdoor patio. The ranch's extensive resort facilities include a gourmet restaurant in the main lodge, casual dining on the riverside patio, a full-service health spa, tennis and basketball courts, a riverside swimming pool, and a full equestrian facility.

Most importantly, from room service to concierge, Sorrel River Ranch is dedicated to exceeding Four-Diamond standards, providing guests with an exceptional experience through personalized service and attention one might expect at a bed & breakfast or intimate inn.

# GOLDENER HIRSCH INN

Located mid-mountain at Deer Valley Resort, this AAA Four-Diamond Hotel Award winner is an intimate, elegant, yet friendly Austrian-style chalet situated in an idyllic mountain setting with four-season beauty.

Throughout the seasons, all the local sports, as well as Park City's shopping, theaters, museums, restaurants, and galleries are minutes from the inn. In the summer mountain-biking and during the winter, due to the location of the Goldener Hirsch, the inn offers ski-in, ski-out access.

The twenty guestrooms are uniquely decorated with hand-carved, hand-painted Austrian furniture. Inviting country prints grace the sofas, chairs, and draperies. All rooms feature king-sized beds with lush down comforters. Three suites have romantic king-size canopy beds. All rooms and suites are spacious, and most have private balconies and wood-burning fireplaces. All bathrooms throughout the hotel were recently renovated and feature the finest travertine tile showers, granite countertops and spa tubs. In addition new couches, easy chairs, coffee tables, lighting and flat screen HDTVs were recently implemented in the upgrade of all the rooms.

The Goldener Hirsch Restaurant features superb Continental and American cuisine in an elegant, yet relaxed Austrian setting. The menu features Austrian specialties and nouveau American cuisine with European influences. In the summer, dinner is served nightly. In the winter, the lounge features an apres ski menu with the broadest selection wines and beers in Park City. The restaurant is open daily for lunch and dinner.

**Address:** 7570 Royal Street E Park City UT 84060
**Phone:** 435-649-7770
**Tollfree:** 800-252-3373
**Fax:** 435-649-7901
**Email:** ghi@goldenerhirschinn.com
**Web:** www.goldenerhirschinn.com
**Room Rates:** 155–839
**Suite Rates:** 230–1,379
**No. of Rooms:** 8
**No. of Suites:** 12
**Credit Cards:** Most CCs Accepted
**Attractions**: Skiing, snow-mobiling, cross-country skiing, snow-boarding, hot-air ballooning, mountain biking, golf, fly-fishing, hiking, shopping, theater, museums, art galleries, restaurants, August art festival, January Sundance Film Festival,
**Services:** Valet service, underground parking, gift shop, TV lounge, newspapers, cable TV, Terry cloth robes, slippers, breakfast, local shuttle service.
**Restrictions:** Children welcome, No pets allowed, One room handicapped-equipped, non-smoking.
**Concierge:** Available from 7:00am–11:00pm
**Room Service:** Available from 7:00am–9:00pm
**Restaurant:** Offers a delicious contemporary Alpine cuisine with a seasonal American spin.
**Bar:** Open from 11:30am–10:00pm
**Business Facilities:** Copiers, Audio-visual
**Conference Room:** 1 room, capacity 25 people
**Sports Facilities:** Small workout room with bike and treadmill.
**Spa Services:** In-room massage available at guest request plus spa sessions that will revitalize and rejuvenate..
**Airport:** Salt Lake Int'l Airport
**Location:** Silver Lake Village, Deer Valley

# GREEN VALLEY SPA & WEIGHT LOSS CLINIC

**Address:** 1871 W Canyon View Dr
Saint George UT 84770
**Phone:** 435-628-8060
**Tollfree:** 800-237-1068
**Fax:** 435-673-4084
**Email:** webmaster@greenvalleyspa.com
**Web:** www.greenvalleyspa.com
**Suite Rates:** 99 per person
**No. of Suites:** 50
**Credit Cards:** Most CCs Accepted
**Attractions**: Daily hiking in Red
Rock Canyons, Grand Canyon,
Zion National Park, Bryce Canyon,
1½ hours from Las Vegas.
**Services:** Rose Gardens, Hi-
Speed wireless Internet, 2 gift
shops (the clubhouse and the spa
shop) & much more
**Restrictions:** Pets allowed
**Concierge:** Yes: available (daily)
7:00am – 7:00pm
**Room Service:** Yes: meals can be
served in room
**Restaurant:** Casual dining in an
elegant atmosphere.
**Business Facilities:** Limited
**Conference Room:** 1 room /
capacity: up to 60 people
**Sports Facilities:** 4 indoor tennis
courts, 2 racquetball courts, 6
swimming pools, golf/tennis
camps
**Spa Services:** Green Valley's
award winning spa treatments
were created to both refresh your
spirit and calm your mind.
**Airport:** Las Vegas Int'l Airport
**Location:** In Southern Utah

The marvelous accommodations at Green Valley Spa have received raves from guests and travel critics.

Each room is meticulously detailed with large whirlpool baths, fireplace, four poster bed, goose down comforters & pillows and freshly ground Starbucks coffee.

Green Valley offers hikes for all fitness levels; Trails include Zion National Park, Bryce Canyon, and the Red rock trails of Snow Canyon State Park. The Vic Braden Tennis College offers year round Tennis Camps. The world famous Spa offers 70 different treatments. Guests can choose from All-Inclusive packages which include, four diamond accommodations, meals, spa treatments & guided hikes or the option of reserving a room only and selecting from the A la Carte menu the activities & spa treatments of your choice.

This intimate resort (only 45 rooms) should be on the list of every discriminating traveler.

# ARLINGTON'S WEST MOUNTAIN INN

Arlington's West Mountain Inn is a charming 1850s Colonial-style farmhouse with white clapboard, green shutters and seven gables. Furnished with country antiques, a wood-stove and high beamed ceilings, the Inn offers a warm, hospitable environment. Enjoy fabulous views of the Battenkill Valley, the Green and Red Mountains, and miles and miles of lush country meadows. Located close to the historic village of Arlington, guests can enjoy outlet shopping, historic Hildene, and other outdoor adventures.

All of the rooms are individually decorated with antiques, comfortable reading chairs, canopy beds and fireplaces. Each bathroom is individually decorated and contains a full bath with tub and shower.

After an afternoon of exploring 150 acres of gardens, lawns, hiking trails and meadows, relax with a snack of homemade cookies or muffins while sipping the Inn's special hot spiced cider with spiced rum. For those special occasions, there is a country barn which seats 125 people. It has a dance floor where guests can dance the night away while celebrating that special occasion. After a fun-filled day, luxuriate in a hot bath using the complimentary toiletries.

Dine by candlelight in the wood-paneled dining room adorned with fresh-cut flowers and wood-burning fireplace. Maybe start with baked brie in filo dough with walnuts, followed by Black Angus filet mignon with wild mushroom jus. To top of the delicious meal, how about maple-pecan pie ala mode.

At the Arlington West Mountain Inn, take pleasure in a fabulous setting, wonderful views, and a warm, friendly staff.

**Address:** 144 W Mountain Inn Rd Arlington VT 05250
**Phone:** 802-375-6516
**Fax:** 802-375-6553
**Email:** info@westmountaininn.com
**Web:** www.westmountaininn.com
**Room Rates:** 155–221
**Suite Rates:** 155–269
**No. of Rooms:** 18
**No. of Suites:** 7
**Credit Cards:** Most CCs Accepted
**Attractions**: Historic village and shopping, Outlet shopping, Historic Hildene, Golf, Skiing. Canoeing, River tubing and swimming, Mountain biking
**Services:** Gift shop, TV lounge, Game area, Library, Baby-sitting upon request. Some kitchen facilities, fireplaces & balconies, Some rooms w/ cable TV and/or telephones, toiletries, Individual climate controls, snacks all day
**Restrictions:** No Pets Allowed; 2 Rms w/Handicap Access/ Equipped
**Concierge:** 7:30am–10:30pm (daily)
**Room Service:** No
**Restaurant:** West Mountain Inn Restaurant, serving breakfast from 8:00-10:00 a.m.; and serving dinner from 6:00-9:00 p.m. (Evening-casual dress code)
**Bar:** Noon – 11:00pm; Hors d'oeuvres served 6:00 – 7:00pm
**Business Facilities:** Copiers, Fax, Modem ports
**Conference Room:** 2 rooms, capacity 35
**Sports Facilities:** No on-site workout room
**Spa Services:** Front desk will be able to assist you with an in-house massage or arrange appointments to the nearest spa.
**Airport:** Albany Int'l Airport
**Location:** In the Country

# THE GOVERNOR'S INN

**Address:** 86 Main Street
Ludlow VT 05149
**Phone:** 802-228-8830
**Tollfree:** 800-468-3766
**Fax:** 802-228-2961
**Email:** innkeeper@thegovernorsinn.com
**Web:** www.thegovernorsinn.com
**Room Rates:** 164–279
**Suite Rates:** 259–319
**No. of Rooms:** 7
**No. of Suites:** 1
**Credit Cards:** Most CCs Accepted
**Attractions**: Golf, hiking, arts
and crafts school, professional
summer theater, country stores,
antique stores, art galleries,
downhill and cross country skiing,
snowshoeing, Green Mountain
National Forest, Weston Priory,
Plymouth Notch Historical Site
**Services:** TV lounge; Cable TV
with DVD/VHS in most rooms;
Video/DVD lending library; Gas
fireplaces (most rooms); Air
conditioned; Luxurious robes;
Thermo Masseur whirlpool tubs
(some rooms); Afternoon Tea,
Cooking Seminars, Innkeeping
Classes
**Restrictions:** Recommended
for children twelve and over; No
smoking; No pets allowed.
**Concierge:** 8:00 am – 10:00 pm
**Restaurant:** Coffee/Tea Service
always available in foyer. Full
Breakfast 8:00–9:30am (earlier
by request). Afternoon tea:
4:00–5:00pm. Dining: by advanced
reservation, Saturdays & special
occasions.
**Bar:** 4:00 – 10:00 pm (wine & beer
available)
**Conference Room:** 1 room/
capacity 6 people
**Business Facilities:** Wireless
Internet
**Sports Facilities:** No
**Spa Facilities:** Will refer to local
establishments
**Airport:** Hartford, CT;
Manchester, NH
**Location:** Central Vermont

From the moment you step into this historic Victorian country house, you are surrounded by gracious elegance and warm hospitality befitting Governor's Stickney's home. The Governor's Inn is a late 19th century country home located on the Ludlow village green just one mile from Okemo Mountain. Innkeepers Jim and Cathy Kubec welcome you to a haven for enjoying life's pleasures and a base for exploring Vermont.

Awake to a bountiful breakfast—perhaps apple cinnamon pancakes or our Governor's souffle—served on antique china, with crystal, and silver. Tea lovers delight in our extensive tea menu, featuring over 40 different blends.

Chat with the innkeepers and other guests in one of the inn's common rooms, or enjoy the privacy of your own room, where you can watch TV or enjoy the whirlpool tub. Many guestrooms have spectacular views of nearby Okemo Mountain.

Take advantage of our "concierge service" by letting your innkeepers assist you with reservations, directions, and suggestions for your visit to the area. Then, set out for the day, perhaps with a Vermont country picnic prepared by the inn's chef. Village shops and restaurants are within walking distance.

Enjoy afternoon tea, sweets and tea sandwiches served in the parlor, which features extraordinary slate fireplaces, polished woodwork, and oriental rugs. The inn has a lounge with wine and beer available. Retire to your luxurious bed chamber, warmed by a gas fireplace in the winter (or comfortably air conditioned in warm weather).

Here you will find outstanding food; comfortable, inviting, and well-appointed guestrooms; gracious surroundings; excellent service and generous hospitality.

# WILBURTON INN

Welcome to the Wilburton Inn, Manchester Vermont's twenty acre grand Victorian estate specializing in holiday vacations, romantic getaways, sport vacations, executive retreats and elegant country weddings.

Located high on the crest of a hill overlooking the Battenkill Valley and Vermont's Green Mountains, the Wilburton Inn was once the largest private estate in Manchester Village. Everything about it is superlative: fabulous location, ambiance and architecture. Since 1902, when the mansion was completed, there have been five owners of the property, each holding fast to a standard of excellence.

Driving past stone-walled estates on River Road, you sense that you are returning to an era of gracious living, undisturbed by the pressures of contemporary life. The day at the Wilburton begins with a full country breakfast served in the terrace dining room, including, of course, blueberry pancakes and genuine Vermont maple syrup. From the wide windows, admire breathtaking panoramic views of the mountains and the valley. After breakfast, take a pleasant stroll through the extensive grounds and the sculpture gardens. During the day, explore the shopping, recreational and cultural activities in town just one mile away. Hike the Green Mountains, or try sports at nearby ski, spa and golf centers. Enjoy a game of tennis at the Inn or relax by the pool. Read a newspaper or a book from the deck off your room.

Afternoon tea is served on the terrace or in the living room. Have a cocktail or glass of wine by the living room fireplace before dinner. Dining at the Wilburton is a wonderful experience. The handsome dining room has a massive fireplace. The menus feature fresh premium ingredients with herbs and salads cut from the garden. The pastry chef creates delicious desserts and artisan breads in the Wilburton kitchen. The wine captain will help select the perfect wine to pair with your dinner.

Experience the best of Vermont—come up to the Wilburton Inn. We look forward to greeting you at the Wilburton Inn and sharing with you all its romance, adventure, history and beauty.

**Address:** 257 Wilburton Drive Manchester Village VT 05254
**Phone:** 802-362-2500
**Tollfree:** 800-648-4944
**Fax:** 802-362-1107
**Email:** wilburtoninn@gmail.com
**Web:** www.wilburton.com
**Room Rates:** 115–345
**Suite Rates:** 200–350
**No. of Rooms:** 26
**No. of Suites:** 3
**Credit Cards:** Visa, MC, Amex
**Attractions**: In winter, ski, snow shoe & cross country ski. In spring, go fishing. In summer, hike our mountains, play tennis, swim, golf, canoe, enjoy concerts and theater. In fall, enjoy the colors of Vermont foliage. Year round shopping, antiquing and dining.
**Services:** Sculpture gardens, a gazebo. We offer guests a shopping discount bookl
**Restrictions:** Pets allowed in out building only.
**Concierge:** Front desk assistance
**Room Service:** Yes
**Restaurant:** Dinner is served by the massive fireplace in the handsome Billiard Room from 6pm–9pm.
**Bar:** Dining Room, Terrace and Living Room
**Business Facilities:** Some AV, Computer, Copy, Fax and wireless connection available
**Conference Room:** Multi areas capacity up to 200 people
**Sports Facilities:** Pool, Tennis Courts
**Spa Services:** We will be happy to make reservations for you at any of the area's local spas or exercise centers. We can also arrange for in-room services.
**Airport:** Albany Airport
**Location:** Manchester, Vermont

# THE BUCCANEER

**Address:** 5007 Estate Shoys Christiansted VI 00824
**Phone:** 340-712-2100
**Tollfree:** 800-255-3881
**Fax:** 340-712-2104
**Email:** reservations@thebuccaneer.com
**Web:** www.thebuccaneer.com
**Room Rates:** 250–680
**Suite Rates:** 450–970
**No. of Rooms:** 138
**No. of Suites:** 5
**Credit Cards:** Visa
**Attractions**: St Croix's beauty has made it a playground for the rich and famous for generations, snorkeling, Buck Island National Park, golf and tennis, wander centuries-old streets of Christiansted, kayak the Salt River, Columbus's landing site, shopping, museum
**Services:** Twice daily maid service with turn-down, kayaks and floating mats, welcome cocktails, Kids Camp for 4–12 year olds, intro to scuba lessons.
**Restrictions:** No Pets, Children welcome
**Concierge:** Full concierge service
**Room Service:** In-room dining 7am–9:30pm.
**Restaurant:** The Terrace offers open-air fine dining and spectacular views. Complimentary breakfast is also served. The Mermaid Restaurant serves salads, burgers, sandwiches and lunch specials.
**Bar:** Three bars
**Business Facilities:** Fax, copier, wireless Internet
**Conference Room:** Multi-areas / capacity up to 125 people
**Sports Facilities:** Fitness room available 24/7
**Spa Services:** The Hideaway Spa pampers guests with massages, body and skin treatments and salon services.
**Airport:** St Croix (STX)
**Location:** Five minutes east of historic Christiansted

The Buccaneer. Gracious. Elegant. Legendary. Founded in the 17th century and family-run for generations, The Buccaneer blends old-world charms with warm hospitality, and the amenities expected by today's traveler.

The Buccaneer is a luxury oceanfront resort located on St. Croix in the United States Virgin Islands. Completely self-contained, The Buccaneer offers a challenging 18 hole golf course, 8 superb tennis courts, 3 exquisite beaches, 3 restaurants, water sports center, health spa, and fitness center, all located on a 340 acre tropical estate.

Spacious, elegant accommodations are placed throughout the property with expansive terraces and impressive views. The Great House main building sits atop a hillside overlooking the Caribbean Sea and the Christiansted Harbor.

The resort is constructed around buildings which date to 1653; its architecture and history reflect the rich heritage of St. Croix. It is located less than a five minute drive to the historic town of Christiansted, where sightseeing, duty-free shopping and fine dining can be found.

### Distinctions
- "One of the World's Top Fifty Tropical Resorts?"
  - *Condé Nast Traveler Readers' Poll Awards*
- "One of the Top 25 Hotels in the Caribbean, Bahamas, and Bermuda?"
  - *Travel and Leisure Magazine*
- "One of the Top 10 Best Values in the Caribbean, the Bahamas and Bermuda?"
  - *Travel and Leisure Magazine*

# ESTATE CONCORDIA PRESERVE ECO-RESORT

Concordia is a retreat eco-resort for a quiet getaway in an upscale camping environment with spectacular open ocean views. Our unpopulated location provides an extremely quiet retreat. Estate Concordia Preserve includes 2 types of accommodations: Concordia Eco-Tents and Concordia Studios.

25 extraordinary multi-level tents each with private toilet, shower, kitchen & deck. Eco-tents are powered by solar energy and include running water and refrigerator Tents large enough for 4–5 adults to sleep on twin beds in a loft and a day bed. Screened windows allow nature lovers to be as close to St. John's flora and fauna as possible without actually sleeping outside. There are 9 Concordia Studios which feature large open-air rooms similar to a spacious hotel room. Each studio includes fully equipped kitchens and private bathroom and are unique in design and decor. The eco-resort now has 8 new Concordia Eco-Studios able to accommodate four people with queen-sized bed plus sleep sofa as well as kitchen facilities, bathroom with solar-heated shower and comfortable private deck. Location of the new studios allows guests the closest access to Salt Pond beach trail, Pavilion and Café Concordia.

**Address:** 20-27 Estate Concordia St. John VI 00831
**Phone:** 340-693-5855
**Tollfree:** 800-392-9004
**Fax:** 340-693-5960
**Email:** reservations@maho.org
**Web:** www.maho.org/EstateConcordiaPreserve.cfm
**Room Rates:** 155–250
**No. of Rooms:** 42
**Credit Cards:** Most CCs Accepted
**Attractions**: Each day at Maho, you'll find a full venue of activities to choose from. Visit our Activities Desk to consult with one of our dedicated staff members who can provide you with the best options to fit your needs.
**Services:** Luxury camping in green tent-cottages and the villas, towels & bedding
**Restrictions:** 7 night minimum during select holidays. No pets, handicap accessible
**Concierge:** Front desk assistance
**Room Service:** No
**Restaurant:** The Maho Pavilion Restaurant and Café Concordia are unique outdoor restaurant with spectacular ocean views.
**Bar:** Cafe Concordia
**Business Facilities:** Limited, Internet access
**Conference Room:** Yes
**Spa Services**: Yoga classes
**Sport Facilities:** No on site gym or workout room
**Airport:** St. Thomas STT
**Location:** near Coral Bay

# THE GOODSTONE INN & ESTATE

**Address:** 36205 Snake Hill Road
Middleburg VA 20117
**Phone:** 540-687-4645
**Tollfree:** 877-219-4663
**Fax:** 540-687-6115
**Email:** information@goodstone.com
**Web:** www.goodstone.com
**Room Rates:** 285–385
**Suite Rates:** 375–770
**No. of Rooms:** 12
**No. of Suites:** 6
**Credit Cards:** Visa, MC, Amex
**Attractions**: Bike, hike, canoe,
read, dine, get a spa treatment or
just sit by the pool.
**Services:** High-speed
Internet, bathrobes & slippers,
complimentary water & soda,
fireplaces in common area, in-
room safe, iron/ironing board,
binoculars, umbrellas & walking
sticks, fully equipped kitchen,
phones, TV in common rooms
**Restrictions:** Children 10 and
older are welcome. No pets.
Restricted smoking areas.
**Concierge:** Available from
8am – 10pm (daily)
**Room Service:** Yes: available
from 4–9pm /limited In-Room
menu
**Restaurant:** Goodstone Inn &
Estate seeks to provide its guests
with an unparalleled dining
experience.
**Bar:** Yes: open from 4 – 9pm
(daily)
**Business Facilities:** Limited
access to fax/copier; high-speed
Internet in rooms.
**Conference Room:** 3 rooms /
capacity: up to 55 people
**Sports Facilities:** None on site
**Spa Services:** Recently
renovated one of our farmstead
barns to offer our guests the
perfect balance of relaxation.
**Airport:** Dulles Int'l Airport
**Location:** just on the out-skirts
of town

Escape to a place untouched by time, where pristine pastures gently roll past breathtaking views of the Blue Ridge
Mountains. Here our quaint luxury inn is surrounded by
265 unspoiled acres of Virginia's Hunt and Wine Country in
Middleburg, Virginia. Whether you're here for a romantic luxury bed and breakfast weekend, an exquisite dining experience,
a corporate retreat, or renting a cottage for a girl's weekend,
our gracious staff is here to assist you.

In the 1700s, Middleburg, Virginia was a stopping point for
weary travelers. Not much has changed. Tucked away on the
outskirts of Loudoun County, our hospitable Virginia estate
has welcomed visitors from all over the world. Some come
for the hunt. Some come for the steeple chase, some come
to enjoy the beautiful landscape while hiking our many acres.
While others come to rest their minds and bodies in our cozy
English, French and Virginia style cottage retreats. Who says
you have to rough it in the country? The Goodstone Inn &
Estate Manor House, Spring House, Carriage House, Dutch
Cottage and French Farm Cottage provide luxury suites and
deluxe bedrooms that evoke the feeling of an earlier time,
tempered with the amenities you expect from a contemporary
luxury Southern retreat. Complimentary homemade cookies,
fine bathroom amenities and the softest robes and slippers
are at your fingertips to make you feel at home.

Executive Chef William Walden brings years of experience
and expertise to the Goodstone Inn. He has a refined approach to French cuisine keeping to traditional and classical
preparations. Chef Walden states: My *"raison d'etre"* is artistic
cuisine with the greatest depth of flavor.

# BEST WESTERN PIONEER SQUARE SEATTLE HOTEL

This elegant, thoroughly restored turn-of-the-century hotel, listed on the National Register of Historic Places, 3 diamond AAA, is conveniently located in the heart of downtown Seattle's Pioneer Square Historic District, just one block from the waterfront and takes guests back to a bygone era of style, grace and comfort.

The seventy-five romantic rooms and suites come in a variety of classic decors updated to the needs and comforts of today's guests. All rooms have individual heating and air-conditioning; direct-dial, fax/modem; data port telephones; color cable TV with remote control; and beautifully appointed individual bathrooms with Corian counters, hair dryers and Neutrogena products and amenities. For an excellent night's sleep, Serta Perfect Sleeper mattresses and soundproof double-pane wood windows are standard. Some rooms have wrought iron, New Orleans-style balconies and French doors overlooking Yesler Way, while others have a view of the Puget Sound. Room rates include evening turndown service and a complimentary deluxe continental breakfast.

The Pioneer Square Hotel is the perfect location for wedding parties, receptions, meetings, and family reunions or simply for that romantic weekend get-away.

The many nearby attractions include Seattle's historic Pioneer Square, Safeco Field "Home of the Seattle Mariners, the Stadium Exhibition Center, the new Seahawks Football Stadium, the world famous Pike Place Market, Bell Harbor Cruise Terminal, the Washington State Ferry system and Aquarium, shopping and art galleries, and Seattle's famous restaurants and night life.

The Pioneer Square Hotel, where the style, grace and comfort of a bygone era, are just a fashionable—today!

**Address:** 77 Yesler Way
Seattle WA 98104
**Phone:** 206-340-1234
**Tollfree:** 800-800-5514
**Fax:** 206-467-0707
**Email:** info@pioneersquare.com
**Web:** pioneersquare.com
**Room Rates:** 99–199
**Suite Rates:** 179–279
**No. of Rooms:** 72
**No. of Suites:** 3
**Credit Cards:** Most CCs Accepted
**Attractions:** Safeco Field, Seahawks Stadium, Historic Pioneer Square, Klondike Gold Rush Museum, Waterfront, Smith Tower, WA State Ferry System, Cruise ship Terminals, Aquarium
**Services:** Garage/Parking, Car hire, Valet Service, Laundry, Baby-sitting service, Library, Fireplace, Balconies, Individual bathrooms w/hair dryers, In-room climate control, Cable TV, Radio, continental breakfast, Turndown
**Restrictions:** Service Animals Only, 3 Rooms Handicap Equipped, Non-Smoking
**Concierge:** Yes: (daily) 6:00am–10:00pm
**Room Service:** Yes: (daily) 5:00pm–10:00pm
**Restaurant:** Al Boccalino (next door). Reservations are suggested. Closed on Mondays.
**Bar:** Yes: (next door) Pioneer Square Saloon, Noon–2:00am.
**Business Facilities:** Boardroom with DSL Internet, Copiers, Fax, Fax Modems, Voicemail, Dataports
**Conference Room:** 1 room / capacity: up to 10 people
**Sports Facilities:** Privileges at Pure Fitness Health Club.
**Spa Facilities:** Will refer to local establishments
**Airport:** Seattle/Tacoma Int'l
**Location:** In Historic Downtown

# MARCUS WHITMAN HOTEL & CONFERENCE CENTER

**Address:** Six West Rose
Walla Walla WA 99362
**Phone:** 509-525-2200
**Tollfree:** 866-826-9422
**Fax:** 509-529-9282
**Email:** reservations@
marcuswhitmanhotel.com
**Web:** www.marcuswhitmanhotel.com
**Room Rates:** 109–184
**Suite Rates:** 179–274
**No. of Rooms:** 127
**No. of Suites:** 22
**Credit Cards:** Most CCs Accepted
**Attractions**: Walla Walla offers
the oldest continuous symphony
west of the Mississippi. Museums,
historic sites and homes, unique
shops, more than 100 wineries
and tasting rooms, as well as the
hotel's public gallery depicting
the life of Marcus and Narcissa
Whit
**Services:** Wired and wireless
access, airport transportation,
breakfast is complimentary.
**Restrictions:** Pet friendly, 8
handicap accessible
**Concierge:** Yes: available (daily)
from 9am–5pm
**Room Service:** No
**Restaurant:** The Marc Restaurant
offers a sense of place with Pacific
Northwest Cuisine.
**Bar:** Yes: Vineyard Lounge—
open daily
**Business Facilities:** Business
center with free WiFi access,
laptop hookups, PCs, copy and
fax capabilities.
**Conference Room:** 7 rooms /
capacity: up to 400 people
**Sports Facilities:** No on-site gym
or workout room
**Spa Facilities:** Referrals to local
facilities
**Airport:** Walla Walla Regional
**Location:** Downtown

Pleasures unexpected await guests at the Marcus Whitman Hotel & Conference Center, nestled in the heart of downtown Walla Walla in Washington wine country. Within walking distance, guests will find a variety of wine tasting rooms, eclectic shops and art galleries.

Opening in 1928, the hotel was completely renovated and restored to its original elegance before reopening in 2001. From the quaint Georgian Room complete with fireplace to the Grand Lobby, guests will enjoy the rich décor and comfortable atmosphere.

Each guestroom is richly appointed in Italian Renaissance styling, featuring handcrafted furnishings. Guests may choose between deluxe guestrooms in the adjoining West Wing or Spa Suites, Executive Tower King Rooms or Luxury Suites in the historic tower.

The Marc Restaurant, located just off the hotel's main lobby, offers a sense of place through Pacific Northwest Cuisine.

With more than 10,000 square feet of event space, the ballrooms of The Marcus Whitman Hotel & Conference Center are the largest and most technologically advanced in Eastern Washington. Offering complete banquet and catering services, the hotel offers flexible options for small, intimate gatherings to large groups of 400.

As Walla Walla's destination hotel and restaurant, guests will find a comfortable, indulgent atmosphere with genuine hospitality and excellent service.

Exceptional Guest Experiences for Every Guest!

# THE WASHINGTON HOUSE INN

The Washington House Inn was Cedarburg's first inn, built in 1846 on this site. In 1886, the present Victorian cream-city brick building replaced the original structure. From 1886 until the 1920s The Washington House Inn existed as a hotel at which time it was converted into offices and apartments. In 1983 the ownership of the inn changed hands and work began to restore and transform the building back to its original use as an inn. The Washington House Inn is now listed on the National Register of Historic Places.

The romance of country Victorian style is captivating as one enters the Washington House Inn, the ultimate in bed and breakfast accommodations. A lovely collection of antique Victorian furniture and a marble-trimmed fireplace offer a warm reception. Tastefully appointed, the comfortable, elegant guestrooms feature antiques, cozy down quilts, whirlpool and steam baths and fireplaces.

A delicious expanded continental breakfast buffet is served each morning in welcoming Gathering Room. Homemade muffins, cakes and breads are baked in the Inn's kitchen using recipes from an authentic turn-of-the-century Cedarburg cookbook. Fresh fruit, cereal, freshly squeezed juices, and a fine selection of tea and coffee are also offered. Each evening guests may join one another for a complimentary social hour featuring award winning Cedar Creek wines and local cheeses. There are several excellent local Cedarburg restaurants and the Innkeeper will be happy to make reservations for you.

The staff is friendly and helpful, with attention to detail their foremost concern.

**Address:** W62 N573 Washington Ave, Cedarburg WI 53012
**Phone:** 262-375-3550
**Tollfree:** 800-554-4717
**Fax:** 262-375-9422
**Email:** whinn@execpc.com
**Web:** www.washingtonhouseinn.com
**Room Rates:** 100–315
**Suite Rates:** 236–315
**No. of Rooms:** 34
**No. of Suites:** 3
**Credit Cards:** Most CCs Accepted
**Attractions**: Unique shops, Historic Cedar Creek Settlement, Cedar Creek Winery, Cedar Creek Park, Interurban Bike Trail. antiquing, farmers markets, nature center, golf
**Services:** In-room TV/DVD/VCR Telephones, Individual heat & A/C control, fireplaces, free WiFi access in guest rooms, Gift Certificates available.
**Restrictions:** No pets allowed, Handicapped facilities & elevator available
**Concierge:** Yes—available 24/7
**Room Service:** Yes: available 7-10:00am
**Restaurant:** Walking distance to restaurants… menus available at front desk and we would be happy to make suggestions or help with reservations and directions.
**Bar:** No: Wine & Cheese reception from 5-6pm (daily)
**Business Facilities:** Copier, Audio-Visual, Fax, Wireless Internet
**Conference Room:** 1 room / capacity: up to 40 people
**Sports Facilities:** Whirlpool & Sauna
**Spa Services:** Whirlpool and sauna available. In-house massage packages available.
**Airport:** Mitchell Int'l Airport
**Location:** Downtown Cedarburg

# SPRING CREEK RANCH

**Address:** 1800 Spirit Dance Road
Jackson WY 83001
**Phone:** 307-733-8833
**Tollfree:** 800-443-6139
**Fax:** 307-733-1524
**Email:** info@springcreekresort.com
**Web:** www.springcreekresort.com
**Room Rates:** 170–340
**Suite Rates:** 180–360
**No. of Rooms:** 125
**No. of Suites:** 27
**Credit Cards:** Most CCs Accepted
**Attractions**: Fishing, hunting,
Yellowstone and Grand Teton
National Park, Jackson Hole Mt
Resort (skiing, wildlife viewing,
white water rafting, rodeos, cross
country skiing, hiking and biking,
guided tours, horseback riding.
**Services:** Evening turndown,
Wood burning fireplaces, airport
shuttle, outdoor heated pool,
indoor hot tub, tennis courts.
**Restrictions:** No Pets, Smoking
designated area, Children
Welcome!
**Concierge:** Yes: available 24/7
**Room Service:** Yes: available
7am–9:00pm Limited In-Room
menu
**Restaurant:** The Granary
Restaurant serving breakfast,
lunch, and dinner nightly. The
Granary Bar serving lunch, light
dinner, and drinks.
**Bar:** Yes: our lounge (daily)
4:00pm–Closing
**Business Facilities:** Full
Business Center: computer, fax,
copies & Admin Assist.
**Conference Room:** 4 rooms /
capacity: up to 500 people
**Sports Facilities:** Full gym &
workout room
**Spa Services:** Our spa is the
ideal place to disconnect from
the outside world and reconnect.
Steam Room.
**Airport:** Jackson Hole Airport
**Location:** Mountain resort

Spring Creek Ranch, a year-round luxury resort, is located on a wildlife sanctuary, almost 1,000 feet above the town of Jackson, with spectacular views of the Teton Mountain Range, including the world famous 13,700 foot Grand Teton.

Our luxury resort gives guests the choice of Inn Rooms, Condominiums, or Mountain Villas to provide the right accommodations to suit your needs. Whether exploring Grand Teton or Yellowstone National Parks, or experiencing Jackson Hole's countless recreational opportunities, Spring Creek Ranch is a destination luxury resort for any type of guest. Our resort is the proud recipient of the prestigious *Condé Nast Traveler* Gold List designation. We pride ourselves on our tradition of integrity, innovation and our ability to provide services that exceed expectations.

Haute cuisine and room service are available from the four-star Granary Restaurant, along with daily maid service, a private outdoor Jacuzzi, full-sized outdoor pool and tennis courts. In addition, the open space of East Gros Ventre Butte is yours for horseback riding, hiking, and cross country skiing.

With the addition of the Wilderness Adventure Spa, treatment rooms and weight room, Spring Creek Ranch now has the facilities to match it's unsurpassed views.

# ADDITIONAL MEMBERS - USA

## Alaska

**Cape Fox Lodge**
Ketchikan
907-225-8001
www.capefoxlodge.com

## Arizona

**Inn At Eagle Mountain**
Fountain Hills
480-816-3000
www.innateaglemountain.com

**Lodge At Sedona - A Luxury Bed and Breakfast**
Sedona
928-204-1942
www.lodgeatsedona.com

**Tanque Verde Ranch Resort**
Tucson
520-296-6275
www.tvgr.com

## Arkansas

**The 1886 Crescent Hotel & Spa**
Eureka Springs
479-253-9766
www.crescent-hotel.com

## California

**Albion River Inn**
Albion
707-937-1919
www.albionriverinn.com

**Post Ranch Inn**
Big Sur
831-667-2200
www.postranchinn.com

**Ventana Inn & Spa**
Big Sur
831-667-2331
www.ventanainn.com

**Bristol Hotel**
Campbell
408-559-3330
www.bristol-hotel.com

**Carlyle Hotel**
Campbell
408-559-3600
www.carlyle-hotel.com

**Inn At Depot Hill**
Capitola
831-462-3376
www.innatdepothill.com

**La Playa Hotel Carmel-by-the-Sea**
Carmel
831-624-6476
www.laplayahotel.com

**Duchamp Hotel**
Healdsburg
707-431-1300
www.duchamphotel.com

**The Honor Mansion**
Healdsburg
707-433-4277
honormansion.com

**Hopland Inn**
Hopland
707-744-1890
www.hoplandinn.com

**Orchard Hill Country Inn**
Julian
760-765-1700
orchardhill.com

**La Valencia Hotel**
La Jolla
858-454-0771
www.lavalencia.com

**Surf & Sand Resort**
Laguna Beach
949-497-4477
www.surfandsandresort.com

**Wine & Roses Hotel & Restaurant**
Lodi
209-334-6988
www.winerose.com

**Sunset Marquis Hotel**
Los Angeles
310-657-1333
www.sunsetmarquishotel.com

**The Orlando**
Los Angeles
323-658-6600
theorlando.com

**Fess Parker's Wine Country Inn & Spa**
Los Olivos
805-688-1545
www.fessparker.com

**The Sanctuary Beach Resort**
Marina
831-883-9478
www.thesanctuarybeachresort.com

**The Marina Del Rey Hotel**
Marina Del Rey
310-301-1000
www.marinadelreyhotel.com

**Sea Rock Inn**
Mendocino
707-937-0926
www.searockinn.com

**Stevenswood Spa Resort**
Mendocino
707-937-2810
www.stevenswood.com

**La Residence**
Napa
707-253-0337
www.laresidence.com/

**Doryman's Inn**
Newport Beach
949-675-7300
www.dorymansinn.com

**Olema Druids Hall**
Olema
415-663-8727
www.olemadruidshall.com

**Lighthouse Lodge & Suites**
Pacific Grove
831-655-2111
www.lhls.com

**Martine Inn**
Pacific Grove
831-373-3388
www.martineinn.com

**The Willows Historic Palm Springs Inn**
Palm Springs
760-320-0771
www.thewillowspalmsprings.com

**Villa Royale Inn**
Palm Springs
760-327-2314
www.villaroyale.com

**Garden Court Hotel**
Palo Alto
650-322-9000
www.gardencourt.com

**Summerwood Winery & Inn**
Paso Robles
805-227-1111
www.summerwoodwine.com

**Rancho Valencia Resort & Spa**
Rancho Santa Fe
858-756-1123
www.ranchovalencia.com

**The Mission Inn Hotel & Spa**
Riverside
951-784-0300
www.missioninn.com

**Rancho Bernardo Inn**
San Diego
858-675-8500
www.ranchobernardoinn.com

**Hotel Abri**
San Francisco
415-392-8800
larkspurhotels.com/collection/abri

**Hotel Griffon**
San Francisco
415-495-2100
www.hotelgriffon.com

**Stanyan Park Hotel**
San Francisco
415-751-1000
www.stanyanpark.com

**SW Hotel**
San Francisco
415-362-2999
www.swhotel.com

**The Inn At Union Square**
San Francisco
415-397-3510
unionsquare.com

**The Orchard Hotel - San Francisco**
San Francisco
415-362-8878
www.theorchardhotel.com

**Villa Florence**
San Francisco
415-397-7700
www.villaflorence.com

**Hotel Valencia - Santana Row**
San Jose
408-551-0010
www.hotelvalencia-santanarow.com/

**Harbor View Inn**
Santa Barbara
805-963-0780
www.harborviewinnsb.com

**Montecito Inn**
Santa Barbara
805-969-7854
www.montecitoinn.com

**Santa Barbara Inn**
Santa Barbara
805-966-5305
www.SantaBarbaraInn.com

**The Upham Hotel**
Santa Barbara
805-962-0058
www.uphamhotel.com

The Upham Hotel's Country House
Santa Barbara
805-963-2283
countryhousesantabarbara.com

Shutters On The Beach
Santa Monica
310-458-0030
www.shuttersonthebeach.com

Hotel Sausalito
Sausalito
415-332-0700
www.hotelsausalito.com

The Inn Above Tide
Sausalito
415-332-9535
www.innabovetide.com

The Alisal Guest Ranch and Resort
Solvang
805-688-6411
www.alisal.com

The Inn at Peterson Village
Solvang
805-688-3121
www.peterseninn.com

MacArthur Place
Sonoma
707-938-2929
www.macarthurplace.com

The Fairmont Sonoma Mission Inn
  And Spa
Sonoma
707-938-9000
fairmont.com/Sonoma

Meadowood Napa Valley
St Helena
707-963-3646
www.meadowood.com

The Wine Country Inn & Gardens
St Helena
707-963-7077
wine-country-inn.com

Sutter Creek Inn
Sutter Creek
209-267-5606
www.suttercreekinn.com

Cal-a-Vie Health Spa
Vista
760-945-2055
www.cal-a-vie.com

Le Montrose Suite Hotel
West Hollywood
310-855-1115
www.lemontrose.com

The Ahwahnee Hotel
Yosemite National Park
209-372-1407
www.yosemitepark.com/Accommodations_
TheAhwahnee.aspx

Napa Valley Lodge
Yountville
707-944-2468
www.napavalleylodge.com

## Colorado

Hotel Jerome - A Rock Resort
Aspen
970-920-1000
hoteljerome.rockresorts.com

The Burnsley All Suite Hotel
Denver
303-830-1000
www.burnsley.com

The Golden Hotel
Golden
303-279-0100
www.thegoldenhotel.com

Keystone Resorts
Keystone
970-496-3712
www.keystoneresort.com

The Galatyn Lodge
Vail
970-479-2418
www.vail.net/galatyn

## Connecticut

The Griswold Inn
Essex
860-767-1776
www.griswoldinn.com

Delamar Greenwich Harbor
Greenwich
203-661-9800
www.thedelamar.com

West Lane Inn
Ridgefield
203-438-7323
www.westlaneinn.com

## District of Columbia

The Morrison - Clark Inn
Washington
202-898-1200
www.morrisonclark.com

## Florida

The Westin Colonnade - Coral Gables
Coral Gables
305-441-2600
www.starwoodhotels.com/westin

**Greyfield Inn - Cumberland Island**
Fernandina Beach
904-261-6408
www.greyfieldinn.com

**Casa Morada**
Islamorada
305-664-0044
www.casamorada.com

**Kona Kai Resort and Gallery**
Key Largo
305-852-7200
www.konakairesort.com

**Heron House**
Key West
305-294-9227
www.heronhouse.com

**Hotel Nash South Beach**
Miami Beach
305-674-7800
www.nashsouthbeach.com

**Hotel Ocean**
Miami Beach
305-672-2579
www.hotelocean.com

**Courtyard At Lake Lucerne**
Orlando
407-648-5188
www.orlandohistoricinn.com

**The Lodge & Club - Ponte Vedra**
Ponte Vedra Beach
904-273-9500
www.pvresorts.com

**Casa Monica Hotel**
St Augustine
904-827-1888
www.casamonica.com

**Governors Inn**
Tallahassee
850-681-6855
www.thegovinn.com

## Georgia

**AVIA Hotels - Savannah**
Savannah
912-233-2116
www.aviahotels.com/hotels/savannah

**East Bay Inn**
Savannah
912-238-1225
www.eastbayinn.com

**Eliza Thompson House**
Savannah
912-236-3620
www.elizathompsonhouse.com

**Foley House Inn**
Savannah
912-232-6622
www.foleyinn.com

**Kehoe House**
Savannah
912-232-1020
www.kehoehouse.com

**Olde Harbour Inn**
Savannah
912-234-4100
www.oldeharbourinn.com

**Planters Inn - Savannah**
Savannah
912-232-5678
www.plantersinnsavannah.com

**The Gastonian**
Savannah
912-232-2869
www.gastonian.com

**The Marshall House**
Savannah
912-644-7896
www.marshallhouse.com

**Ocean Lodge**
St Simons Island
912-291-4300
oceanlodgessi.com

**The King and Prince Beach & Golf Resort**
St Simons Island
912-638-3631
www.kingandprince.com

## Idaho

**Old Northern Inn**
Coolin (Priest Lake)
208-443-2426
www.oldnortherninn.com

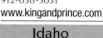
**Hearthstone Lodge - Elegant By The River**
Kamiah
208-935 1492
www.hearthstone-lodge.com

## Illinois

**Hotel Indigo Chicago - Downtown Gold Coast**
Chicago
312-787-4980
www.chicagogoldcoast.hotelindigo.com

**The Talbott Hotel**
Chicago
312-944-4970
www.talbotthotel.com

**The Homestead**
Evanston
847-475-3300
www.thehomestead.net

## Iowa

**Mont Rest Bed & Breakfast**
Bellevue
563-872-4220
www.montrest.com

## Louisiana

**Bienville House Hotel**
New Orleans
504-529-2345
www.bienvillehouse.com

**Dauphine Orleans Hotel**
New Orleans
504-586-1800
www.dauphineorleans.com

**Hotel Provincial**
New Orleans
504-581-4995
www.hotelprovincial.com

**International House**
New Orleans
504-553-9550
www.ihhotel.com

**Soniat House Hotel**
New Orleans
504-522-0570
www.soniathouse.com

## Maine

**Balance Rock Inn of Bar Harbor Maine**
Bar Harbor
207-288-2610
balancerockinn.com

**Bar Harbor Hotel - Bluenose Inn**
Bar Harbor
207-288-3348
www.barharborhotel.com

**Inn By The Sea**
Cape Elizabeth
207-799-3134
www.innbythesea.com

**The Harraseeket Inn**
Freeport
207-865-9377
www.harraseeketinn.com

**The Captain Lord Mansion and
    Garden House**
Kennebunkport
207-967-3141
www.captainlord.com

**The Colony Hotel**
Kennebunkport
207-967-3331
www.thecolonyhotel.com

**Pomegranate Inn**
Portland
207-772-1006
www.pomegranateinn.com

**Black Point Inn Resort**
Prouts Neck
207-883-2500
www.blackpointinn.com

**The Claremont Hotel**
Southwest Harbor
207-244-5036
www.theclaremonthotel.com

**York Harbor Inn**
York Harbor
207-363-5119
www.yorkharborinn.com

## Maryland

**Intercontinental Harbor Court Hotel**
Baltimore
410-234-0550
www.harborcourt.com

**Bethesda Court Hotel**
Bethesda
301-656-2100
www.bethesdacourtwashdc.com

**Savage River Lodge**
Frostburg
301-689-3200
www.savageriverlodge.com

## Massachusetts

**Bulfinch Hotel Boston Massachusetts**
Boston
617-624-0202
www.bulfinchhotel.com

**Millennium Bostonian Hotel**
Boston
617-523-3600
www.millenniumhotels.com

**The Charles Street Inn**
Boston
617-314-8900
www.charlesstreetinn.com

**The Lenox Hotel**
Boston
617-536-5300
www.lenoxhotel.com

**The Inn at Harvard**
Cambridge
617-491-2222
www.theinnatharvard.com

The Bradford Inn of Chatham
Chatham
508-945-1030
www.bradfordinn.com

The Chatham Wayside Inn
Chatham
508-945-5550
www.waysideinn.com

Deerfield Inn
Deerfield
413-774-5587
www.deerfieldinn.com

Penny House Inn & Day Spa
Eastham
508-255-6632
www.pennyhouseinn.com

The Charlotte Inn
Edgartown
508-627-4151
charlotteinn.net

Cranwell Resort, Spa & Golf Club
Lenox
413-637-1364
www.cranwell.com

The Wauwinet
Nantucket
508-228-0145
www.wauwinet.com

The Porches Inn at MASS MoCA
North Adams
413-664-0400
www.porches.com

Emerson Inn By The Sea
Rockport
978-546-6321
www.emersoninnbythesea.com

Yankee Clipper Inn
Rockport
978-546-0001
www.yankeeclipperinn.com

The Dan'l Webster Inn and Spa
Sandwich
508-888-3622
www.danlwebsterinn.com

The Inn At Stockbridge
Stockbridge
413-298-3337
www.stockbridgeinn.com

The Red Lion Inn - Stockbridge
Stockbridge
413-298-5545
www.redlioninn.com

## Michigan

Hotel Iroquois
Mackinac Island
906-847-3321
www.iroquoishotel.com

Stafford's Perry Hotel
Petoskey
231-347-4000
www.staffords.com/perryhotel

## Mississippi

Cedar Grove Mansion Inn &
   Restuarant
Vicksburg
601-636-1000
www.cedargroveinn.com

## New Hampshire

The Mount Washington Hotel
Bretton Woods
603-278-1000
www.omnihotels.com/FindAHotel/
BrettonWoodsMountWashington.aspx

Three Chimneys Inn
Durham
603-868-7800
www.threechimneysinn.com

## New Jersey

The Bernards Inn
Bernardsville
908-766-0002
www.bernardsinn.com

Congress Hall
Cape May
609-884-8421
www.congresshall.com

The Queen Victoria Bed & Breakfast
Cape May
609-884-1613
www.queenvictoria.com

The Virginia Hotel
Cape May
609-884-5700
www.virginiahotel.com

Lambertville House
Lambertville
609-397-0200
www.lambertvillehouse.com

## New Mexico

La Hacienda Grande
Bernalillo
505-867-1887
www.lahaciendagrande.com

**Rancho De San Juan**
Espanola
505-753-6818
www.ranchodesanjuan.com

**Hacienda Del Cerezo**
Santa Fe
505-982-8000
www.haciendadelcerezo.com

**Hotel Plaza Real**
Santa Fe
505-988-4900
www.santafehotelplazareal.com

**Inn Of The Anasazi**
Santa Fe
505-988-3030
www.innoftheanasazi.com

**Inn On The Alameda**
Santa Fe
505-984-2121
www.innonthealameda.com

**La Posada De Santa Fe Resort & Spa**
Santa Fe
505-986-0000
laposada.rockresorts.com

## New York

**Riveredge Resort Hotel**
Alexandria Bay
315-482-9917
www.riveredge.com

**The 1770 House Restaurant & Inn**
East Hampton
631-324-1770
www.1770house.com

**Lake Placid Lodge on the Water's Edge**
Lake Placid
518-523-2700
www.lakeplacidlodge.com

**Mirror Lake Inn Resort and Spa**
Lake Placid
518-523-2544
www.mirrorlakeinn.com

**Montauk Yacht Club**
Montauk
631-668-3100
www.montaukyachtclub.com

**Beekman Tower Hotel**
New York City
212-355-7300
www.thebeekmanhotel.com

**Fitzpatrick Grand Central Hotel**
New York City
212-351-6800
www.fitzpatrickhotels.com

**Fitzpatrick Manhattan Hotel**
New York City
212-355-0100
www.fitzpatrickhotels.com

**The Benjamin**
New York City
212-715-2500
www.thebenjamin.com

**The Mandarin Oriental - New York**
New York City
212-805-8800
www.mandarinoriental.com/newyork/

**The Michelangelo Hotel**
New York City
212-765-1900
www.michelangelohotel.com

**The Surrey**
New York City
212-905-1477
www.thesurrey.com

**Beekman Arms - Delamater Inn**
Rhinebeck
845-876-7077
www.beekmandelamaterinn.com

## North Carolina

**Richmond Hill Inn**
Asheville
828-252-7313
www.richmondhillinn.com

**The Umstead Hotel and Spa**
Cary
919-447-4000
www.theumstead.com

**The Siena Hotel**
Chapel Hill
919-929-4000
www.sienahotel.com

**The Sanderling Resort & Spa**
Duck
252-261-4111
www.thesanderling.com

**First Colony Inn**
Nags Head
252-441-2343
www.firstcolonyinn.com

**The Fearrington House Country Inn**
Pittsboro
919-542-2121
www.fearrington.com

**Snowbird Mountain Lodge**
Robbinsville
828-479-3433
www.snowbirdlodge.com

**1906 Pine Crest Inn & Restaurant**
Tryon
828-859-9135
www.pinecrestinn.com

**The Swag**
Waynesville
828-926-0430
www.theswag.com

## Ohio

**Inn & Spa at Honey Run**
Millersburg
330-674-0011
www.innathoneyrun.com

## Oregon

**The Inn at Lithia Springs**
Ashland
541-482-7128
www.ashlandinn.com

**The Hotel Elliott**
Astoria
503-325-2222
www.hotelelliott.com

**The Campbell House Restaurant and Inn**
Eugene
541-343-1119
www.campbellhouse.com

**The O' Dysius Hotel**
Lincoln City
541-994-4121
www.odysius.com

**The Avalon Hotel & Spa**
Portland
503-802-5800
www.avalonhotelandspa.com

**The Heathman Hotel - Portland**
Portland
503-241-4100
www.heathmanhotel.com

## Pennsylvania

**Greystone Manor Bed & Breakfast**
Bird-In-Hand
717-393-4233
www.greystonemanor.com

**Tara - A Country Inn**
Clark
724-962-3535
www.tara-inn.com

**Glasbern**
Fogelsville
610-285-4723
www.glasbern.com

**Barley Sheaf Farm Estate & Spa**
Holicong, Bucks County
215-794-5104
www.barleysheaf.com

**The Inn at Jim Thorpe**
Jim Thorpe
570-325-2599
www.innjt.com

**Lancaster Arts Hotel**
Lancaster
717-299-3000
www.lancasterartshotel.com

**The Inn at Leola Village**
Leola
717-656-7002
www.theinnatleolovillage.com

**Buhl Mansion Guest House**
Sharon
724-346-3046
www.buhlmansion.com

**The Shawnee Inn and Golf Resort**
Shawnee on Delaware
570-424-4000
www.shawneeinn.com

**Skytop Lodge**
Skytop
570-595-7401
www.skytop.com

## Puerto Rico

**Villa Montana Beach Resort**
Isabela
787-872-9554
www.villamontana.com

## Rhode Island

**The 1661 Inn & Hotel Manisses**
Block Island
401-466-2421
www.blockislandresorts.com/

**Cliffside Inn**
Newport
401-847-1811
www.cliffsideinn.com

**The Francis Malbone House**
Newport
401-846-0392
www.malbone.com

**Vanderbilt Hall Hotel**
Newport
401-846-6200
www.vanderbilthall.com

## South Carolina

**John Rutledge House Inn**
Charleston
843-723-7999
www.johnrutledgehouseinn.com

**King's Courtyard Inn**
Charleston
843-723-7000
www.kingscourtyardinn.com

**Market Pavilion Hotel**
Charleston
843-723-0500
www.marketpavilion.com

**Mills House Hotel**
Charleston
803-577-2400
www.millshouse.com

**Planters Inn**
Charleston
843-722-2345
www.plantersinn.com

**The Governor's House Inn**
Charleston
843-720-2070
www.governorshouse.com

**The Inn at Middleton Place**
Charleston
843-556-0500
www.theinnatmiddletonplace.com

**Wentworth Mansion**
Charleston
843-853-1886
www.wentworthmansion.com

**Litchfield Plantation**
Pawleys Island
843-237-9121
www.litchfieldplantation.com

## Tennessee

**General Morgan Inn & Conference Center**
Greeneville
423-787-1000
www.generalmorganinn.com

**Historic Eureka Hotel**
Jonesborough
423-913-6100
www.eurekajonesborough.com

**Inn At Blackberry Farm**
Walland
865-984-8166
www.blackberryfarm.com

## Texas

**The Sanford House Inn and Spa**
Arlington
817-861-2129
www.thesanfordhouse.com

**Mansion at Judges' Hill**
Austin
512-495-1800
www.judgeshill.com

**Hotel ZaZa - Dallas**
Dallas
214-468-8399
www.hotelzazadallas.com

**Rosewood Crescent Hotel**
Dallas
214-871-3200
www.crescentcourt.com

**Rosewood Mansion On Turtle Creek**
Dallas
214-559-2100
www.mansiononturtlecreek.com

**The Tremont House - A Wyndham Historic Hotel**
Galveston
409-763-0300
wyndham.com/hotels/GLSTH/main.wnt

**The Lancaster - Houston**
Houston
713-228-9500
www.thelancaster.com

**Emily Morgan Hotel**
San Antonio
210-225-5100
www.emilymorganhotel.com

**Hotel Valencia - San Antonio Riverwalk**
San Antonio
210-227-9700
www.hotelvalencia.com

**The Fairmount Hotel - San Antonio**
San Antonio
210-224-8800
www.thefairmounthotel-sanantonio.com

## Vermont

**The Castle Hill Resort and Spa**
Cavendish
802-226-7361
www.castlehillresort.com

**The Point At Castle Hill Resort**
Cavendish
802-226-7688
www.cavendishpointe.com

**Three Mountain Inn**
Jamaica
802-874-4140
www.threemountaininn.com

**The Charles Orvis Inn**
Manchester Village
802-362-4700
www.equinoxresort.com

**The Mountain Road Resort**
Stowe
802-253-4566
www.mountainroadresort.com

**Topnotch Resort & Spa**
Stowe
802-253-8585
www.topnotchresort.com

**Woodstock Inn & Resort**
Woodstock
802-457-1100
www.woodstockinn.com

## Virgin Islands

**Hibiscus Beach Hotel**
St Croix
340-773-4042
www.hibiscusbeachresort.com

**Secret Harbour Beach Resort**
St Thomas
340-775-6550
www.secretharbourvi.com

## Virginia

**The Berkeley Hotel**
Richmond
804-780-1300
www.berkeleyhotel.com

**Stonewall Jackson Hotel & Conference Center**
Staunton
540-885-4848
www.stonewalljacksonhotel.com

**Inn At Gristmill Square**
Warm Springs
540-839-2231
www.gristmillsquare.com

**Williamsburg Inn**
Williamsburg
757-253-2277
www.colonialwilliamsburg.com

## Washington

**Hotel Bellwether**
Bellingham
360-392-3100
www.hotelbellwether.com

**Turtleback Farm Inn**
Eastsound
360-376-4914
www.turtlebackinn.com

**Alexis Hotel - Seattle**
Seattle
206-624-4844
www.alexishotel.com

**Mayflower Park Hotel**
Seattle
206-623-8700
www.mayflowerpark.com

**Sorrento Hotel**
Seattle
206-622-6400
www.hotelsorrento.com

**Montvale Hotel**
Spokane
509-747-1919
www.montvalehotel.com

**Sun Mountain Lodge**
Winthrop
509-996-2211
www.sunmountainlodge.com

**Willows Lodge**
Woodinville
425-424-3900
www.willowslodge.com

**Birchfield Manor Country Inn**
Yakima
509-452-1960
www.birchfieldmanor.com

## West Virginia

**Blennerhassett Hotel**
Parkersburg
304-422-3131
www.theblennerhassett.com

## Wisconsin

**The Geneva Inn**
Lake Geneva
262-248-5680
www.genevainn.com

**The Mansion Hill Inn**
Madison
608-255-0172
www.mansionhillinn.com

# ALFSTADTHOTEL AMADEUS

The Amadeus Hotel is a small, traditional and exclusive Hotel, located directly in the historic city center of Salzburg. The Hotel is in a quiet street, directly in the pedestrian area.

We serve a great — all you can eat — breakfast buffet in the morning and free afternoon coffee or tea every day. For centuries, our guests have delighted in first-class service, together with dishes reflecting international and Austrian cuisine. An international wine list and an array of popular beers provide the perfect complement to our rich selection of dishes. Famous Austrian writer, Stefan Zweig, once praised our "**Salzburger Nockerl**" dessert as being "the very best."

Most of the sights, such as Getreidegasse, Mozart Museem, Festival halls as well as the Salzburgs Congress Center are easy to reach within a few minutes walking distance. The fairgrounds are about 10 minutes car ride away. At our front desk we will be happy to help you with sightseeing tours and other information you need.

In 1965 Salzburg was the scenery of a film which would become famous: "The Sound of Music" starring Julie Andrews and Christopher Plummer. Our busses were used by the film crew and our limousines carried the stars. After the release of the film, many fans came to Salzburg asking for the original sites — and our drivers could naturally guide them. That's how the "Original Sound of Music Tour" started.

Enjoy your stay in Salzburg Old-Town in enchanting traditional furnished rooms with all the comfort you need.

**Address:** Walketseder Ges.m.b.H
Linzergasse 43 45
Salzburg A-5020
**Phone:** 43-6628-71401
**Fax:** 43-6628-714017
**Email:** salzburg@hotelamadeus.at
**Web:** www.hotelamadeus.at
**Room Rates:** 100–200€
**Suite Rates:** 200–260€
**No. of Rooms:** 22
**No. of Suites:** 4
**Credit Cards:** Most CCs Accepted
**Attractions:** St. Peter cemetery, Mozart square, Getreidegasse, Mozarts birthplace, Collegiate church, Franciscan church, Mirabell gardens, Linzer alley, St. Sebastian
**Services:** The charming hotel rooms are equipped with Cable-TV, Telephone, room safe and the bathrooms are fully equipped.
**Restrictions:** Latest arrival 6pm! Children up to 6 yrs old stay free.
**Concierge:** No
**Room Service:** No
**Restaurant:** First-class service together with dishes reflecting international and Austrian cuisine.
**Bar:** No
**Business Facilities:** Yes
**Conference Room:** No
**Sports Facilities:** No
**Spa Facilities:** We will happily refer you to a local establishment
**Airport:** Salzburg Airport
**Location:** Downtown

# HOTEL HERITAGE BRUGES

**Address:** Niklaas
Desparsstraat 11
Bruges 8000 Belgium
**Phone:** 32-0-50-444-444
**Fax:** 32-0-50-444-440
**Email:** info@hotel-heritage.com
**Web:** www.hotel-heritage.com
**Room Rates:** 151 – 265 ¤
**Suite Rates:** 375 – 451 ¤
**No. of Rooms:** 20
**No. of Suites:** 4
**Credit Cards:** Visa, MC, Amex
**Attractions:** Cozy restaurants, Interesting museums, Elegant shops, Romantic carriage rides, Boat rides on Bruge's famous canals, Chocolate tasting . . .
**Services:** Private baths, Hairdryer, Cosmetic mirror, flat screen TV, Minibar, 2 direct dial telephones, Safe, Trouser press and ironing facilities, PC and modem line, Air conditioning, Buffet breakfast, Wireless-Internet access (WiFi), DVD-&CD player.
**Restrictions:** No pets allowed, no handicap equipped rooms, Adults only.
**Concierge:** Yes: (daily) 7:00am – 11:00pm
**Room Service:** Yes (daily) 24/7
**Restaurant:** In May 2009, our four star Hotel Heritage opened its own restaurant: "Le Mystique."
**Bar:** Yes: our lounge (daily) 7:00am – 1:00am (closing)
**Business Facilities:** Fax, copies, Wifi
**Conference Room:** Seminar and business meeting facilities
**Sports Facilities:** Fitness room.
**Spa Services:** Healthcentre with sauna and Turkish steam bath and Sunbed.
**Airport:** Local Bruges airport
**Location:** In the heart of medieval Bruges.

Originally built as a private mansion in 1869, the Hotel Heritage later fell into hands of bankers who renovated and converted this magnificent 19th century Classical building into a fine four star luxury hotel.

The Hotel Heritage offers its guests elegant, stylish rooms, all characterized by individual decoration, nice soft furnishings, and well appointed bathrooms with all the modern amenities. The hotel has four suites where the rooms overlook the unique city skyline of Bruges and have marble bathrooms with a Jacuzzi and separate showers.

This four star hotel has many attractive features, such as a health centre with sauna, Turkish steam bath, relaxation area and solarium, and a fitness room installed in a marvelous 14th Century cellar. In the attractive welcoming lounge with bar is an open fireplace and Italian fabrics where guests can relax for afternoon tea or coffee, or get their pre-dinner drinks. And a splendid buffet breakfast, a light lunch or a romantic dinner are served in the charming 1869 room, which reflects the glorious past of the house.

Experience a pampering your richly deserve!

# TROUT POINT LODGE OF NOVA SCOTIA

Luxury in the heart of the Canadian wilderness, nestled next to the Tusket River, immediately adjacent to the Tobeatic Wilderness Area of southern Nova Scotia—Trout Point is undoubtedly the most luxurious wilderness lodge in Atlantic Canada, offering impeccable service and designed for absolute Haute Rustic comfort.

An architectural master piece made from giant Eastern Spruce logs, chiseled granite and sandstone, with full scribe notch and dovetail joinery, Trout Point's owners built the Lodge in celebration of the Great Camps erected along the U.S. & Canadian Eastern Seaboard in the early 20th century.

Fifteen varied accommodation options await guests, including the superb Great Lodge, riverside River Bend Lodge, and lakeside Black Bear Cottage & Cub Cottage. Each spacious lodging features luxurious bedding, comfortable seating areas, and tasteful bathrooms with access to truly relaxing public areas with fireplaces. This three-story structure houses guest facilities, the Great Room, mezzanine library, dining room, kitchen, two bars, and recreational facilities on the banks of the Tusket River. Replete with mica and Tiffany lamps, oriental rugs, log furniture, and extensive indoor and outdoor public areas, Trout Point is the ideal nature retreat.

The kitchen at Trout Point Lodge deftly brings to fruition savory creations by drawing from traditional cooking techniques combined with fresh local ingredients.

Enchanting. Extraordinary . . . and, Very Exclusive. The Lodge, open from mid-May to late-October, provides access to unique experiences.

**Address:** 189 Trout Point Road Kemptville Nova Scotia BOW 1YO
**Phone:** 902-761-2142
**Tollfree:** 902-482-8360
**Fax:** 800-980-0713
**Email:** troutpoint@foodvacation.com
**Web:** www.troutpoint.com
**Room Rates:** 165–310 CAN$
**Suite Rates:** 225–350 CAN$
**No. of Rooms:** 9
**No. of Suites:** 3
**Credit Cards:** Visa
**Attractions:** Outdoor recreation beckons, including river & lake swimming, canoeing, kayaking, cedar hot tub & barrel sauna, & guided fishing. Hike the woodland trails the Tobeatic wilderness. The Lodge borders the largest pristine nature area in Nova Scotia.
**Services:** Fishing & wilderness guides, BVLGARI amenities, cooking & wine classes.
**Restrictions:** Cancellation & no-show penalties from 10% to 100% of the total value of the reservation.
**Concierge:** Yes
**Room Service:** Yes–Snack Menu. Open until 10pm
**Restaurant:** The Lodge serves fresh Nova Scotia seafood in prix-fixe menus inspired by the French New World.
**Bar:** Yes–Open until 11pm
**Business Facilities:** WiFi
**Conference Room:** 2 Rooms with capacity of 24
**Spa Services:** Cedar wood-fired hot tub and cedar barrel sauna. Also In-room massages.
**Airport:** Halifax Airport
**Location:** Adjacent to the Tobeatic Wilderness at the confluence of two rivers

# SWISS HOTEL

**Address:** 89 Daly Avenue
Ottawa Ontario K1N 6E6
**Phone:** 613 -237-0335
**Tollfree:** 888-663-0000
**Fax:** 613-594-3327
**Email:** info@swisshotel.ca
**Web:** www.swisshotel.ca
**Room Rates:** 99–258
**No. of Rooms:** 22
**Credit Cards:** Visa, MC, Amex
**Attractions:** Ottawa Convention
Centre, University of Ottawa,
Conference Centre, Rideau Canal
and Byward Market. National
Gallery of Canada, Parliament
Hill, US Embassy.
**Services:** Optional Swiss
breakfast buffet. A/C, FREE
Internet. Private bathrooms,
hardwood flooring, iPad in every
room.
**Restrictions:** Non-smoking,
Children over 12 years of age, No
pets. No wheelchair access.
**Room Service:** Breakfast served
to the honeymoon suites
**Concierge:** Front Desk assistance
**Restaurant:** You are right at the
center of all the best Ottawa has
to offer, superb restaurants, and
exciting night spots.
**Bar:** Just around the corner to the
Byward Market
**Business Facilities:** WiFi,
computer, fax, copier, audio-visual
equipment
**Conference Room:** 1 room f/p
and piano up to 12 people
**Sports Facilities:** No on site gym
or workout room
**Spa Services:** Nearby
**Airport:** Ontario Airport
**Location:** Right Downtown

Located right downtown, Swiss Hotel offers some of the most unique accommodations in Ottawa. Developed with an original European design and portraying Swiss modernity at its finest including free Internet, Swiss Hotel caters to both businesses and leisure. Walking distance from Ottawa's greatest attractions, Swiss Hotel offers rooms equipped with unparalleled amenities.

Built in 1872 from limestone in a 19th Century Vernacular Classical Revival. Swiss Hotel has undergone several changes over the years. Formerly known as the Gasthaus Switzerland Inn, the Swiss Hotel has transformed the beautiful bed and breakfast into a modern hotel while still retaining its historic charm.

Back then in 1867 when Canada was born, Daly Ave was the most popular and "fashionable" street in Ottawa. Sandy Hill is one of the oldest neighborhoods. Because of Swiss Hotel's ideal downtown location, consider leaving the car at home and exploring Ottawa by foot, bike or public transit.

European style rooms and suites are simple elegant with all the modern amenities. Bedding at the Swiss Hotel is 100% Egyptian cotton. Guest rooms and romantic suites boast WiFi, use of an Apple iPad, private bathrooms with raindrop shower, hardwood floors, original artwork, flat screen TV and window that open. Optional Swiss buffet breakfast. This intimate, adult only, inn makes an ideal facility for all small events, from business meetings to daily gatherings.

The Swiss Hotel is dedicated to a green world and encourages eco-friendly activities.

# LAKESIDE ILLAHEE INN & NATURE PARK

This exquisite waterfront boutique Inn rises regally on the shores of beautiful Lake Kalamalka, known as "The Lake of Ten Thousand Colors" and rated as one of the top ten most beautiful lakes in the world by the National Geographic Society. Situated in the Top of the Okanagan Valley we are easily accessible by car, by boat or float plane. The Lakeside Illahee Inn offers, within the wonders and colors of the four seasons, quality accommodations for vacation and business travelers, waterfront sunset and Grand Room fine dining, wedding and reception services, corporate retreats, group meetings & family reunions amid relaxation and serenity; all in its nature park surroundings.

The Inn is characterized by a modern spacious open plan design, accessorized by an awe-inspiring unobstructed 180° view of beautiful Lake Kalamalka and complemented by a stunning British Columbia Provincial Park literally at the back door. Each room or suite is well appointed and distinctive; named for a wild flower, a tree that grows at Illahee, or a water feature nearby.

Why not enjoy fine hospitality and the many 4 season outdoor recreation opportunities offered in an atmosphere decidedly rural, laid back, relaxing, elegant and unimaginably scenic in its makeup. Enjoy spring blossom times plus see waterfalls 2½ times higher than Niagara Falls, the fall fruit/wine grape harvest times … the splendor of winter plus downhill skiing.

At the end of a beautiful day in the Spring, Summer or Fall Seasons join us for waterfront sunset dining or in the Grand Room & Loft for "Powder Snow" time.

**Address:** 15010 Tamarack Drive Vernon British Columbia V1B 2E1
**Phone:** 250-260-7896
**Tollfree:** 888-260-7896
**Email:** stay@illahee.com
**Web:** www.illahee.com
**Room Rates:** 114−209 $
**Suite Rates:** 164−379 $
**No. of Rooms:** 5
**No. of Suites:** 3
**Credit Cards:** Visa, MC
**Attractions:** Golf, Estate Wineries, Cruise Okanagan, Downhill & Nordic Skiing, Aspengrove Equestrian Academy, Village Cheese Factory, Mountain Biking, Swimming, Boating, Canoeing & Kayaking, Fishing, Wind Sailing, Ice Skating, Ice Fishing, Dog Sledding.
**Services:** Music/reading lounge, lakeview hot-tub, WiFi, on-site parking, Boat dock, boat buoys, lakeview patio, full service breakfast included in room rate
**Restrictions:** No smoking or pets. Limited handicap access.
**Concierge:** Yes: available (daily) from 8:00am−8:00pm
**Room Service:** No
**Restaurant:** Waterfront sunset dining in the "Upper Room." or "Grand Room & Loft," for Inn guests and members of the Illahee Diners Club by reservation.
**Bar:** No
**Business Facilities:** Admin assistance available
**Conference Room:** 1 "high tech" boardroom/ 22 person capacity
**Sports Facilities:** No onsite gym or workout room
**Spa Services:** Mountainside lakeview hot tub onsite and open year-round.
**Airport:** Kelowna Int'l Airport
**Location:** Okanagan Valley Golf, Ski & Wine Country

# ABIGAIL'S HOTEL

**Address:** 906 McClure Street
Victoria British Columbia V8V 3E7
**Phone:** 250-388-5363
**Tollfree:** 800-561-6565
**Fax:** 250-388-7787
**Email:** innkeeper@abigailshotel.com
**Web:** www.abigailshotel.com
**Room Rates:** 172–350 CAN$
**No. of Rooms:** 23
**Credit Cards:** Visa, MC, Amex
**Attractions:** Experience the sights, sounds & tastes of breathtaking Victoria! Stroll Government & Wharf Streets to the Inner Harbour. The Royal BC Museum, Craigdarroch Castle.
**Services:** 24 hr parking, wireless Internet and local calls. Endless coffee & tea, freshly baked cookies upon arrival and gourmet breakfasts included in your stay.
**Restrictions:** Abigail's is a heritage building with no elevator access. Pets welcome in select rooms, $30 charge.
**Concierge:** 24 hour Service
**Room Service:** Breakfast in Bed option
**Restaurant:** Abigail's Hotel provides a decadent three course gourmet breakfast included in the room rates. Enjoy evening hors d'oeuvres compliments of the Chef.
**Bar:** Licensed – Champagne, Wine and beer service in Library Lounge
**Business Facilities:** 24 hr business station with Internet, fax and printer. Free wireless.
**Conference Room:** Based on availability.
**Sports Facilities:** No – Pass offered to local YMCA
**Spa Services:** Abigail's Hotel offers on-site spa services 7 days a week for your relaxation.
**Airport:** Vancouver Int'l Airport
**Location:** Downtown Victoria

Of the many special places Vancouver Island offers, this unique and romantic boutique bed and breakfast hotel is conveniently nestled at the end of a tranquil cul-de-sac surrounded by quaint English gardens and friendly residential homes. The enchanting setting at Abigail's makes it an ideal locale for relaxing getaways, intimate weddings and receptions and the hotels reputation for excellence in amenities and service clearly precedes it, on an international scale. Tourists are drawn to Abigail's for its cozy, communal atmosphere.

Intimately housed in a 1930s heritage Tudor mansion, Abigail's blends the romance and charm of the past with all the comforts and conveniences of the present. Each of the 23 beautifully appointed guestrooms has its own characteristic and flair. Many rooms feature marvelous soaker baths, cozy spa robes, down duvets, rich linens and signature wood-burning fireplaces. Wireless Internet service, local calling, coffee and tea 24 hours a day and parking are all inclusive during your stay with us.

Each morning the hotel fills with the irresistible aroma of freshly prepared baked goods, and gourmet breakfasts, interactively presented by Abigail's Executive Chef. Complimentary appetizers are served each evening in our Library Lounge which guests can pair with local award winning wine & champagne. Offering a balance between luxury and adventure, Abigail's is walking distance to must-see ocean or city tours, classic horse-drawn carriage rides, galleries, museums, and fine dining establishments for your choice of global cuisine.

Abigail's is a family owned and operated business that has had the privilege of being voted Best of the City nine years in a row and has been the recipient of a long list of awards

# AMETHYST INN AT REGENTS PARK

Amethyst Inn is a fully-restored historic mansion dating from 1890. A few of our many features are 13 foot ceilings, period furniture and antiques. There are cozy fireplaces in most rooms. In the parlor we serve a full English breakfast on antique crystal and china. To help you unwind there are several Jacuzzis on the premises. And don't worry about your car: we have lots of secure, free parking on our property.

Start your day with a steaming cup of freshly grounded coffee or choose from our wide selection of herbals teas in the parlor. Then, proceed into the Victorian dining room to enjoy a three course hotels breakfast enhanced by fine china and silver. Be part of the conversation or sit privately at one of the many tables.

All our dishes are prepared by our bed and breakfast award winning hostess, using organic, farm fresh, and seasonal produce when available. It is served in our elegant dining room, and tables are set with linen, fine china and crystal. We will make your honeymoon or anniversary unforgettable.

Amethyst Inn at Regents Park is located right between Downtown Victoria and Oak Bay Town Centre. We're less than two kilometers (20 minute walk) to downtown shopping centers and Victoria's China Town.

The inner harbor of Victoria, British Columbia is truly beautiful. You can stroll around and enjoy the views as you walk past the Legislative Building, Empress Hotel, Royal British Columbia Museum and Beacon Hill Park; these are just some of the landmarks that you'll see. In the summer there are many street performers. Some will entertain you, some create wonderful paintings, while others are carve little totem poles.

This is something you won't want to miss!

**Address:** 1501 Fort Street Victoria British Columbia V8S 1Z6
**Phone:** 250-595-2053
**Tollfree:** 888-265-6499
**Fax:** 250-595-2054
**Email:** innkeeper@amethyst-inn.com
**Web:** www.amethyst-inn.com
**Room Rates:** 149 – 399$
**No. of Rooms:** 13
**Credit Cards:** Visa, MC, Amex
**Attractions:** Craigdarroch Castle, Victoria Jubilee Hospital, BC Museum, inner harbor, Antique Row and quaint shops on Government Street, the Lieutenant-Governor's French Gardens
**Services:** High-ceilinged rooms and suites with four-poster beds, fireplaces, Jacuzzis and hydrotherapy spa-tubs-for-two, wide screen LCD TVs with cable/ up to 60 channels, DVD players and movie library, wireless Internet.
**Restrictions:** Recommended for Adults. Smoking allowed "outside" only. No Pets
**Concierge:** Our front desk will be happy to assist you
**Room Service:** No
**Restaurant:** All our dishes are prepared by our award winning hostess, using organic, farm fresh-seasonal produce when available.
**Bar:** No
**Business Facilities:** Computer/ wireless Internet
**Sports Facilities:** Jacuzzi / soaking tubs in rooms
**Spa Services:** Jacuzzis on the premises. Several types of spa treatments are available.
**Airport:** Local facilities
**Location:** 15 minutes South of Downtown Vancouver

# POINT GRACE RESORT & SPA

**Address:** Grace Bay Providenciales, Turks & Caicos
**Phone:** 649-941-7743
**Tollfree:** 888-209-5582
**Fax:** 649-946-8255
**Email:** reservations@pointgrace.com
**Web:** www.pointgrace.com
**Suite Rates:** 425–3,400 US$
**No. of Suites:** 28
**Credit Cards:** Most CCs Accepted
**Attractions:** Scuba diving, parasailing, boat charters, deep sea, bottom and bone fishing, water sports instruction, golf, tennis at Provo Golf and Country Club, bicycles, picnic hampers.
**Services:** Airport transfers & arrival drink. Twice daily maid service, bath amenities by Asprey of London, 100% Egyptian Cotton linen, NY *Times Digest*, TV lounge, small DVD library.
**Concierge:** Yes
**Room Service:** Yes
**Restaurant:** Grace's Cottage presents a unique blend of Caribbean ingredients and gourmet cuisine. Hutchings Restaurant, serving casual food as well as Caribbean renditions of the classics
**Bar:** Yes
**Business Facilities:** Yes: computer and printer access
**Conference Room:** Nearby
**Sports Facilities:** No
**Spa Services:** The Thalasso Spa at Point Grace Resort on Providenciales is a full-service European-style Thalassotherapy spa.
**Airport:** Providenciales Int'l
**Location:** Halfway between Florida and Puerto Rico

Point Grace derives its name from its singular location on the "Point" of "Grace Bay." Grace Bay derived its name from a lady, Grace Hutchings, who visited here on her honeymoon in 1892. Inspired by classic, turn-of-the-century British Colonial architecture, the beach front setting looks out upon a shimmering vista of turquoise sea and alabaster beach.

Here, in a setting seemingly untouched by time, each suite has been designed to include every luxury, leaving you free to encounter your own personal state of grace. Point Grace offers a selection of beachfront one, two, three and four bedroom suites and penthouses, plus one bedroom pool-front or ocean view cottage suites, magnificently furnished and decorated; each suite captures the flavor of West Indies yester-years. A unique collection of African tribal crafts and artwork, in the tradition of the great expressionist masters, is thoughtfully utilize to lend an exotic and refined insight.

The Thalasso Spa at Point Grace Resort on Providenciales is a full-service European-style Thalassotherapy spa. We have combined our knowledge of famous Thalgo Spas of France and have created a relaxing Caribbean ocean front environment for your enjoyment.

Grace's Cottage, the elegant restaurant at Point Grace, is poised to take its place on the Caribbean culinary landscape.

An extraordinary Caribbean retreat located on the pristine twelve-mile beach of Grace Bay.

# RONDEL VILLAGE

Rondel Village is a fascinating beach front retreat, located on Jamaica's romantic west coast, Negril!

Rondel Village is our family owned and operated exclusive villa resort on Negril's beautiful seven mile beach. This unique property offers privacy and tranquility in spacious, elegant accommodations, amidst lush tropical gardens. An enchanting paradise where service is personalized and the surroundings are comfortable and relaxing. Our spacious villas offer 1, 2 or 3 bedrooms with 2, 3 or 4 bathrooms. Each villa has a private enclosed whirlpool spa, living room and kitchen including a housekeeper who will cook a meal per day (guests purchase the food). Attractive beachfront, superior and garden rooms provide a comfortable home away from home.

If you are looking for that quiet vacation in a central location, with easy access to the towns facilities, Rondel Village is the place to go.

An environmentally friendly hotel, Rondel Village operates under an Environmental Management System and asks our guests to assist us in this program.

We invite you all to enjoy the incomparable experience that is Rondel Village.- Winner of the Jamaica Hotel & Tourist Association Small Hotel of the Year Award 2008.

**Address:** Norman Manley Blvd. Negril, Westmoreland, Jamaica
**Phone:** (876) 957-4413
**Tollfree:** 800-544-5979
**Fax:** 876-957-4915
**Email:** info@rondelvillage.com
**Web:** www.rondelvillage.com
**Room Rates:** 75–180 US$
**Suite Rates:** 145–470 US$
**No. of Rooms:** 32
**No. of Suites:** 8
**Credit Cards:** Most CCs Accepted
**Attractions:** Water and land sports are a feature of Negril. Visit the Historic Negril Lighthouse and mini-museum inside with artifacts dating back to 1894. Kool Runnings Water Park.
**Services:** Air conditioning, cable TV, In-room safes, 2 Pools & 2 Jacuzzis, Internet Cafe, Wireless Internet, 24 hour Security, DVD Player-villas, CD Player-rooms, Hair Dryer, Telephone, Beach towels, Beach and pool lounge chairs
**Restrictions:** No Pets Allowed
**Concierge:** Yes: available (daily) 8:00am–10:00pm
**Room Service:** Yes: available (daily) 8:00am–10:00pm
**Restaurant:** Island Twist Restaurant offers some of the most mouth watering and authentic Jamaican style meals. 7:30am–10:00pm
**Bar:** Island Twist experienced bartenders will serve you one of their specials with a twist!
**Business Facilities:** Internet "cafe" / wireless Internet (fee)
**Conference Room:** No
**Sports Facilities:** No on site gym or workout room
**Spa Services:** We have 2 swimming pools & Jacuzzis.
**Airport:** Negril Airport
**Location:** 7 mile beach Negril

# AVILA HOTEL - CURAÇAO

**Address:** Penstraat 130
Willemstad, Curaçao,
Netherlands Antilles
**Phone:** 599-9-461-4377
**Tollfree:** 800-747-8162 (USA)
**Fax:** 599-9-461-1493
**Email:** info@avilahotel.com
**Web:** www.avilahotel.com
**Room Rates:** 220–360 $
**Suite Rates:** 350–1,300 $
**No. of Rooms:** 154
**No. of Suites:** 10
**Credit Cards:** Visa, MC, Amex
**Attractions:** Curaçao offers a
comprehensive array of activities
ranging from world-class golf,
shopping, gambling and scuba
diving to 4 × 4 safaris, swimming
with dolphins, ocean kayaking.
**Services:** Café Barista offering
the finest selection of coffees.
Hairdresser "De Parel" for your
perfect hair make-over. NPM
Fashionality: Latest Fashion
boutique. Explore Curaçao:
Tour Desk. Van Dorp-Eddine:
Convenience shop. Avila
boutique: Gift shop.
**Restrictions:** Call for details
**Concierge:** Front desk or Mgr on
Duty
**Room Service:** 7–10am for
Breakfast only; Off hours—per
restaurant availability
**Restaurant:** Our restaurants offer
a variety of quality, fresh food day
and night.
**Bar:** Yes: the Blues Bar, Schooner
Bar, & Pool Bar
**Business Facilities:** 2 Business
Centers: copiers, fax / Internet
**Conference Room:** 5 rooms /
capacity: up to 160 people
**Sports Facilities:** Tennis Court,
Avila Fitness Club
**Spa Services:** Santai Spa: Santai
means "relaxation" in Indonesian.
**Airport:** Local airport
**Location:** On beach near
Willemstad, Curaçao

Avila creates an atmosphere for its guests, by generating and creating time for the special things in life. It is a house, a home, your favorite bar, your first choice for dinner, your beach, your escape and a great friend. Family run, the Avila Hotel boasts a history that covers more than two hundred years. Time seems to stand still here. Ceiling fans whirl slowly. The air smells sweetly of hibiscus and trinitaria (bougainvillea). The resident cat "Choller" stretches lazily on a sofa. Another perfect day magically evolves into yet another balmy, star-studded night. Friendly. Intimate. Understated. Welcoming. It is famous for its quiet, restful tranquility and yet it is only a short distance from Willemstad (Curaçao's capital).

The heart of the Avila Hotel is a beautiful Dutch Colonial style mansion. It is estimated that the original building was built at the end of the 18th century.

The east wing, La Belle Alliance, with its beautiful pastel-colored buildings reflects the style and architecture of the historical Dutch Colonial mansion. This wing houses the deluxe rooms and suites, all with balconies and ocean view and it combines modern conveniences and amenities with the charm of a bygone era. The west wing, called the Blues Wing, was built to a new and unique concept. It is an all wooden structure, a first for a Curaçao hotel, and two stories high, housing 20 premium deluxe rooms. All feature a private terrace or balcony overlooking the ocean. The grandest addition to the Avila Hotel is the Octagon Wing. It features 68 spacious rooms decorated in sophisticated neutrals with splashes Caribbean colors.

Our aim is to deliver to our guests a sense of timeless elegance, a bygone age delivered in a modern package. Avila is not only a location, but also a destination.

# HOTEL MAKANDA BY THE SEA, VILLAS AND STUDIOS

Makanda by the Sea is the ideal location for visitors wishing to experience Costa Rica's natural splendor and variety while enjoying the comforts of first-class jungle lodging. All of the Villas are contoured into the jungle and descending mountain terrain with the abruptly inclining hillsides allowing dramatic ocean views from all locations.

In July 1985, Makanda by the Sea was started by the designer and owner, Joe McNichols. Inspired by his dream, Makanda has been built in balance with its natural surroundings. Using nature as the backdrop, the architectural openness allows the rich tropical flora to become a part of the living environment. Selection of flora was based on the ability to attract a mix of butterflies, birds, monkeys, sloths and other local fauna, making a stay here a heightened jungle experience.

Dazzling late-afternoon sunsets and tantalizing tropical breezes greet you as you stroll the beaches of Costa Rica's Pacific Coast. A splash of color catches your eye as an unnamed species of bird or butterfly wings it's way through the rain forest. A challenging hike through the jungle paths lead to a secluded rocky beach cove where guests can explore the tide pools as well as rare pre-Columbian fish traps.

At Makanda by the Sea you will find a number of ways of keeping comfortable on even the hottest of tropical days. The geometrically designed infinity pool. Spacious viewing decks. Enjoy delicious poolside appetizers.

Or, unwind in the Jacuzzi while the wildlife watches you! These are only a few of the many wonders that have captured the imaginations of visitors from around the world as they are quietly seduced by the natural splendor of a visit to Hotel Makanda by the Sea. Makanda, the name once said to mean "essence" or "nectar" in ancient Sanscrit, is a paradise found!

**Address:** 3K Main Road 2, Manuel Antonio Park, Puntarenas, Costa Rica
**Phone:** 506-2777-0442
**Tollfree:** 888-625-2632
**Fax:** 506-2777-1032
**Email:** info@makanda.com
**Web:** www.makanda.com/EN
**Room Rates:** 200 – 460 US$
**Suite Rates:** 200 – 460 US$
**No. of Rooms:** 11
**No. of Suites:** 11
**Credit Cards:** Most CCs Accepted
**Attractions:** • Manuel Antonio Park Hike • Mangrove Boat • Whitewater Rafting • Canopy Zipline • Jet Skis • Snorkel/ Dolphin & Whale Tour • Horseback Riding • ATV Tour • Kayak Excursions • Butterfly/ Reptile Farm • Vanilla Spice Farm • Surfing • Inshore/Offshore Sportfishing
**Services:** • Welcome Cocktail Breakfast In-Room • Coffee Maker • A/C • Cable TV • Stereo & iPod dock • Mini Bar • Full Kitchen • Safe • Secure Parking • Free Internet/Int Calls • Tour Desk • Wedding Plan
**Restrictions:** Adults Only – Regretfully we do not accept children under the age of 14 yrs.
**Concierge:** Available 7am to 8pm
**Room Service:** Available 7am to 10pm Daily
**Restaurant:** Sunspot Bar & Grill, located poolside.
**Bar:** Sunspot Bar & Grill
**Business Facilities:** Available
**Conference Room:** No
**Sports Facilities:** No
**Spa Services:** We are proud to offer a complete range of Spa Services in the comfort of your luxury Villa.
**Airport:** Local airport
**Location:** Manuel Antonio-Quepos

# THE ALTA HOTEL

**Address:** Alto de las Palomas
Santa Ana Costa Rica
**Phone:** 506-2282-4160
**Tollfree:** 888-388-2582
**Fax:** 506-2282-4162
**Email:** hotlalta@racsa.co.cr
**Web:** www.thealtahotel.com
**Room Rates:** 99 -155 $
**Suite Rates:** 125 – 600 $
**No. of Rooms:** 18
**No. of Suites:** 5
**Credit Cards:** Most CCs Accepted
**Attractions:** Irazu Volcano, La
Paz Waterfall Gardens, Cafe
Britt Coffee Tour, Poas Volcano,
sightseeing, shopping
**Services:** Tour & car rental
service, High-speed & wireless
Internet, laundry & dry cleaning,
Baby Crib, luggage storage,
limited exchange (dollars to
colones),Continental Breakfast
(included with room rate)
**Restrictions:** No Pets, Children
Welcome!
**Concierge:** Yes: available 24/7
**Room Service:** Yes: (daily) from
7am – 9:45pm
**Restaurant:** La Luz restaurant in
1997, created what was perhaps
the first true "fusion" cuisine.
**Business Facilities:** Full
business center: computer, fax,
copier—available 24/7
**Conference Room:** 3 rooms /
capacity: up to 255 people
**Sports Facilities:** Full fitness
center, pool and sauna
**Spa Services:** The Alta Hotel has
built a special relationship with
a nearby Spa so that guests may
receive full spa treatments.
**Airport:** Juan Santamaria Int'l
**Location:** A suburb of San Jose

Small, special, and intimate. The Alta Hotel is beautifully
sculpted hotel which cascades down Alto de Las Palomas
(the Hill of the Doves), providing exquisite views of the vol-
canoes, mountains and valley that surround San Jose. The
carved look melds different styles—Spanish-Moorish medieval, countryside elegant—into one graceful structure. The
vaulted ceilings in the paseo and wide stone stairway lead
castle-like from the reclusive guest rooms to the warm glow of
La Luz Restaurant.

The hotel has an old-world ambiance, offering a sharp contrast to the modern, hotel look. When you arrive you feel like
you've entered an elegant hacienda in 17th Century Spain.
The setting is warm and welcoming, but not pretentious. The
rooms have the overall look of elegant austerity as if an old
monastery had been converted into an art academy. They are
clean and simple, almost humble in design. The finishes are
rustic. Sculpted pedestals serve as television stands; rustic,
exposed copper plumbing decorates the bathrooms; terra-
cotta tiles cover the bathroom and bedroom floors. Perhaps
the finest features of the hotel are the large balconies that
overlook the Valley of the Sun and bring the exquisite view
into the room. Pristine Egyptian cotton sheets and duvets
cover the beds. Bathrooms offer exquisitely tiled vanities and
a host of thoughtful amenities. Five years or twenty years
from now, the hotel will not have changed much because of
the timeless style and the incorporation of fine design and
fabrics.

Go up to your room, relax and savor the view, soon an exquisite feast will be served in La Luz.

# LOS ALTOS DE EROS LUXURY INN, SPA & YOGA

We are a 5-Star Costa Rica Luxury Hotel Resort and we sit on a 27 acre estate atop a small mountain with views to the Pacific Ocean. To some, the ideal vacation or holiday is spent in total relaxation, far from the crowds, the noise, and the hustle and bustle of organized civilization (and tourism) as we know it. For those people, we are the ultimate destination. We are sited on a serene mountaintop estate with 360 degrees of view including the Pacific ocean—complete with tropical birds, monkeys, amazing butterflies, and many more sights and sounds of the Costa Rica flora and fauna. Day trips are available for whitewater tubing, rappelling down waterfalls, hot volcanic mud baths, and river experiences with crocodiles and with white faced monkeys in your boat!

We are in a very private and secure location from which you can do everything in Costa Rica … or nothing at all.

We are an extremely popular Costa Rica romantic honeymoon destination, yet many come here just to propose to their mate! If you want the perfect setting for your Costa Rica romantic interlude or celebration you will appreciate the fact that we are "adults only-no children."

And while you are here enjoy the "Sunset Massage and Romantic Dinner For 2" in our Spa. It is as good as it gets anywhere. One guest said "This experience was better than my wedding!" By the way, we would love to host your wedding or other special romantic celebration.

More than 95% of our "5-Star Costa Rica Hotel" success is a direct result of our Costa Rican staff. Approximately 3 to 1 staff-to-guest ratio, no staff turnover whatsoever, with the average tenure almost 4 years. They truly love their work here and you will experience it every day.

**Address:** Altos de Pinilla Tamarindo Costa Rica
**Phone:** 506-8850-4222
**Tollfree:** 786-866-7039
**Email:** info@losaltosdeeros.com
**Web:** www.losaltosdeeros.com
**Suite Rates:** 395–595 US$
**No. of Suites:** 5
**Credit Cards:** Most CCs Accepted
**Attractions:** Within a 20 minute drive (which we provide to you as a courtesy) you can surf, swim at two beaches, shop, take a canopy tour, go sport fishing, ride horses or ATV's, play golf, visit nearby towns, nightlife, restaurants.
**Services:** FREE Cuban cigars, laundry service, complimentary breakfast & lunch, limited time—cooking classes! Free smoothies, wine and beer are available at any time, Yoga center
**Restrictions:** Adults only, please.
**Room Service:** Yes
**Concierge:** Front Desk assistance
**Restaurant:** We feature Costa Rica Grass-Fed Beef, Free-Range Chicken, Organic Fruits & Vegetables, and Seafood Packed in Shaved Ice that comes directly to us from the fishing boat. Special diets welcome.
**Bar:** Yes
**Business Facilities:** Fax, copier
**Conference Room:** No
**Sport Facilities:** Yoga
**Spa Services:** Think beyond a darkened room with a couple of candles. Our acclaimed Spa de Eros is open air. Views from the 5 private treatment rooms feature the mountains, jungle, the Pacific Ocean. Enjoy the Balinese Soaking Tub, large heated hydrotherapy pool
**Airport:** Tamarindo Airport
**Location:** Hillside outside Tamarindo

# HOTEL KLAUSK K

**Address:** Bulevardi 2/4
Helsinki Finland 00120
**Phone:** 358-40-900-3771
**Fax:** 358-20-770-4730
**Email:** rooms@klauskhotel.com
**Web:** www.klauskhotel.com
**No. of Rooms:** 63
**Credit Cards:** Most CCs Accepted
**Attractions:** Our hotel is located
at the heart of the city centre.
The city has ample offerings
for visitors who look for new
experiences and nightlife.
Museums, shopping, music clubs,
orchestras, restaurants, clubs,
and festivals.
**Services:** A good bed and
delicious food are essential for
travelers. Parking.
**Room Service:** Yes, room service
is available
**Restrictions:** No smoking, No
pets, handicap accessible
**Concierge:** Available 7am–11pm
**Restaurant:** Our restaurants
have received their cheerful and
relaxed atmosphere from Tuscany,
Italy.
**Bar:** Yes; we have a trendy
nightclub
**Business Facilities:** Internet, fax,
copier, event assistance
**Conference Room:** 4 meeting
rooms
**Sports Facilities:** On site gym
**Spa Services:** Helsinki Day
Spa is a new kind of urban spa,
which offers a soothing place of
relaxation. With the historical
architecture, the modern design
of the spa offers a unique
atmosphere.
**Airport:** Helsinki Airport
**Location:** Top of the Espanada
on a tree lined street

In 1938, the Board of Rake decided to combine the premises of the restaurant and the boarding house, and named them Klaus Kurki. The expanded hotel became a significant accommodation business in Helsinki, featuring proper premises such as an elegant dining hall and renovated rooms. After the renovation, the hotel included 63 rooms, all equipped with a toilet and most with a bathroom.

The former Klaus Kurki hotel underwent a massive 15 million euros renovation in 2005 and it has transformed into a modern, upscale lifestyle oasis. Inspired by Finland's national epic, The Kalevala, the interiors of Klaus K express the emotional themes of mysticism, passion, desire and envy.

Four different guest room motifs feature cutting edge design and comfort customized for today's traveler. Thoroughly individual and decidedly contemporary, design hotel Klaus K is a hotel with a soul and a story, waiting for you discover it and all of its riches.

In the 1970s, the hotel was a family-run business, until it was sold to a hotel chain at the end of the decade. Three decades later, in 2005, the same family, represented by Mia and Marc, return to manage the hotel.

# HOTEL BRITANNIQUE

The Britannique is a genuine charming hotel. Its site, close to Place du Chatelet, in the historical center of Paris is ideal for visiting by foot the oldest districts such as the Louvre, Les Halles, Le Marais, Saint Germain des Prés and the Latin quarter, the islands of la Cité and Saint Louis.

Since 1861, The Britannique has cultivated the great courtesy of the English art of living tinted with elegance which makes the Parisian charm. It has also added to it the refinements of a top of the range comfort and the conviviality of traditional French hospitality. Stroll down the most beautiful avenue in the world, the Champs Élysées, climb the Eiffel Tower for a wonderful view of the city. Visit the historic monuments, from Notre Dame to Montamartre and countless others. See Paris by night as you dine by candle-light, floating down the Seine on a river boat.

From the moment you arrive your stay at the Hotel Britannique will be memorable. Our concierge will be able to assist you with all your needs, both inside and outside our hotel, whether you are staying with us for business or pleasure.

Remember—there is no place like Paris!

**Address:** 20 Avenue Victoria Paris France F-75001
**Phone:** 33-1-42-33-74-59
**Fax:** 33-1-42-33-82-65
**Email:** mailbox@hotel-britannique.fr
**Web:** www.hotel-britannique.fr
**Room Rates:** 135 – 221 ¤
**Suite Rates:** 229 – 325 ¤
**No. of Rooms:** 39
**No. of Suites:** 1
**Credit Cards:** Most CCs Accepted
**Attractions:** It's Paris! Enjoy the Grand Louvre Museum, Notre Dame Cathedral, Modern art Pompidou center, Picasso Gallery, le Marais, Quartier Latin, Eiffel Tower, near railway stations, Seine River and much more.
**Services:** A/C, Reading Room, Private bathrooms with hair dryers, Direct dial telephone, Internet, WiFi, Minibar, Flat screen TV & movies from US, UK, Germany & Italy, Lobby safe, buffet breakfast, electronic keys, newspaper, laundry service
**Restrictions:** Call for details
**Concierge:** Yes—available 24/7
**Room Service:** No
**Restaurant:** The hotel will serve you a generous and hearty breakfast.
**Bar:** Bar service with fine champagnes, wines
**Business Facilities:** Full business assistance available
**Conference Room:** No
**Sports Facilities:** No
**Spa Services:** Our friendly staff will be able to assist you with recommendations, appointments and directions to the facilities in the local area.
**Airport:** Orly Airport
**Location:** In the historic heart of Paris near Seine river

# LA VILLA MAURESQUE - BOUTIQUE HOTEL RIVIERA

**Address:** 1792 Route de la Corniche Boulouris, Saint Raphael France 83700
**Phone:** 33-4-94-83-02-42
**Fax:** 33-4-94-83-02-02
**Email:** info@villa-mauresque.com
**Web:** www.hotelsfrench-riviera.com/en/boutique-hotel-st-tropez-french-riviera
**No. of Rooms:** 6
**Credit Cards:** Most CCs Accepted
**Attractions:** diving, sailing, kayaking, jet skiing, wakeboarding or waterskiing, the Verdon Grand Canyon, Thoronet Abbey, the "Calanques de Cassis," sightseeing—medieval hilltop villages, rent boats/yacht with or without a crew, horse riding, tennis, beach.
**Services:** La Villa Mauresque's two hotels, Boutique Hotel Riviera and Spa French Riviera both enjoy fitness room, personal trainers, yoga teachers, massages in your room or on the seafront … you name it, and we are pleased to help you find what you desire.
**Restrictions:** Children & Pets welcome.
**Concierge:** Yes: available 24/7
**Room Service:** Yes: available 24/7
**Restaurant:** Culinary delights complemented by the panoramic views of the French Riviera coast, inspired by magnificent flavors & colours of local produce, our Chef acclaimed for his delicate-but-generous Mediterranean-style dishes spiced with Provencal flair
**Bar:** Yes: available 24/7
**Business Facilities:** Yes
**Conference Room:** Yes
**Sports Facilities:** Fitness room
**Spa Services:** Massages, beauty treatments etc...on site enjoy the Jacuzzis and sea front hot tubs as well as the Turkish bath (steam room)
**Airport:** Nice, Marseille or Toulon Airports
**Location:** The French Riviera

The Villa Mauresque is composed of 2 of the most romantic luxury hotels on pristine park on the seafront, tucked away in one of the most enchanting locations near Saint Tropez and Cannes with breathtaking sea views over the Mediterranean.

The Villa Mauresque is composed of two luxury hotels in the same grounds—the "Boutique Hotel French Riviera" and the "Spa French Riviera," both hotels with their own pools and own external Jacuzzis and stunning sea views from everywhere! The Boutique Hotel Riviera is a 6 room luxury boutique hotel right on the seafront, with stunning views in every direction and a pool and Jacuzzi spa overlooking the sea. Each room has been individually decorated with every attention to detail.

The hotel chef's culinary delights are complemented only by the panoramic views of the French Riviera coast. Inspired by the magnificent flavours and colors of our local produce, Chef Phillippe Joffroy is acclaimed for his delicate-but-generous Mediterranean-style dishes spiced with Provençale flair. Philippe brings out the very best of each individual ingredient. Whether you are staying at the Spa Hotel Riviera or the Boutique Hotel Riviera we offer an exceptional service in that we allow the guest to choose where to lunch or dine. Watch the sun go down whilst you savor mouth-watering food and sip deliciously refreshing rosé wine from Provençe.

Of all the Boutique hotels in France, La Villa Mauresque is unique in its architecture and sense of peace and quiet.… Enjoy a drink from the external seaview Jacuzzi spa, get ready to unwind completely.…

# CHAPSLEE HOUSE

Evocative of a bygone era, Chapslee, formerly the summer residence of the late Hon'ble Raja Charanjit Singh of Kapurthala, is now a small, exclusive Hotel. The Hon'ble Raja Charanjit Singh of Kapurthala was a member of the erstwhile Council of States and had the distinction and privilege of being an invitee to the coronations of both King George V and King Edward VIII. He was a host and gourmet extraordinaire and his table was considered to be one of the finest in northern India. Built in 1835, Chapslee was acquired by Lord Auckland, then Governor General of the East India Company. The declaration of the first war against Afghanistan known as 'The Afghan Manifesto,' was signed at Chapslee on the first of October, 1838. Sir Edward Buck writes in his famous book.

Kanwar Ratanjit Singh, son of the late Lt.Col. Rajkumar Ripjit Singh, C.I.E., and grandson of Raja Charanjit Singh, opened Chapslee to visitors in 1976. He continues to reside there and Chapslee is still the family home it was, but he now shares it with his guests. Resplendent with heirlooms such as Gobelin tapestries, rare textiles and cabinetry from the Doge's palace in Venice, chandeliers from Murano, blue pottery jardinieres from Multan, Peshwa vases, Persian carpets, marble statuary and a collection of Indian object d'arts.

Chapslee offers six elegantly appointed suites, a library and card room, tennis court and croquet lawn. It is also known for its cuisine and has found pride of place in almost all leading articles and publications on travel and architecture. An ambiance of gentility pervades the atmosphere and the tradition of hospitality for which the royal house of Kapurthala is known. Chapslee exudes old world charm.

**Address:** Shimla India 171 001 (H.P)
**Phone:** 91-177-2658663
**Tollfree:** 91-177-2802542
**Fax:** 91-177-2653085
**Email:** chapsleesm@gmail.com
**Web:** www.chapslee.com
**No. of Rooms:** 5
**No. of Suites:** 5
**Credit Cards:** Visa, MC
**Attractions:** Shimla has many attractions; superb views and delightful walks; the Vice-regal Lodge, the State Museum, Jakhoo Temple, the Mall and Maria Bros., the famous shop for books and antiquities.
**Services:** Old world antiques, services and dining as a member of the Raja's family
**Restrictions:** Children welcome, smoking allowed, no pets, no handicap access
**Room Service:** By pre-arrangement
**Concierge:** Front Desk assistance
**Restaurant:** Traditional Royal Indian cuisine from the Palaces of the Maharajas and Nawabs of India. Anglo-Indian . . . Cuisine of the Raj.
**Bar:** Various — served with dinner
**Conference Room:** No
**Business Facilities:** Limited
**Sport Facilities:** No on site gym or workout room
**Spa Facilities:** Will refer to the local establishments
**Airport:** Local airport
**Location:** A Rajah's Palace

# HOTEL MONNA LISA

**Address:** Via Borgo Pinti 27
Florence Tuscany Italy I-50121
**Phone:** 39-0-55-247-97-51
**Fax:** 39-0-55-247-97-55
**Email:** info@monnalisa.it
**Web:** www.monnalisa.it
**Room Rates:** 240,000 ¤
**No. of Rooms:** 45
**Credit Cards:** Most CCs Accepted
**Attractions:** Giotto's Bell Tower,
National Museum of Bargello,
Uffizi Gallery, antique gold shops,
high fashion boutique shopping,
renowned pastries—eateries/
restaurants, antiques galore!,
sightseeing, guided tours,
**Services:** Satellite TV, minibar,
safe deposit box, Internet & WiFi,
pay per view TV, newspapers,
laundry & ironing service,
elevator, luggage storage.
**Restrictions:** Children welcome,
smoking allowed, pets welcome,
handicap access
**Concierge:** Yes: available (daily)
24/7
**Room Service:** No
**Restaurant:** Buffet breakfast is
served (daily) from 7:30am until
10:00am.
**Bar:** Yes: open (daily) from
10:00am–11:00pm
**Business Facilities:** Limited:
Internet & WiFi (fee)
**Conference Room:** 2 rooms /
capacity: up to 38 people
**Sports Facilities:** On site gym
**Spa Services:** If a workout in
our gym is not "your thing," our
helpful staff will be happy to
assist you with recommendations,
appointments and directions to
the local spa facilities.
**Airport:** Amerigo Vespucci
**Location:** Downtown

The Hotel Monna Lisa offers the atmosphere of another age as one of the best 4-star hotels in the historical center of Florence, the extraordinary birthplace of Italian art. Inside the hotel—period decor, sculptures and original paintings are conserved in an ambience of irresistible charm, surrounded by discrete and charming luxury, complete with the most modern comforts.

Located in the historical center of Florence, the 45 rooms, all completely different from each other in terms of space and furnishings, enjoy the pleasant tranquility that characterizes the hotel. Several have balconies overlooking the gracious garden and offered in a variety of layouts, the rooms are furnished with antique furniture and period paintings. Charming in the attention to detail and the quality of *passamenterie*, they come complete with air conditioning, flat-screen satellite TV, mini bar and bathroom with whirlpool tub (Superior and Suite). The hotel is equipped with a gym, which is free to use, and also a solarium.

The staff of the Hotel Monna Lisa will be happy to assist you during your stay, providing information and valuable suggestions; at reception you can book guided tours and excursions and rent a car, even with a driver. In the lush Italian garden during the warm months, after a day of visits to museums and shopping, you can relax by enjoying a drink or reading a newspaper.

# ALBERGO VILLA MARTA

The Hotel Albergo Villa Marta is a nineteenth-century hunting lodge which has recently been restored. The villa is surrounded by a spacious Renaissance Lucchese garden, where guests can enjoy unique serenity. On the facing hillside is an impressive view of the peaceful Convent of San Cerbone, still in use today.

Hotel Albergo Villa Marta has classic and deluxe double rooms; each room has its own character, created with a combination of elegant furnishings, subtle color schemes and simple architecture.

Guests at the Hotel Albergo Villa Marta are invited to enjoy an extensive buffet breakfast served in summer in the villa's garden and in winter in the comfortable and elegant Breakfast Room with its welcoming open fire. The "Good Awakening" menu offers food prepared in the traditional way, with care and boundless enthusiasm.

The Hotel Albergo Villa Marta, with its elegance and crystal-clear swimming pool, promises an unforgettable holiday for those looking for relaxation, warm Tuscan hospitality and culture. Similarly, for those traveling on business, Hotel Albergo Villa Marta is the ideal place to relax from the stresses and strains of the day. This exclusive site includes a small, private neo-classical chapel, the ideal location for an intimate and romantic wedding.

Our aim is to make your stay unforgettable and satisfy your every need.

**Address:** Via del Ponte Guasperini, 873 Lucca Italy 55100
**Phone:** 39-0583-370101
**Fax:** 39-0583-379999
**Email:** info@albergovillamarta.it
**Web:** www.albergovillamarta.it
**Room Rates:** 156 – 262 $
**No. of Rooms:** 15
**Credit Cards:** Most CCs Accepted
**Attractions:** The hotel is located near the beautiful town of Lucca, which still preserves its romantic and mysterious fascination. In the surrounding area there are ancient gardens, castles, churches and historical places to visit, for example: Puccini's House.
**Services:** Wine & Oil Tasting, Transfer Service, Conference Organization, Tours, Painting Course, Cookery Course, Swimming pool, Chapel, Bicycles, Safety Deposit Box, Internet point and WiFi, Baby sitting services.
**Restrictions:** Call for details
**Concierge:** Located at our front desk
**Room Service:** Room service and laundry service are available.
**Restaurant:** Ristorante Botton d'Oro is open from 7pm until 10pm (except Sundays). Tuscan and Italian cuisine is served. Reservations are needed.
**Bar:** Bar is open daily from 11:00am until 11:00pm
**Business Facilities:** Fax service, conference organization
**Conference Room:** 1 meeting room—capacity/up to 20 people
**Sports Facilities:** No on-site facilities
**Spa Services:** The front desk will be happy to assist you by connecting you to the local area health club and spas.
**Airport:** Balilei Pisa, Vespucci Firenze Int'l Airports
**Location:** Only 5 km from the historical town of Lucca.

# VILLA DEL FARO

**Address:** 64 Camino Costero de San Jose a La Rivera
Baja Baja California Sur 23400
**Email:** rental@villadelfaro.net
**Web:** www.villadelfaro.net
**Room Rates:** 140–425 US$
**Suite Rates:** 265–425 US$
**No. of Rooms:** 5
**No. of Suites:** 4
**Credit Cards:** Visa, MC
**Attractions:** Villa del Faro is 3 miles from some of the best East Cape surf breaks. There are miles of empty beach, trails into the mountains, ocean swimming, bird watching, snorkeling, scuba-diving, fishing trips available, whale watching from your private balcony.
**Services:** The friendly, discreet staff at Villa del Faro will be glad to arrange day trips, and help you with our local expertise. Maid service.
**Restrictions:** Call for details
**Concierge:** Yes
**Room Service:** Yes
**Restaurant:** Villa del Faro is known for its gourmet International Cuisine. The restaurant and bar are private and serve the hotel's clientele exclusively.
**Bar:** Yes
**Business Facilities:** No
**Conference Room:** No
**Sports Facilities:** Large elegant freestyle swimming pool, Ocean
**Spa Services:**
**Airport:** San Jose del Cabo
**Location:** is a hidden oasis nestled on the Sea of Cortez endless private beach.One ho

Exquisitely off the Grid !!
Imagine yourself in the middle of nowhere … in the lap of luxury…. White sand, waving palms, spectacular sunsets and it's all eco-friendly.

Villa del Faro is a hidden oasis nestled on the Sea of Cortez with acres of private beach. The Villa was created as a labor of love by artisans and architects and is a family enterprise. It is one of the most beautiful venues on the East Cape of Baja Sur and is now offering exclusive and exquisite accommodations and cuisine.

We offer five separate accommodations, Casa Palapa, Casita Tres, Casita Dos á North & South Suites, and the Stone Beach Cottage. They all share a large mosaic pool and all have spectacular ocean views. Each is unique with hand crafted furnishings, stone fireplaces, and private terraces set in a world of gardens, fountains and a dramatic ocean side Baja environment. A lovely breakfast is included with all rentals. Exceptional International Table d'Hôte gourmet dinners are available.

Villa del Faro is just 45 minutes from the shops of San Jose del Cabo and the Los Cabos Airport, an hour and a half from cosmopolitan Cabo San Lucas—but it is a world away in seclusion and serenity. Villa del Faro is a writer's retreat, a secluded romantic getaway, a beachcomber's paradise, a private garden enclave, an artist's hideaway, and a culinary Mecca.

We invite you to enjoy a level of vacation excellence that is not lost and gone forever, but is increasingly hard to find.

# CABO SURF HOTEL & SPA

A boutique beach resort located on one of the most privileged beaches in Los Cabos and has rooms, suites and villas available.

The architecture resembles a California style beach house with white stucco walls, arches and red tile roofs. Luscious vegetation enhances gardens and surroundings. Well thought out decoration details and functionality ensure our guests get inspired throughout their stay. All rooms face the ocean with superb views and the soothing sounds of rolling waves are heard all around the resort for our guests to enjoy.

All hotel accommodations include marble floors, cedar carpentry, palm thatch on some balconies, duvet covers, comforters, L'Occitane bath amenities, flat screen TV with prime channel programming, round table with chairs, mini fridge, wireless internet connection and terrace.

The pool is conveniently located in the center of the resort facing the beach. Located on the pool deck is a heated Jacuzzi tub, for your enjoyment. It is great for relaxation after a grueling surf session or a daily workout.

**Address:** Playa Acapulquito, Km. 28 San Jose del Cabo
**Phone:** 52-624-142-2666
**Tollfree:** 858-964-5117
**Email:** info@cabosurfhotel.com
**Web:** www.cabosurfhotel.com/en
**Room Rates:** 265 $
**Suite Rates:** 295 $
**No. of Rooms:** 22
**No. of Suites:** 4
**Credit Cards:** Most CCs Accepted
**Attractions:** Sightseeing, Relaxing, Shopping, Fine Dining, Golf, Tennis, Sportfishing, Scuba Diving & Snorkeling, Graywhale Watching
**Services:** L'Occitane bath amenities, flat screen TV, satellite programming, mini fridge, wireless internet, terraces, beach front rooms, jacuzzi, iron and board, safe deposit box, bath robes.
**Restrictions:** Call for details
**Concierge:** Yes
**Room Service:** Yes
**Restaurant:** 7 Seas Seafood Grille where the house specialty is fresh sea bass. Our executive chef Alejandro Rodriguez offers unique dishes found nowhere else.
**Bar:** Yes
**Business Facilities:** Wireless Internet, fax, copies
**Conference Facilities:** Limited
**Sport Facilities:** No gym or workout room.
**Spa Services:** Spa Services: the Sea Spa & Salon has a menu of therapies and treatments to astound you including facials, massage therapies and body treatment options.
**Airport:** Cabo San Lucas
**Location:** Playa Acapulquito

# CASA LUCILA HOTEL BOUTIQUE

**Address:** Olas Alas No 16
Mazatlan Sinaloa C.P. 82000
**Phone:** 52-669-982-1100
**Fax:** 52-669-982-1150
**Email:** frontdesk@casalucila.com
**Web:** casalucila.com
**Room Rates:** 115 – 295 $
**No. of Rooms:** 8
**Credit Cards:** Visa, MC, Amex
**Attractions:** Casa Lucila is a destination boutique hotel ideally located on the oceanfront in the Historic Center of Old Mazatlan. Casa Lucila is within a short walk to the area's art galleries, restaurants, nightlife, and a variety of boutiques.
**Services:** Oceanfront location in the Historic Center of Old Mazatlan, luxurious private baths, complimentary wireless Internet access, a flat-screen plasma TV, and Bvlgari bath amenities.
**Restrictions:** Adults-only, non-smoking. Young adults 15 years and older must have their own room.
**Room Service:** Yes: available (daily) 7:00pm – 11:00
**Concierge:** Front Desk assistance
**Restaurant:** Enjoy a quiet breakfast, lunch or an intimate dinner in our quaint, comfortable restaurant.
**Bar:** Yes
**Business Facilities:** Yes
**Conference Facilities:** 2 areas/ capacity up to 40 people
**Spa Services:** Relieve your stress and regenerate vital energy wellness with an hour long massage. Swedish, Sport (Deep Tissue), Reflexology, Shiatsu or Hot Stone. Reservations are required at least 24 hours prior.
**Airport:** Rafael Buelna Int'l & Mazatlan Airports
**Location:** Oceanfront

A rich and storied past surrounds Casa Lucila Hotel Boutique, located in the heart of Viejo Mazatlan. Its restoration is dedicated to the memory of a loving mother and father, Lucila Valades Valdez and Fernando Valades Lejarza. The building has endured several incarnations during its lifetime, from a mansion for wealthy German immigrants to a Jazz-Age hot spot O'Brien's frequented by John Wayne, Robert Mitchum, and Ernest Hemingway. Throughout its many manifestations, the buildings Victorian facade has remained a constant. After two long grueling years of construction, Casa Lucila Hotel Boutique opened in 2007 but not without the help of all the talented individuals who helped restore the building.

The hotel has eight beautifully designed and individually different rooms, each named of the eight daughters of Lucila Valades Valdez. Each guestroom offers ocean or courtyard views and is accented with custom-made Italian doors and windows, tiled floors and bathroom fixtures. Each was installed in the hotel to offer our guests a place to relax.

From annual meetings, corporate celebrations, or holiday parties, Casa Lucila Boutique Hotel can provide the finest accommodations and personalized menus for your event. Our Event Planners can help you organize an intimate event of twelve people up to a larger group of 80. Modern and chic, yet simple, Casa Lucila's various sections can provide a sizeable courtyard for intimate weddings, birthday parties or anniversaries. From complete menus, flowers, music, plan layout, and wedding documents, we can guide you through the process and organize every detail with you.

EWW 9498 25TH ED

# HOTEL HACIENDA LOS LAURELES - SPA

This intimate 5 star hotel, boasting just 23 guest rooms, imparts the look and feel of a private hacienda. Thick stucco walls, terra-cotta floors, ornate wrought iron furniture and colorful Mexican fabrics give the hotel an inviting, informal appeal. Outdoors, points of interest include colorful gardens and the fine laurel trees that were preserved during the renovation. Relax in the hotel's newly expanded Petit Spa with a traditional "temazcal," or indigenous steam bath, and enjoy fine traditional Mexican fare and international cuisine in its award-winning restaurant.

A quick trip into Oaxaca, designated by UNESCO as one of Mexico's World Heritage sites, will bring you to the breathtaking archaeological digs at Monte Alban, home of the ancient Zapotecs. Browse the open markets for a keepsake of Oaxacan green or black pottery; ornate colonial churches; or museums that house the treasures of Mexico's past.

Spacious rooms and suites recreate the gentle atmosphere of the haciendas from colonial times. Every terrace and patio overlooks lush gardens, the mountains and the nearby town of Oaxaca. The city is full of magnificent buildings and churches. We are one of the most sought after places for weddings. With the Sierra Mountains as a backdrop, our wedding planner can assist you with all the "little" details and managing your guest list of up to 500 people.

"After the wedding" or just as a "get away"—Hotel Hacienda Los Laureles-Spa awaits you.

**Address:** Hildago #21, San Felipe Del Agua Oaxaca Oaxaca CP 68020
**Phone:** 52-951-501-5300
**Fax:** 52-951-501-5301
**Email:** bookings@ hotelhaciendaloslaureles.com
**Web:** www.hotelhaciendaloslaureles.com
**Room Rates:** 247–268 $
**Suite Rates:** 331–389 $
**No. of Rooms:** 23
**No. of Suites:** 8
**Credit Cards:** Visa, MC, Amex
**Attractions:** Oaxaca cooking classes, historic pyramids, Monte Alban, Mitla, museums, historic city tours & churches, mountain hiking, tennis, horseback riding, golf.
**Services:** Soaps, shampoos, hairdryers, facial mirrors, robes, color TV, A/C-heating, mini bars, car rental service, baby sitter, safe deposit box, shoe shine, wireless Internet.
**Restrictions:** International or local holidays, a 3 or 4 night minimum stay is required.
**Concierge:** Yes—available 24/7
**Room Service:** Yes—House Special menu
**Restaurant:** Los Cipresse serves Oaxaca, Mexican and international foods. Open 7am–11pm. Special barbeques and Mexican nights..
**Bar:** Yes—open 7am till 11pm (daily)
**Business Facilities:** Computer, fax, copier available 7am until 8pm (daily)
**Conference Room:** 1 room / capacity up to 80 people
**Sports Facilities:** Gym area
**Spa Services:** Aromatherapy, various types of massages.
**Airport:** Mexico City Int'l
**Location:** Residential area.

# LAS ALAMANDAS

**Address:** Km. 83 Carretera Federal # 200 Quemaro Jalisco 48850
**Phone:** 52-322-285-5500
**Tollfree:** 888-882-9616
**Fax:** 52-322-285-5027
**Email:** info@alamandas.com
**Web:** www.alamandas.com
**Suite Rates:** 371 – 2,070 $
**No. of Suites:** 16
**Credit Cards:** Most CCs Accepted
**Attractions:** Explore the views and unspoiled acreage by horseback, mountain bike, or hiking trails. Tennis court, Boogie boards, surfing, croquet, ping pong and beach volleyball
**Services:** Tile baths, oversized tub/shower, private terraces, mini bar
**Restrictions:** Call for details
**Concierge:** Yes: available 24/7
**Room Service:** Yes: available (by special arrangement) from 8:00am – 11:00pm
**Restaurant:** All of the ingredients are fresh;the fish and seafood are the best of the daily catch from local fishermen. Many of the fruits and vegetables & all of the herbs are grown organically in property.
**Bar:** Yes: open 7am – 11pm (daily) our Oasis Bar & Estrella Azul Rooftop Lounge
**Business Facilities:** Media Room, Conference Facilities, Internet
**Conference Room:** 1 room / capacity up to 80 people
**Sports Facilities:** Fully equipped gym
**Spa Services:** Oceanfront massage/yoga Palapa offering a host of massage treatments, salon services, and yoga instruction.
**Airport:** Manzanillo Airport or our own landing strip (plane restrictions)
**Location:** Midway between Puerto Vallarta and Manzanillo along the famed "Costalegre."

A luxury boutique hotel and Mexico's most private resort, Las Alamandas is a romantic retreat on the Pacific Coast ideal for a honeymoon, a family get-together, a corporate retreat or the ultimate beach getaway. This secluded haven is located midway between Puerto Vallarta and Manzanillo, along the famed "Costalegre" coast of the state of Jalisco. Managed as an elegant, private estate where guests are accorded the highest standards of hospitality, this exclusive beachfront hideaway is situated on over 1,500 acres of unspoiled tropical paradise.

The seven-villa hideaway (which accommodates a maximum of 42 guests) is managed like an elegant, private estate where guests feel completely at home. The villas have high-pitched tile roofs, shaded terraces and white ceramic floors. Walkways decorated with stone Mosaic wind though lush tropical gardens. Each room is decorated in the jewel-like colors chosen by owner/developer Isabel Goldsmith-Patio. A pleasing mix of designs, fabrics, and crafts were selected from all over Mexico. Rattan sofas upholstered in canary yellow or shocking pink hold bright-colored embroidered cushions on which to take a siesta. Mexican folk art hand-painted artifacts enliven each room. Accommodations include large, hand-painted, Mexican tile baths featuring oversized tub and shower, bidet, double sinks and large open shelving, as well as private terraces and full-sized living/dining areas.

Dine to the strains of Mexican music in a palm grove right next to the ocean! Las Alamandas, full-service Oasis Restaurant, serves fresh and healthy cuisine along with a variety of liquors and fine wines. In the evening, the terrace is candlelit and the surrounding gardens are illuminated.

The romantic paradise is located on the Mexican Riviera, south of Puerto Vallarta and north of Manzanillo.

# KVIKNE'S HOTEL

At Kvikne's the best traditions of innkeeping go right back to 1752. The Kvikne family, who still own the hotel today, took over in 1877 and a continuous process of development has been going on from that day to this.

The hotel was built in the "Swiss" style. Much new building, reconstruction and extension has gone on since, but none of it has altered the special character of this place. The hotel is graced with an extensive collection of artworks and antiques, which give it its special style.

Kvikne's is a modern hotel with old world charm and atmosphere and with 200 guest rooms is one of the largest tourist hotels in Norway. With its long verandas overlooking the Sognefjord, the main building of Kvikne's Hotel is the largest and most impressive of our old wooden hotel structures in Norway. It is one of the most beautiful examples of the building style which the Norwegians call "Swiss."

One cannot live on beautiful views and atmosphere alone. Food is an important part of your stay and at Kvikne's we emphasize sensual experiences which will stay with you for life. The cuisine is international, as are our chefs. We use local ingredients as far as possible and the fjord is an outstanding larder. The hotel manager and head waiter can offer wines from our extensive cellar to complement your dining experience. The list of prominent guests is a long one. Keiser Wilhelm II of Germany was a frequent guest in Balestrand. Royalty, emperors, presidents, prime ministers, film stars and artists from many countries can be found on the guest list.

Come stay with us and experience!

**Address:** Kviknevegen 8 Balestrand Norway N-6898
**Phone:** 47-57-69-4200
**Fax:** 47-57-69-4201
**Email:** bookings@kviknes.no
**Web:** www.kviknes.no
**Room Rates:** NOK 1080–1580
**No. of Rooms:** 190
**Credit Cards:** Most CCs Accepted
**Attractions:** With so much to do you can enjoy local or regional adventures while visiting: Wine tasting, hikes in the Jostedal Glacier National Park, touring downtown, or a game of golf.
**Services:** Free wireless Internet, TV, hair dryer, telephone, laundry service on request
**Concierge:** No
**Room Service:** Yes
**Restrictions:** Call for details
**Restaurant:** Full service gourmet restaurant on site. The cuisine is international, as are our chefs. We use local ingredients as far as possible and the fjord is an outstanding larder.
**Bar:** Yes
**Business Facilities:** Yes
**Conference Room:** Yes / capacity up to 450 people
**Sports Facilities:** No on site gym or workout room
**Spa Facilities:** No
**Airport:** Forde and Sogndal Airports
**Location:** Peninsula surrounded by majestic mountains

# HOTEL CONTINENTAL

**Address:** Stortingsgaten 24/26
Oslo Norway 0117
**Phone:** 47-22-82-40-00
**Fax:** 47-22-82-40-65
**Email:** booking@hotel-continental.no
**Web:** www.hotel-continental.no
**Room Rates:** 1750–2150 Norway¤
**No. of Rooms:** 155
**No. of Suites:** 8
**Credit Cards:** Most CCs Accepted
**Attractions:** Here is a handful of
things to do and attractions to
take in while visiting the capital
of Norway, The sculpture park
Vigelandsparken, Holmenkollen
ski jump, The Viking Ships
Museum, The Norwegian National
Opera and Ballet, and The Kon-
Tiki Museum.
**Services:** Parking, car rental,
currency exchange, Barber,
message center, copier, Audio/
Visual
**Restrictions:** No pets allowed
**Concierge:** Yes
**Room Service:** Yes
**Restaurant:** Full restaurant and
bar.
**Bar:** Yes
**Business Facilities:** Yes
**Conference Room:** Yes
**Sports Facilities:** Yes
**Spa Services:** Full range of spa
services available.
**Airport:** Oslo Airport
Gardermoen
**Location:** In the heart of Oslo,
the capital of Norwway

A stay at Hotel Continental is an experience in its own
right. The hotels unique history, the individually designed
rooms and suites, and our impressive collection of art attract
guests from around the world. All our staff do all they can to
give all our guests that something extra. We have a selection
of special offers and package deals, ranging from romantic
weekends to an evening at one of the city's theaters. At the
heart of all our special offers is an unforgettable experience—
a stay at the venerable Hotel Continental.

The history of Hotel Continental sounds like an old-fashioned fairy tale. It's a tale about poor people who, through
hard work and sheer talent, created a lasting monument.
Today, with the hotel owned and run by the fourth genera-
tion, Hotel Continental is Norway's' only five-star hotel and a
paradigm of quality in the hospitality industry. A single family,
over four generations has built up and developed the hotel
into the world-class business we know today. Hotel guests
from all over the world choose Hotel Continental when they
visit Oslo. Companies of all sizes choose the hotel for their
conferences and meetings, and many private individuals
choose us as the backdrop for their special celebrations.

Our attention to detail, discretion, first-class service, delicious food and drinks, unique art collection and our unusual
history and special atmosphere all serve to make a stay
at Hotel Continental a five-star experience. We call it "The
Continental Experience."

# DDG RETREATS

We would like to offer you a very special and unique opportunity for Europe—to relax and recuperate in absolutely private and luxurious 5 star Retreat. It consists of 5 outstanding 1-bedroom private Casas and a luxury 5-bedroom designer Villa Daria.

This retreat has been designed mainly for adults but we are happy to accept children over the age of 11–12 years old. The Casas are intended for romantic spa breaks, for couples or families who wish to enjoy a total get away within a private setting. Each property has breathtaking views over the sea or mountains. They have been built using only eco-friendly materials and equipped to the highest standard. Every house was designed as its own individual project, so each property is unique in its decor and design. Our facilities can be rented on a self-catering basis or if you prefer to have a totally relaxing experience then we would be happy to serve you food on a daily basis.

While you are staying with us there are many things for your enjoyment. We have a library of books, magazines, CDs and DVDs for your enjoyment or you could relax in the hammock, swim, play tennis, use our gym and spa facilities, go horse riding to the local farm, ride a bike, play golf, drink great wines and enjoy outside dining and scenic views, or just enjoy walking around the lovely local area.

The DDG Retreat is located within a territory of preserved natural park. At DDG Retreat our guests can experience a great variety of plants and animals to see.

We will celebrate your arrival with flowers, basket of fruits and a bottle of French Champagne. !!!Welcome!!!

**Address:** Albarrada, Finca, La Pavusena, Casa Daria s/n Casares Malaga Spain 29690
**Phone:** 34-659-168-217
**Fax:** 34-659-168-217
**Email:** info@ddgworld.com
**Web:** www.ddgretreatcom
**Suite Rates:** 142–555€
**No. of Suites:** 5
**Credit Cards:** Most CCs Accepted
**Attractions:** Museums, carnivals, motorcycle & car racing events, explore ruins, tour the city on foot, restaurants and shops, golf, tennis.
**Services:** Hob/stove, fridge/freezer, microwave, coffee machine, iron/ironing board, TV, DVD, CD, bathrobes, slippers, hairdryer, toiletries, safe deposit box, mini bar, hammock, air fans
**Restrictions:** Children 11 years of age or older. Younger children can be accepted. Please check with the office first.
**Concierge:** Front Desk assistance
**Room Service:** Yes
**Restaurant:** For those who prefer a care free holiday, we serve breakfast, light lunch or dinner on a daily basis from our delicious home menu. Couples may choose a romantic dinner for two.
**Bar:** Yes
**Business Facilities:** Limited
**Conference Room:** Limited
**Sports Facilities:** Heated infinity pool, sauna, steam room, gym and tennis court
**Spa Services:** Our spa is located in the tropical garden in private and comfortable setting where you can truly relax and escape the tension of everyday life.
**Airport:** Malaga Airport
**Location:** Costa del Sol, Casares

# VICTORY HOTEL

**Address:** Lilla Nygatan 5,
Gamla Stan SE-111 28
Stockholm Sweden
**Phone:** 46-8-506-400-00
**Tollfree:** 46-8-506-400-50
**Fax:** 46-8-506-400-10
**Email:** info@victoryhotel.se
**Web:** www.victoryhotel.se
**Room Rates:** 1375 Sweden ¤
**No. of Rooms:** 48
**No. of Suites:** 4
**Credit Cards:** Most CCs Accepted
**Attractions:** Centrally located in
the historical and entertainment
districts of Stockholm, area
attractions include (within
walking distance): Stortorget,
Stockholm Stock Exchange
Building, Riddarholmen
Church, The Great Cathedral of
Stockholm.
**Services:** In-room amenities
and service: Air conditioning,
Internet access (surcharge),
Premium television channel(s),
Flat-panel television, In-room
safe, Complimentary newspaper,
Phone, Minibar, Wake-up.
**Restrictions:** Call for details
**Concierge:** Yes
**Room Service:** Yes
**Restaurant:** Victory Hotel has
2 restaurants and also features
a bar/lounge. A complimentary
breakfast is served each morning.
**BAR:** Yes: located in restaurants
**Business Facilities:** Wireless
Internet, Fax.
**Conference Room:** Yes
**Sport Facilities:** No
**Spa Services:** Sauna and
relaxation area available by
appointment only.
**Airport:** Stockholm Arlanda
**Location:** In Old Town Stockholm

The Victory Hotel is a welcoming and exclusive hotel with a personal atmosphere in a perfect location in Gamla Stan, Stockholm's charming Old Town. The fact is that the hotel is a tourist attraction in itself. It contains a unique, private collection of marine antiques, passionately selected by the collector himself, the hotel's founder and owner Gunnar Bengtsson.

Victory Hotel offers 45 guestrooms. Rooms feature city views. Beds feature down comforters. Plasma televisions come with premium satellite channels. Wireless Internet access (surcharge) is provided along with phones, complimentary newspapers, and in-room safes. Bathrooms include bathrobes, slippers, complimentary toiletries, and hair dryers. Mini bars, air conditioning, and trouser presses are also included. Irons/ironing boards and wake-up calls can be requested.

Whether you are planning a small conference meeting or a family reunion, the personal service, the historic surroundings and the familiar atmosphere makes this an ideal setting. Experience elegance like never before!

# TONGSAI BAY COTTAGES & HOTEL

The land of Tongsai Bay is undoubtedly one of the most beautiful in Thailand. The cottages were built around the beauty and kept as much of what Mother Nature gave them as possible. Their philosophy is "living in harmony with nature."

In order to appreciate nature, guests need to be in open space; not just watching from inside an air conditioned box. The concept of great outdoor living then followed. There are spacious outdoor spaces for all suites and villas all overlooking the sea. First you can start with the bathtub on the balcony for bathing with a sea view. Then you can eat, take a bath with a view, and even sunbathe and sleep (mosquito netting provided) all in open space while you are safe with the knowledge that you only have to step inside for air-condition and cover if it is too hot or if it rains.

If that isn't enough, there is Prana Spa which consists of 3 private cottages where you may experience unique relaxation techniques combined with a variety of original herbal recipes that help relieve stress. The massages offer their own effective but harmless techniques that combine the traditional Thai massage with the scientific study of the human body.

If you never want to leave your suite, room service is available all day. But do venture out, because the restaurants are superb. Chef Chom's Thai Restaurant by the Lobby offers spectacular views out over the bay with an International Breakfast Buffet and Thai dinner. Po-Lad Beach Bistro on the Beach offers open-air international cuisine for lunch and dinner. The Butler's Restaurant on the hillside just a few minutes' walk from the Grand Villas, specializes in Pan-Asian and European food with a menu created seasonal.

This resort has thought of everything to renew and restore your mind, body and soul. You may never want to go home.

EWW 266 25TH ED

**Address:** 84 Moo 5, Bophut Ko Samui Suratthani 84320
**Phone:** 66-0-77-245-462
**Fax:** 66-0-77-425-462
**Email:** info@tongsaibay.co.th
**Web:** www.tongsaibay.co.th
**Suite Rates:** 11000-52000 THB ¤
**No. of Suites:** 83
**Credit Cards:** Most CCs Accepted
**Attractions:** Scuba diving, Deep sea fishing, 25 acres of gardens, Snorkeling, Golf, Visit Local Temples
**Services:** Car rental, Taxi service, Gift shop, Minibar, DVD/CD & VCD library, IDD telephone, Safety box, Hairdryer, Coffee & tea making facilities, Satellite TV, DVD/VCD/CD player.
**Restrictions:** Call for details
**Room Service:** Yes — available 7:00am – Midnight
**Restaurant:** Chef Chom's Thai Restaurant - 7:00-10:30am for breakfast and 7:00-10:00pm for dinner; Po-Lad Beach Bistro (daily) from 11:00am – Midnight serving lunch and dinner; The Butler's serves dinner (nightly) 7:00–10:00pm
**Bar:** Po-Lad Beach Bar — 11:00am–2:00am and our Lobby Lounge Bar —10:00am–Midnight
**Business Facilities:** Internet
**Conference Facilities:** Limited
**Sports Facilities:** Swimming pools, wading pool & Jacuzzi, Gym, Tennis court.
**Spa Services:** Prana Spa opens 11:00am–10:00pm (daily).
**Airport:** Local facilities
**Location:** Northeastern coast of Samui Island in the Gulf of Thailand

# PERA PALACE HOTEL

**Address:** Mesrutiyet
Caddesi No 52
Tepebasi Beyoglu Turkey 34430
**Phone:** 90-212-377-40-00
**Fax:** 90-212-377-40-77
**Email:** reservations@perapalace.com
**Web:** www.perapalace.com
**Room Rates:** 315 – 725€
**No. of Rooms:** 115
**Credit Cards:** Most CCs Accepted
**Attractions:** Istanbul, capital
to three major empires of their
times—Roman, Byzantium and
Ottoman empires—is like an
open air museum where ruins
of all three empires are still
exhibited.
**Services:** 24 hour room service,
Concierge service, Baby sitting,
Dry cleaning, Shoe shine service,
Car rental, Airport transfer
(transfers by classic cars are also
available), Complimentary WiFi
access
**Restrictions:** Call for details
**Concerige:** Front Desk assistance
**Room Service:** 24 Hour room
service
**Restaurant:** Yes—restaurant, bar
and lounge on site
**Bar:** Yes
**Business Facilities:** Fax, copier,
WiFi
**Conference Room:** Yes—10
rooms, various capacities
**Sports Facilities:** Yes—fully
equipped gym
**Spa Services:** Yes—Steam bath,
Jacuzzi, sauna, etc.
**Airport:** Istanbul Int'l Airport
**Location:** Heart of the city

Pera Palace Hotel, was home to many firsts. Apart from the Ottoman Palaces, it was the first building to have electricity as well as the first electric elevator. British writer Daniel Farson described the elevator in these words: "It is the most beautiful elevator in the world made of cast iron and wood … It ascends like a lady who curtsies. Tourists cannot take their eyes off this utterly pretty and aristocrat elevator." Pera Palace Hotel, a significant prominent symbol of Istanbul's urban culture for over a hundred years, was also witness to many historical events such as World War I, the Occupation of Istanbul, the Turkish War of Independence, the founding of the Turkish Republic and World War II.

Pera was once the heart of Istanbul, a cosmopolitan hub—where people of many nations lived, where many languages and dialects were spoken. And at the heart of Pera was Pera Palace Hotel.

Pera Palace Hotel welcomes its guests back to the glamour of nostalgic Istanbul with a visit to its classic and uniquely furnished rooms and suites. Original 19th Century features, including precious "White Carrara" marbles and exquisite "Murano-glass" chandeliers make Pera Palace Hotel suites the ideal place to experience century-old heritage. At the same time, expertly installed state-of-the-art technology and new technological services guarantee the comfort of a luxury-class hotel.

Unique facilities and expert services help turn both business and leisure trips into the ultimate experience of comfort and luxury. Enjoy flawless service and first-class facilities throughout your stay at Pera Palace Hotel.

# SUMAHAN ON THE WATER

Sumahan sits on the very edge of the Bosphorus Straits which separate Europe from Asia and link the cold waters of the Black Sea to the warm waters of the Sea of Marmara and the Aegean beyond. The Bosphorus feeds the heart and spirit of the city.

It is a rare Bosphorus-front property that has remained in the hands of the original family. Turkish-American owner-architects Nedret and Mark Butler have transformed an unlikely family heirloom—a derelict late Ottoman alcohol factory, into a special retreat for visitors to the modern city. Its aim is to provide the highest degree of service to the independent traveler in the intimacy of a family-owned hotel.

Status in Istanbul has long been determined not by the horsepower of your car but by the magnificence of your living room view. Every bedroom in the hotel offers an ever-changing seascape of fishermen and ferryboats and ships gliding through the night. It's a view of myth and of history. Odysseus, Jason and his Argonauts all passed in front of the Sumahan as did Soviet submarines. The busy city of Istanbul is there on display—on a clear day, close enough to touch—but guests of the Sumahan enjoy this panorama from the quiet privacy of a secluded waterfront.

The word guest is not a euphemism at Sumahan. Afternoon tea, a snack to greet you off a late night plane, a cup of coffee if you choose to check your e-mails in the library (all rooms have Internet access)—these are the sort of things we are delighted to offer not as an "extra" but as a matter of basic hospitality. We will press a pleated skirt, find a guide who specializes in Byzantine mosaics or arrange an experienced driver to get you through a busy schedule of meetings- and do just about anything to make your stay a pleasant one.

**Address:** Kuleli Caddesi No: 51 Cengelkoy Istanbul Turkey 34684
**Phone:** 90-216-422-8000
**Fax:** 90-216-422-8008
**Email:** info@sumahan.com
**Web:** www.sumahan.com
**No. of Rooms:** 7
**No. of Suites:** 13
**Credit Cards:** Visa, MC, Amex
**Attractions:** Sightseeing Tours
**Services:** Baby sitting/child Services, Full Breakfast, Currency Exchange Services, Doctor On Call, Dry Cleaning, Evening Turn Down Service, Garden/Terrace, Maid Service Daily, Porter/Bellmen, Reading room, Shoeshine, Theater Ticket Desk
**Restrictions:** Wheelchair accessible, 1 handicap equipped room
**Concierge:** 24/7 assistance
**Room Service:** Available 24/7
**Restaurant:** KORDON- Award winning a la carte restaurant featuring seafood and Mediterranean cuisine. Waterfront Terrace Restaurant- Serving Turkish and International cuisine. Both are open for lunch & dinner.
**Bar:** Full Bar serves light snacks & soft drinks
**Business Facilities:** Business Center
**Conference Room:** 35 people maximum
**Sports Facilities:** State-of-the-art equipment & free weights
**Spa Services:** Sumahan's Wellness center offers Hamam, traditional Turkish bath, and specialized massage treatments (deep tissue, Swedish, Shiatsu, reflexology, aromatherapy, cellulite treatment, 4 hand massage).
**Airport:** Cengelkoy Airport
**Location:** 15 minutes from Kabatas

# HOTEL SELCUKLU EVI

**Address:** Yunak Mah PK 55
Urgup Cappadocia Turkey 50400
**Phone:** 90-384-341-7460
**Fax:** 90-384-341-7463
**Email:** selcukluevi@gmail.com
**Web:** www.selcukluevi.com
**Room Rates:** 90–150€
**Suite Rates:** 150–350€
**No. of Rooms:** 8
**No. of Suites:** 10
**Credit Cards:** Most CCs Accepted
**Attractions:** Hot air balloon
flight, ritual dancing performance
of whirling dervishes, Bivouac
and barbecue diner around the
fire, Turkish Bath, mountain
biking, horse / donkey back riding,
pottery workshops, cooking
lessons, Goreme Churches,
Uchisar Castle
**Services:** Baby sitting, wedding
planning, car rental with or
without driver, TV w/international
channels available in rooms,
Free Internet access, Gift Shop,
Handcrafts Shop, Laundry
service, Tour Booking
**Restrictions:** Call for details
**Concierge:** Yes
**Room Service:** Yes
**Restaurant:** Turkish specialties
are prepared on a daily basis.
Turkish dishes, deserts, coffee
or tea. For breakfast, ladies
will prepare G'zleme (Turkish
pancakes) in front of you.
**Bar:** Turkish wine from our cave
cellar available
**Business Facilities:** Wireless
Internet
**Conference Room:** I room —
meeting style
**Sports Facilities:** No
**Spa Services:** Selcuklu Evi
Boutique offers the following type
of massages: Serail, Cappadocia,
Anatolian, Harmony, Face and
Hair, Flower, Anti-Stress, and
Honeymoon (traditional couple).
**Airport:** Istanbul-Kayseri Airports
**Location:** In the heart of
Cappadocia

More than a hotel, Selcuklu Evi is a historic Seljuk house lovingly restored, arranged in an Oriental style combining authentic charm with great comfort. Located in the heart of Cappadocia, the Country of the Fairy Chimneys, in a small lane surrounded by gardens and local houses, it offers panoramic views of rock hewn caves and the old village.

After 3 years the restoration was complete by the master craftsmen of Cappadocia, these 5 houses together compose 20 rooms and luxurious suites settled around a delightful garden crimped in the rock.

The typical architecture with local stones keeps the hotel warm in winter and cool in summer in a natural way. Near the Oriental room in the garden, there is a wine container with two taps, where you can choose the red or white local wines.

In this paradise of peace and tranquility the private balconies provide privacy and a perfect place to relax. Hospitality is the motto of our house! In our arched dining room you will taste, always served on ceramic plates, the local cuisine and its large variety of flavors, one of our strongest points. The many types of Turkish wine chosen from our cave cellar will guarantee more pleasure to your meal.

Just a short distance from Selcuklu Evi is an ample and nice swimming pool (paying access) which awaits you to refresh yourself after a full day of activities. In the Oriental room you can have relaxing moments reading, chatting, or playing the board games available in a friendly and warm atmosphere.

A good opportunity to rest!

# ADDITIONAL MEMBERS – INTERNATIONAL

## Argentina

Finca Adalgisa
Mendoza, Lujan
54-261-4960713
www.fincaadalgisa.com.ar

## Bermuda

Rosedon Hotel - Bermuda
Pembroke
441-295-1640
www.rosedonbermuda.com

Cambridge Beaches Resort and Spa
Sandy's
441-234-0331
www.cambridgebeaches.com

## Canada

Hotel Du Lac Carling
Brownsburg-Chatham, Quebec
450-533-9211
www.laccarling.com

The International Hotel Suites
 Calgary
Calgary, Alberta
403-265-9600
www.internationalhotel.ca

Galiano Inn - Oceanfront Inn and Spa
Galiano Island, British Columbia
250-539-3388
www.galianoinn.com

Sooke Harbour House
Sooke, British Columbia
250-642-3421
www.sookeharbourhouse.com

The Wickaninnish Inn
Tofino, British Columbia
250-725-3100
www.wickinn.com

Wedgewood Hotel & Spa
Vancouver, British Columbia
604-689-7777
www.wedgewoodhotel.com

Amore by the Sea - A BB Inn and
 Seaside Spa
Victoria, British Columbia
250-474-5505
www.amorebythesea.com

Rosewood Victoria Inn
Victoria, British Columbia
250-384-6644
www.rosewoodvictoria.com

The Victoria Regent Hotel
Victoria, British Columbia
250-412-8101
www.victoriaregent.com

## Costa Rica

Los Heroes Hotel & Restaurant
Tilaran
284-6315
www.travelguides.com/home/losheroes

## England, U.K.

Villa Magdala Hotel
Bath
44-1225-466329
www.villamagdala.co.uk

London Elizabeth
London
44-20-7402 6641
www.londonelizabethhotel.com

The Beaufort
London, Knightsbridge
44-207-584-5252
www.thebeaufort.co.uk

The Claverley on Beaufort Gardens
London, Knightsbridge
44-0-20-7589-8541
www.claverleyhotel.co.uk

Hotel Endsleigh
Tavistock, Devon
44-0-1822-870-000
www.hotelendsleigh.com

Linthwaite House Hotel
Windermere, Cumbria
44-0-15394-88600
www.linthwaite.com

## Fiji

Maravu Plantation Resort
Tavenui Island - Matei
679-3324-303
www.maravu.net

## France

Hotel Du Palais
Biarritz
33-559-416400
www.hotel-du-palais.com

La Maison Bord'eaux
Bordeaux
33-5-56-44-00-45
www.lamaisonbordeaux.com

Le Hameau Albert
Chamonix
33-50-53-05-09
www.hameaualbert.fr

Hotel Mont Blanc
Megeve
33-4-50-21-20-02
www.hotelmontblanc.com

**La Bastide de Marie**
Menerbes
33-4-90-72-30-20
www.c-h-m.com

**Hotel Bourgogne & Montana**
Paris
33-1-45-51-20-22
www.bourgogne-montana.com

**Hotel De Banville**
Paris
33-1-42-67-70-16
www.hotelbanville.fr

**Hotel Des Tuileries**
Paris
33-1-42-61-04-17
www.hotel-des-tuileries.com

**The Madison Hotel**
Paris
33-1-40-51-60-00
www.hotel-madison.com

**Le Relais de Franc Mayne**
Saint Emilion
33-0-246-261
www.relaisfrancmayne.com

**Le Beauvallon**
Sainte-Maxime, Beauvallon-Grimaud
33-4-94-55-78-88
www.hotel-lebeauvallon.com

## Greece

**St Nicolas Bay Resort Hotel & Villas**
Aghios Nikolaos, Crete
30-28410-25041
www.stnicolasbay.gr

**Harmony Boutique Hotel**
Mykonos Town
30-22890-28980-1
www.harmonyhotel.gr

## Grenada

**Spice Island Inn**
St George's, West Indies
473-444-4258
www.spiceislandbeachresort.com

## Ireland

**Seaview House Hotel**
Bantry, County Cork
353-27-50073
www.seaviewhousehotel.com

**The Fitzwilliam Hotel - Dublin**
Dublin
353-1-478-7000
www.fitzwilliamhotel.com

**Ballinkeele House**
Enniscorthy, County Wexford
353-53-9138105
www.ballinkeele.com

## Italy

**Capri Palace Hotel & Spa**
Anacapri
39-081-9780-111
www.capri-palace.com

**Hotel "3Esse" Country House**
Assisi
39-75816363
www.countryhousetreesse.com

**Is Morus Relais**
Cagliari, Sardegna
39-0-70-921171
www.ismorus.it

**Villa Gaidello Club**
Castelfranco Emilia
39-59-926806
www.gaidello.com

**Tenuta Di Ricavo**
Castellina in Chianti (Siena), Toscana
39-0577-740-221
www.ricavo.com

**Hotel La Vecchia Cartiera**
Colle Val d'Elsa (Siena)
39-0577-92-11-07
www.hotelvecchiamilan.com

**Relais Della Rovere**
Colle Val d'Elsa (Siena)
39-0577-92-46-96
www.chiantiturismo.it

**Villa Giulia**
Fano
39-0721-823159
www.relaisvillagiulia.com

**Villa Le Piazzole**
Firenze
39-055-22-3520
www.lepiazzole.com

**Hotel Montebello Splendid**
Florence
39
www.montebellosplendid.com

**Hotel Villa Del Sogno**
Gardone Riviera, Lago di Garda
39-0-365-290181
www.villadelsogno.it

**Hotel Universo**
Lucca, Toscana
39-0-583-493678
www.universolucca.com

**Villa La Principessa**
Lucca, Toscana
39-0583-37-0037
www.hotelprincipessa.com

**Le Torri di Bagnara - Country Resort**
Perugia
39-075 579-2001
www.letorridibagnara.it

**Ca' P'a**
Praiano
39-089-874078
www.casaprivata.it

**Grand Hotel de la Minerve**
Rome
39-06-695-201
www.hotel-invest.com

**Hotel D'Este**
Rome
39-06-446-5607
www.hoteldeste.it

**Hotel Romae**
Rome
39-06-446-3554
www.hotelromae.com

**Hotel Villa Del Parco**
Rome
39-6-44237773
www.hotelvilladelparco.it

**Parkhotel Sole Paradiso**
San Candido
39-474-913120
www.sole-paradiso.com

**Hotel Villa Carlotta**
Taormina
39-942-626058
www.hotelvillacarlottataormina.com

**Hotel Villa Ducale**
Taormina
39-0-942-28153
www.villaducale.com

## Jamaica

**The Tryall Club**
Hanover, Jamaica
876-956-5660
www.tryallclub.com

**Charela Inn Hotel**
Negirl, Westmoreland
876-957-4648
www.charela.com

## Madagascar

**Loharano Hotel**
Nosy Be
261-20-86-92-190
www.loharanohotel.com

## Maldives

**Soneva Fushi by Six Senses**
Kunfunadhoo Island, Baa Atoll
960-660-0304
www.sixsenses.com/soneva-fushi

## Mexico

**El Tamarindo Beach & Golf Resort**
Cihuatlan, Jalisco
52-315-351-5031
www.eltamarindoresort.com

**Las Rosas Hotel & Spa**
Ensenada, Baja
52-646-174-4320
www.lasrosas.com

**Ceiba del Mar Beach & Spa Resort**
Puerto Morelos, Quintana Roo
52-998-872-8063
www.ceibadelmar.com

**Casa Quetzal Hotel**
San Miguel De Allende, Guanajuato
52-415-152-0501
www.casaquetzalhotel.com

**Hacienda De Las Flores**
San Miguel De Allende, Guanajuato
52-415-152-1808
www.haciendadelasflores.com

**Casa Bichu Boutique Hotel**
San Pedro Pochutla, Oaxaca
52-958-584-3489
www.casabichu.com

**The Tides Zihuatanejo**
Zihuatanejo
52-755-55 5 55 00
www.tideszihuatanejo.com

## Morocco

**Dar Ayniwen Villa Hotel**
Marrakech
212-44-32-9684
www.dar-ayniwen.com

## Nigeria

**Planet One**
Maryland, Ikeja, Lagos
234-1-2713910
www.planet1ng.com

## Panama

**Gamboa Rainforest Resort**
Panama City
507-314-9000
www.gamboaresort.com

## Portugal

**Monte do Casal**
Estoi
351-289-991503
www.montedocasal.pt

## South Africa

**Villa St James**
Cape Town
27-21-782-9356
www.villastjames.com

**Tswalu Kalahari**
Kuruman
27-53-781-9234
www.tswalu.com

## Spain

**Duquesa de Cardona**
Barcelona
34-93-268-9090
www.hduquesadecardona.com

**Hotel La Quinta Roja**
Garachico
34-922-133-377
www.quintaroja.com

**El Raco de Madremanya**
Gerona
34-972-49-06-49
www.turismoruralgirona.com

**Torre Del Remei**
Girona, Bolvir (Girona)
34-972-14-0182
www.torredelremei.com

**Hotel Reina Cristina**
Granada
34-9-58-253211
www.hotelreinacristina.com

**Hotel V**
Vejer de la Frontera
34-956-45-17-57
www.hotelv-vejer.com

## Switzerland

**The Claridge Hotel - Zurich**
Zurich
41-44-267-8787
www.claridge.ch

**Widder Hotel**
Zurich
41-1-224-2526
www.widderhotel.ch

## Thailand

**Tongsai Bay Cottages & Hotel**
Ko Samui, Suratthani
66-0-77-245-480
www.tongsaibay.co.th

## Tortola

**Sebastian's On The Beach Hotel**
Roadtown, Tortola
284-495-4212
www.sebastiansbvi.com

**The Sugar Mill**
Tortola
284-495-4355
www.sugarmillhotel.com

## Turkey

**Almina Hotel Istanbul**
Istanbul, Emimono
90-212-638-38-71
www.alminahotel.com.tr

*There's a small hotel,
with a wishing well,
I wish that we were there
together . . ."*

—Rodgers and Hart

# GOING, GOING, . . . GONE WE'VE GONE GREEN!

*"It's Not Easy – Being Green,"* to quote Kermit the Frog. (and, it really isn't)

It began in the late 1960s when the average person started thinking a little more about recycling. We heard about endangered species and their annihilation and about global warming and the impact on the environment. New words such as "eco-friendly," "sustainability," and "eco-tourism" soon became household words to the lodging industry as they began to look at their impact and ways that they could make improvements while still providing their guests with a pleasurable hotel stay, services and more amenities (than the other guy) without passing on the costs. Just like everyone recycles at home, hoteliers are even more conscience of what it takes for them to become "green." So let's just take a moment to decide what "green" really is—and who verifies that the hotel is really living up to their promise to be "green."

First—there is no single set of rules nor is there only one place to become "green certified." The lodging industry may work with several agencies (local, state, country) and private sector programs to obtain such certifications. Each program will have its own standards, regulations, certification time frame that the hotel must adhere to, and rating system. Some programs are much harder than others to qualify for and yes, there are even some hefty fees that hotels incur to become "green." For instance—a hotel being built, brand new, today can begin the "green" process starting at the building's foundation while a "historic" hotel will have to settle for a different certification of "green." But, both travelers and our planet reap the rewards as each business becomes "green." Travelers must remember that all hotels/inn/guesthouses are trying to do just like they do at home—lessen the impact.

As eco-tourism expands there will, no doubt, be more programs for the lodging industry to choose from. Here are the current leading programs that offer "green friendly" or "green certifications." We have included a brief explanation and their website URL in case you would like further information.

1. **GREEN KEY GLOBAL**

   *Summary*: The Green Key Eco-Rating program began in Canada in the 1990's and currently has over 1,200 hotels certified (Canada & USA). They are focused on hotel operations and best practices. The Green Key audit looks at nine major areas of sustainable hotel operations.
   (www.greenkeyglobal.com)

2. **GREEN GLOBE INTERNATIONAL**

   *Summary*: Green Globe is for hotels and golf courses worldwide and has been used by the travel and tourism industry since 1993. The Green Globe certification looks at behavioral, facility and product issues at the hotel and has a third-party independent auditor work on-site with the hotel for compliance. Hotels with this certification must re-certify each year.
   (www.greenglobercerticiation.com)

3. **ENERGY STAR**

   *Summary*: Created about ten years ago by the US Environmental Protection Agency (EPA). Their focus is to reduce energy consumption and greenhouse gas emissions. Energy Star cover 13 types of commercial buildings. With their online system, Portfolio Manager, Energy Star allows clients to monitor their energy usage on a monthly basis.
   (www.energystar.gov)

**4.** GREEN SEAL

*Summary*: Since 1995, Green Seal has been providing a science-based environment certification. Green Seal is not just a certification program. Green Seal is recognized for more than forty product categories and services. (You may find a hotel is not "green certified" but is "green friendly" because they use Green Seal cleaning products, for example)
(www.greenseal.org)

**5.** AUDUBON GREEN LEAF

*Summary*: Begun in 1998, Audubon Green Leaf was established to provide quality guest services while minimizing the impact on the environment. Hotels are given a) 1–5 "leaf rating" based on the hotels a) saving energy, b) reducing waste, c) conserving water and resources, d) preventing pollution
(http://greenleaf.auduboninternational.org)

**6.** LEADERSHIP IN ENERGY AND ENVIRONMENTAL DESIGN – LEED

*Summary*: LEED focuses on going green from the beginning. LEED provides certification that a facility was designed, built or retro-fitted to improve performance in energy and water conservation, emissions, indoor environmental quality and protection of resources.
(www.usgbc.org)

**7.** ECOROOMS & ECOSUITES

*Summary*: Theirs is the only program that requires 100% compliance with all eight of their requirements. They have two levels – approved and certified (which requires an on-site audit). Its main function was originally to serve as an online directory of the most environmentally responsible lodging facilities worldwide.
(www.ecorooms.com)

**8.** GREEN TOURISM BUSINESS SCHEME (GTBS)

*Summary*: Their criteria is divided into 10 areas. Their certifications are utilized by a wide range of hotels, motels, campsites, and campus housing and many others in the lodging industry. Their focus, since 1997, is offering guidelines on how to make a hotel's operations more sustainable while still delivery quality service.
(www.green-business.co.uk)

**9.** SUSTAINABLE TOURISM ECO-CERTIFICATION PROGRAM – STEP

*Summary*: Developed by a non-profit organization, this eco program is aimed at a worldwide reach. Launched in 2007—they have a rating system of 1–5 stars. They are also the only program that specifically addresses certifications for luxury hotels as a separate program.
(www.ecocertification.org)

**10.** CITY/STATE/COUNTRY

In the United States there are 23 states that have enacted some type of green certification. Many countries, worldwide, have also begun their own certification programs.

As you can see, there are many programs available to assist the hotel and lodging industry. You will find that each of these programs has their own insignia. Hotels have begun to alter their web sites to be more informative to the traveling public about their "green" endeavors. On the following page you will find a sample listing of boutique and luxury accommodations that have turned their eyes to "green."

# KNOW THEM BY THE CROWN

Listed below is just a sample of some of our noteworthy "Going Going ... Gone Green Hotels."

COMING SOON—on our www.ElegantSmallHotel.com Internet directory web site you will be able to clearly search for hotels by their amenities, categories, and services (see page 162 for more details) but you will also be able to distinguish our members—simply by the crown they wear!

## Green Certified 👑  Green Friendly 👑

| Page # | Name | Certified | Friendly |
|---|---|---|---|
| 92 | 1843 Battery Carriage | | 👑 |
| 126 | Abigail's Hotel | | 👑 |
| 101 | Arlington's West Mountain | | 👑 |
| 4 | Bernardus Lodge | | 👑 |
| 8 | Carter House Inns & Restaurant 301 | | 👑 |
| 30 | Dolphin Bay Resort & Spa | | 👑 |
| 14 | Grande Colonial Hotel | 👑 | |
| 143 | Hotel Hacienda Los Laureles-Spa | | 👑 |
| 17 | Hotel Pacific | | 👑 |
| 44 | Hotel Rehoboth | 👑 | |
| 76 | Inn at Great Neck | | 👑 |
| 144 | Las Alamandas | | 👑 |
| 18 | Monterey Bay Inn | | 👑 |
| 78 | Hotel Plaza Athenee | | 👑 |
| 40 | Saybrook Point Inn & Spa | 👑 | |
| 20 | Spindrift Inn | | 👑 |
| 16 | The Stanford Inn by the Sea | | 👑 |
| 38 | Strater Hotel | | 👑 |
| 86 | The Allison Inn & Spa | 👑 | |
| 77 | The Andrew | | 👑 |
| 2 | The Hermosa Inn | | 👑 |
| 69 | The Inns & Spa at Mill Falls | | 👑 |
| 88 | The Morris House Hotel | | 👑 |
| 109 | The Washington House Inn | | 👑 |
| 89 | Thomas Bond House Bed & Breakfast | | 👑 |
| 67 | Triple Creek Ranch - Relais & Chateaux | | 👑 |

# AMENITIES - CATEGORIES - SERVICES INDEX

## Amenities

After speaking with thousands of people every year, I still find that I must clarify that there is a difference between these two words—amenities and services. (You will find a paragraph on services further down on this page.) Most of the traveling public and the hotel industry use the two words, interchangeably. So let's touch on amenities, first.

Exactly what are amenities? How do you determine if the hotel is providing you with the amenity that you are looking for, compared to a service? In the lodging industry, amenities are tangible items. Tangible means that you can touch and feel the item—like antique furnishings, a jetted Jacuzzi tub, the iron and ironing board or a coffee pot in the kitchen of your vacation rental. Always remember that the quantity (how many amenities) you receive when you book your stay at a hotel will be based on the selection of your hotel room or "package." Example: a "regular room" will have fewer amenities than a "suite." Listed below, to help you out, are a few of the most common amenities.

- Alarm Clock
- Antique furnishings
- Bicycle
- Coffee Pot
- Computer
- Crib or playpen
- DVD player
- Golf Course
- iPod docking station
- Luxury bedding
- Pet Items (bed, food bowl, etc)
- Pool
- Radio
- Robes & Slippers
- Stereo System
- Telephone
- Tennis Court
- Toiletries
- TVs (flat screen, color, etc)
- Twin, Queen, or King beds

## Services

There are two things that set an Elegant Small Hotels member apart from the rest of the hotel world. Ambiance is the atmosphere that a traveler feels when they stay at a boutique or luxury accommodation. The other and the more important of the two is the service that they receive as a hotel guest. Earlier I wrote about amenities and how they were tangible items. Service is in non-tangible item. Let me clarify. A hotel that provides their hotel guests with the daily newspaper (the tangible item) is providing them a service (non-tangible item) by delivering the newspaper along with breakfast. Some services may or may not require an additional fee. Perfect example: room upgrade. Listed below is a basic list of services that travelers have come to expect from our members.

- Administrative Assistance
- Babysitter
- Bellhop
- Concierge Assistance
- Dog walking
- Dry Cleaning or Laundry Service
- Internet / WiFi / Wireless / High Speed
- Luggage storage
- Maid Service
- Newspaper delivery
- Parking
- Room Service
- Room Upgrades
- Safe Deposit box
- Taxi or Airport shuttle (to/from) airport
- Tour guide
- Turn-down Service
- Wake-up calls

# Categories

What's in a name? The hotel industry spends thousands of dollars each year on reinventing themselves and "branding." Labeling any hotel into a specific category can often times be misleading. The categories below were based on the independent travelers' perception and expectations and were compiled from many surveys. What could be conceived as an "Affordable Elegance" hotel to me might be viewed as a "City Center Hotel" to you. So—certainly our members, logically, will fit into multiple categories. Our guidebooks have always encompassed five distinct types of boutique and luxury hotel accommodations categories. They have been:

- **Affordable Elegance**: Though one normally expects elegant lodgings to come at higher-than-ordinary rates, we have discovered a select few that offer some of the best of both worlds: comfortable, well-appointed rooms, excellent restaurants and access to sports facilities, with many of the essential amenities associated with Grand Luxe hotels—at surprisingly reasonable prices. Please bear in mind, though, that throughout the world, the very top quality accommodations carry a correspondingly steep price.

- **City Center Hotels**: Designed especially for the business traveler, each of these hotels offer a comfortable, inviting environment where an executive may return each day to lodgings ideally appointed to satisfy business, personal and recreational needs. Special emphasis is placed upon conference facilities and services for executives.

- **Grand Luxe Hotels**: Each of these world-class hotels projects an incomparable aura of tradition and grace. A few of the services provided are superb restaurant and room service, an attentive but very discreet staff with full concierge services, and a sumptuous atmosphere of well-secured luxury.

- **Outstanding Resorts**: The quick weekend trip or brief resort holiday is becoming the new vacation style of the ultra-busy. From a wide range of possibilities, we have selected our resort recommendations with regard for their luxurious ambience, excellent cuisine and sporting facilities. Most also offer excellent conference facilities and are perfect for combining recreation and business meetings in beautiful surroundings.

- **Wonderful Country Inns**: Those great small hideaways we all dream about, the perfect place for restoring body and soul (and romance!) cosseted by a caring staff in a gracious and restful ambiance.

With over twenty-five years of traveling, interviewing all types of travelers, speaking with hoteliers about a constantly evolving industry—it has come time to ADD a few more categories. They are:

- **Historic Luxury:** These hotels are our heritage—both the historical events that took place within and in their stunning architecture reminiscent of days gone by. They have all gone through extensive renovations for modernization and luxury while still retaining their splendor of days gone by.

- **Luxury Bed and Breakfast:** These B&Bs have taken the warmth and feel of your typical "bed and breakfast" establishment and escalated themselves to a whole new meaning of intimacy while still retaining their charm.

# AND … MORE TO COME!

In celebration of our 25th Silver Anniversary, our **www.ElegantSmallHotel.com** website will be expanding their SEARCH BY fields to assist travelers, whether for business or pleasure, to find the perfect boutique and luxury accommodations for their next business meeting or vacation. Listed below are some of the universally recognized, searchable icons we will be using on our **www.ElegantSmallHotel.com** website, in the coming months, to provide you with quick visual information about our members and the services that they offer:

(Spas)

(Pets)

(Business Facilities)

(Museums)

(Fine Dining)

(Local Wineries)

(Sports Facilities)

(Historical Building)

(National Parks)

(Children Welcome)

(Handicap Access)

(Shopping)

## Know them by the Crown they wear!

Eco-Certified

Eco-Friendly

# HOTELS OF THE SEA

Many sailors have succumbed to the "call of the sea" but at no time has it been more enjoyable to adventure past the shores of a land mass than on a cruise ship. Oftentimes called a "floating hotel," these luxury liners are truly an island unto themselves and many of these magnificent ships are designed so that you never set foot back on land once you have boarded because they contain all the aspects of a small city—theaters, pools, restaurants, even sports can be enjoyed among their many decks. Docking at exotic ports of call during the day and embarking for a day of exploration. Viewing countless stars at night amidst a calm sea. Adventure and intimacies. You will find such experiences aboard these fine vessels and is something that every traveler should experience at least once in their lifetime.

**Coming Soon – JOIN US – January 2012!**
for the **Premiere and Launching** of the
**USS Elegant Small Hotels**

In the upcoming months, Elegant Small Hotels, part of the Lanier Travel Guides Network will be ADDING a NEW CHAPTER to their award winning Internet directory website. Scheduled to launch in January 2012 you will find complete information on the selected few cruise ships that meet or exceed the same standards that our boutique and luxury "land" hotels excel in. Listed on the adjoining page are just a few of our favorites—with amenities and services, bar none!

# CRUISE LINES AND INFORMATION

| Cruise Line | Vessels | Travel Area |
|---|---|---|
| Abercrombie & Kent www.abercrombieandkent.com | Privately chartered yachts, intimate river barges and small adventure ships | Worldwide including the Galapagos Islands, Antarctica, The Yangtze River and Alaska |
| Butterfield & Robinson www.butterfield.com | The Isabella II (38 people), The Queen of Karia (10 people), Nostra Vita (10 people) | Asia-Pacific, Europe, Africa/Middle Ease, North America, Latin America |
| Crystal Cruises www.crystalcruises.com | Crystal Symphony (922 people), Crystal Serenity (1,070 people) | Worldwide, including the Panama Canal, New England and New Zealand |
| Hebridean Island Cruises www.hebridean.co.uk | Hebridean Princess (49 people) | Scotland and British Isles |
| Lindblad Expeditions www.expeditions.com | National Geographic Explorer (148), National Geo Endeavor (96), National Geo Sea Bird (62); National Geo Sea Lion (62), National Geo Islander (48), Salacia (47), Panorama (44), Lord of the Glens (48), Delfin II (28), Oceanic Discoverer (68) | Nature-oriented, including Antarctica, Galapagos Islands and Egypt |
| SeaDream Yacht Club www.seadreamyachtclub.com | Seadream I, Seadream II (both 112 people) | Caribbean in Winter and Europe in Summer, Trans-Atlantic |
| Silversea Cruises www.silversea.com | Silver Cloud (296), Silver Wind (296), Silver Whisper (382), Silver Shadow (392), Silver Spirit (540), and Prince Albert II (132) | Worldwide, including the Indian Ocean, Southeast Asia, New England and Canada |
| Viking River Cruises www.vikingrivers.com | 26 river barges and ships (200 people average each) | Europe, Russia, Egypt, China and Southeast Asia |
| Windstar Cruises www.windstarcruises.com | Wind Surf (312), Winds Spirit (148) and Wind Star (148) | Worldwide, including Costa Rica, the Greek Isles, the Caribbean |
| The Yachts of Seabourn www.seabourn.com | Seabourn Pride (208), Seabourn Spirit (208), Seabourn Legend (208), Seabourn Odyssey (450), Seabourn Sojourn (450), Seabourn Quest (225) | Worldwide, including Greece and Turkey, Mediterranean Riviera, Northern Europe, Asia, India and Africa |

# OUR WEBSITE — HOW TO USE

If you enjoyed the information contained in this guidebook—and want to learn more; then visit our Internet directory website at www.ElegantSmallHotel.com. There you will find thousands of pages containing wonderful information about traveling the world over and on each of our member properties.

View the "Carousel of Pictures" **1** and select a member property or use our "Hotel Search" **2** to find a member property by name, state or country.

Use the Tool Bar **3** for even quicker navigation. Be sure to check out our boutique e-Newsletter archive for travel "Tips 'N Tricks" and then sign up for future e-Newsletters. Yes—they are FREE!

Everyone is looking for the best value for their traveling dollar. Search for a "Deal by Interest" **4** because you want an "Active Adventure"; or maybe an upcoming "Deal by Holiday" **5** for a family outing; or just escape to one of our exotic "Destinations"**6**. Gain information about the area and all the local attractions that you will see and can experience.

All the information is there. One "click" and you are directly connected through active URL links **7** to our members and can book your reservation today!

### Visit Us Today!
### at
### www.ElegantSmallHotel.com

Best of all—is knowing that there is an Elegant Small Hotels member nearby where you can experience the exceptional service and amenities that makes each of our member boutique and luxury accommodations uniquely memorable.

> *. . . devoted to pleasing the most discriminating. The photos put you on the scene while the text and side notes offer explicit answers.*
> —Los Angeles Times

# KEEP IN TOUCH
## Sign Up for our Monthly e-Newsletters

There's no better way, to have information delivered, than right to your desktop!

**Bed and Breakfast**

**It's FREE!**

**Elegant Hotels**

**It's FREE!**

**Family Travel**

**It's FREE!**

From our e-Newsletters, read the member hotel "Spotlight," search for those specials and packages under "Featured Specials" and read all about those wonderful, faraway, "Destinations" that really are not so far away. Attending a parade, a Jazz festival, a dog/cat show? Then check out the "Special Events" section in the e-Newsletter and find the best place to stay while at your function. Can't travel? Then bring the travel to your kitchen with recipes from around the globe.

**www.ElegantSmallHotel.com**
**www.LanierBB.com**
**www.FamilyTravelGuides.com**

Travelguides.com network, which features www.ElegantSmallHotel.com, was honored by Yahoo! with a Gold Star Award as "Best in its Category" and as "One of the 10 Best Travel Sites on the Internet." Yahoo!-IL also reported that "Elegant Small Hotels is THE source for Luxury Digs and Inntimate Getaways."

Surprise Gift Included

Give a Gift

for yourself or a friend for FREE!

You pay only the shipping/handling charges.

**See Order Form for details.**

Free Guide or
Cookbook Offer

# Lanier Publishing Int'l. Book Order Form

Give a gift to yourself or a friend. Order one (1) book and receive the 2nd book, chosen from the order form list, for FREE! (Only one (1) free book per order form—you pay only the shipping/handling for the 2nd book.) **Allow 3–4 weeks for delivery. ALL Pre-Order books will be delivered by these dates: PreOrder #1 – Oct 2011; PreOrder #2 – June 2011; PreOrder #3 – Sept 2011; PreOrder #4 – Jan 2012.**

| Title | Price | Qty | Total |
|---|---|---|---|
| Bed and Breakfast Getaways – in the South | $14.95 | | |
| Bed and Breakfast Getaways – in the Northeast  (Pre-Order #1) | $14.95 | | |
| Bed and Breakfast Getaways – on the West Coast  (Pre-Order #2) | $14.95 | | |
| Bed and Breakfast Guide – for Food Lovers | $14.95 | | |
| Cinnamon Mornings and Savory Nights | $19.95 | | |
| Elegant Small Hotels: Boutique and Luxury Accommodations | $19.95 | | |
| Inn Love – Recipes for Romance  (Pre-Order #3) | $14.95 | | |
| The Complete Bed & Breakfasts, Inns and Guesthouses Int'l. | $19.95 | | |
| Wedding at the Inn  (Pre-Order #4) | $19.95 | | |
| U.S./Canadian Address (per book) | $ 4.99 | **Shipping and Handling** | |
| International Shipping (per book) | $16.45 | | |
| Insert FREE book title here:                                **FREE** | | $ 4.99 | |
| | | $16.95 | |
| California Residents include 9% Sales Tax | | | |
| **Total Enclosed** | | | |

**SHIP BOOKS TO** (see below):

Name: _____

Address: _____

City: _____ State: _____ Zip: _____

Phone: _____ Fax: _____

Credit Card Type: _____ Number: _____ Exp. Date: _____

Name on Account: _____ Signature: _____

**FAX OR MAIL BOOK ORDER FORM WITH PAYMENT TO:**
LANIER PUBLISHING INTERNATIONAL
PO Box 2240, Petaluma, CA 94953   ph. 707-763-0271   fax: 707-763-5762

# ABOUT THE AUTHORS

### Pamela Lanier

It all began with a post-college trip to Europe. Pamela Lanier quickly fell in love with the charming small boutique hotels she encountered throughout her travels. Determined to become an advocate for the independent lodging industry back in the United States, she premiered her signature title, upon her return in 1982, the *Complete Guide to Bed & Breakfasts, Inns and Guesthouses*. Soon she was acknowledged as the "undisputed leader in the bed and breakfast industry." Now, 27 years later Pamela continues to advocate on the national and international level for the independent lodging industry. She is the author of fourteen differently themed, travel guides and several cookbooks. As a leading travel expert, Pamela communicates with thousands of inns each year through monthly emails, blogs and newsletters. She has appeared in several travel specials for CNN, gives interviews and contributes to various publications and sits on the SIPAC council of the American Hotel and Lodging Association (AHLA). A very active leader in her company, Pamela still finds time to travel and speaks at lodging and tourism conferences around the world sharing the warmth, hospitality, beauty and charm of the dynamic travel industry.

### Marie Lanier

Exposed to the world of travel as a young child, Marie, became an active participant in the family business, establishing a career for herself in the hospitality industry. Her education and experience includes graduating cum laude with her MBA from the University of Miami, studying in the famed hospitality program at NAU, a Guatemalan tour where she taught entrepreneurs to open their own small businesses, and the successful start-up of a tour operation. Marie rejoined Lanier Publishing as Director of Business Development in 2002 and her first order of business was the creation of the Full House Program with IAC/Expedia. In this program she trained 1,200 innkeepers the art of inventory management to increase their bottom line. During her off time, Marie holds positions on two boards. She is the VP of Membership for Toastmasters International and an active Toastmaster, herself. She is also the Director of Fundraising, for her chapter, of the GFWC Women's Club. Filled with enthusiasm about the hotel industry, she is a delightful speaker and very skilled at teaching new concepts in an easy-to-learn manner. Marie has utilized her speaking skills, both in English and Spanish, for PAII, CABBI, Seminar at Sea, the Southwest Florida Association and dozens of other state and international organizations. She continues to tour many lodging establishments each year offering her consulting services on the changing travel industry.

# ABOUT THE COMPANY

Lanier Publishing International began breaking ground in providing information about hotels and their services to the traveling public in 1982. Moving forward into the electronic age, in 1992 Lanier Publishing became partners with America Online as one of its first ten information providers and worked with them for the next seven years while also providing lodging information to Bloomberg, Hotels.com, Knot, Netscape and over twenty other platforms. Lanier Publishing International, through its state of the art, real time, relational databases, allows users and information contributors alike to keep information on the Lanier Travel Guides Network as up-to-date as "the moment" while remaining on the cutting edge with developments such as multi-level e-commerce and site co-branding. The six web sites (www.LanierBB.com, www.ElegantSmallHotel.com, www.FamilyTravelGuides.com, www.TravelGuides.com, www.BedandBreakfastCollection.com, www.PamelaLanier.com) have been online leaders since 1992.

Today, the Lanier Travel Guides Network has grown to include three distinctly focused travel divisions and annually produces several best selling guides—plus several popular e-newsletters and ancillary publications and manages travel information on several top ranking, award-wining Internet directories.

Since Pamela's landmark lodging publication in 1982, the Lanier Travel Guides Network has expanded to include information on over 70,000 member properties in 132 countries and has over 150,000 web pages indexed.